Drink
Drug
Divorce

One woman's misadventures
in faraway places

Leslie Adams

ISBN 978-0-692-39178-5

Leslie Travels Publishing   Georgetown, Texas USA

Contents

Travel can happen in your head and heart,
even if you can't get on a plane.

Introduction

I picked up my copy of *Eat, Pray, Love* and threw it across the room. I had never thought about putting my travels down on paper until I read that book. Actually, I threw it across the room a few times, frustrated that its author's travel experience seemed too good to be true. I'd met many solo female travelers throughout the years and had never heard of anyone's travels going as smoothly as hers. I laughed a lot while reading it though, and joked that my book would be titled *Drink, Drug, Divorce*. And so it is. Mine is the story of a demographic that, on the surface, can seem rather dull: the blonde, blue-eyed, middle class, white American girl. But my hope in writing this book is to inspire others to take the plunge into travel, and to do so regardless of their backgrounds or life situations.

I have never really known the answer to the question, "What do you want to be when you grow up?" I told my mom when I was eighteen that I just wanted to be happy. She laughed and said, "Get a good job and find a good man." Maybe I've been looking for that all this time because I freely admit that I am restless and never satisfied. Some people don't like change, but I do, and I crave the unknown. I like to see, hear, taste, smell, and feel new things. Travel gives me the opportunity to do that every day.

I want this book to be an inspiration for people, especially women, to go, just go anywhere. And I hope it encourages them to create their own paths and not feel the need to follow someone else's. Travel may not be fun or easy. It may not be a vacation, and I can almost guarantee that "true love" will not be found on some idyllic island. But a life of travel will be a rewarding life of adventure, a private experience of growth and change, and, oh my, the stories you will have to tell!

Travel opens our minds to cultures different from our own, at the same time letting us see just how similar we all are. We all struggle, we all have fears and anxieties, we all have hopes and dreams, we all want to love and be loved, and we all want to know happiness and take exciting adventures whenever and wherever possible. The Chinese philosopher Lao Tzu said, "A good traveler has no fixed plans, and is not intent on arriving." I think this philosophy can be applied to any journey in life.

So now, lets travel!

Japan
1979–1980

"Just please get me the hell out of North Carolina!" I frequently screamed to myself.

When I was sixteen Mom and I left New York and moved to North Carolina for her job as a social worker. On my first day at school the homeroom teacher asked me to introduce myself and then said, "Lordy, Lordy! Listen to how she talks. We'll have to learn from her!" That was the beginning of the end for me there.

I tried to fit in, even joined a church group and went to pep rallies, but it didn't work. I spoke, dressed, and thought differently, so inevitably a rumor spread that I was gay. My only friend was Roderick, and he, it turned out, actually was gay. I knew I had to get out of there, so for my senior year of high school I applied to the American Field Service (AFS) exchange student program and passed all their interviews. I told them I didn't care where I went.

They ended up sending me to Japan with one of the first groups ever to go there. The year was bound to have challenges for all involved. The first of these was being told I wasn't allowed to smoke. I wasn't a heavy smoker but I could not imagine facing the stress of being thrown into an alien culture without this crutch.

After we arrived all the students had to go to a campus to take a two-week intensive language course. We were allowed to speak English to each other but the moment we stepped into a classroom we were taught exclusively in Japanese.

After the two-week course, at which point I could only manage to say, "Hello" in Japanese, I was placed in Numazu on the Izu peninsula. Numazu is on the main island of Honshu, about two hours south of Tokyo. It is a "small" fishing village of 300,000 people. It was near the beach, which was not sandy, but instead was hard black rocks and full of trash. The streets were lined with racks of fish that had been split open so they could dry. The smell of rotting fish seemed to never leave the air —and I didn't even eat fish.

There were five members in my host family: a father, a mother, a son and two daughters. The older daughter had moved out of the house and was living with her husband's family. The younger daughter still lived at home and spoke a little English. My host's son also lived in our house and helped his father with the small car repair business they ran in the driveway. The son rarely spoke. He just grunted a lot and shoveled food into his mouth.

The first night my host mother took me into the bathroom to show me how to use the facilities. The bathroom didn't have a toilet in it, was completely tiled from floor to ceiling, and had a small but high-rimmed metal tub in it. You were supposed to scrub yourself outside the tub, rinse off the soap and then get in to soak in the hot water. The water wasn't changed between each bather because by the time you sat in the tub you were supposed to be clean and free of soap. We only had hot water in the evening after it had been warmed all day by the sun in a black tank on the roof. The toilet was in a separate room that had a tiled hole in the floor with foot pads on either side so you could squat over it, hoping your knees didn't buckle. I felt weird being naked in the tub room with my host mother, still a stranger, bathing me. That was the last time I got to bathe first, because in Japan women always come second. It was also the last time the water didn't have hair and dead skin floating in it. The men got to do a lot of things the girls weren't allowed to do, like whistle, or open the refrigerator door between meals. We girls could only open it if we were preparing dinner. There were more rules too. I couldn't smoke or wear make-up or jewelry. My curfew at night was nine o'clock, and I wasn't supposed to get a job.

My host family was not well educated. My host father said he'd fought in World War II and would describe to me how the Japanese army's commanding officers would beat him. He had clubbed fingertips and would rub his bald head, giggling and sucking saliva through his teeth. He and my host mother had an arranged marriage. She was so little and worked so hard around the house, but was always smiling. I could understand some of what was being said, but my Japanese was never good enough to hold a coherent conversation.

One night my host father told me the oldest daughter had given birth to a baby girl and how disappointed everyone was. He said that he told her, "Don't worry, because now when you have a boy, he'll have an older sister to take care of him." I didn't really like my host family much and I wondered if AFS had read the notes from my interviews. I had told them I was from a progressive family, even by American standards.

I rode a small bike to school every day and people gathered on the roadside to stare, point and yell, "Gaijin, Gaijin!" That meant foreigner. Some days it didn't bother me, but there were times when it would have been nice just to be invisible. I had to wear a uniform with a pleated skirt, white bobby socks, and black patent leather shoes. My friends and family back home would never have believed this was me at seventeen years old.

My school was for girls only and I think the teachers were training us to become housewives. Every morning we had to wash the floors on our hands and knees. We also had to stand up in assemblies where the teachers would go on and on and on about all sorts of things like rules and announcements that I couldn't really understand. The teachers walked around with bamboo sticks to smack girls when they'd lean on each other, back to front, and close their eyes. They put me and the other exchange student, Sarah, in special classes since we didn't speak the language fluently. Sarah was from Australia and was with the Rotary exchange program, which required her to change families every three months, rather than stay with the same family for a whole year. Her families, when compared to mine, seemed to have more of a world view, were more free thinking, and were wealthier. And they lived in large homes, drove nice cars and could take her to many cultural events.

Without Sarah I don't know if I could have survived for a year in Japan. We got along well and broke all the rules together. Our classes consisted of Japanese language, flower arranging, hand sewing kimonos, and playing the koto, a long wooden stringed instrument that sits on the floor, and playing the shamisen, a three stringed guitar-like instrument. But my favorite class was Zen meditation, even though I had a hard time sitting still and controlling my thoughts, which just raced or got stuck on something seemingly meaningless, unproductive, or painful. But I loved the teacher: He was so tiny and was missing most of his teeth, but when he smiled his eyes would squint shut and he just glowed. He drew a picture of a bucket full of water and said we were all mere drops in the bucket. He said that when he died, like a leaf falling from a tree, he would become part of the earth and therefore, wherever I was, he would be a part of me.

The girls at the school were constantly giggling with their hands over their mouths. And it was impossible to carry on a conversation about anything substantial with them since they seemed to have never heard of any world figure more relevant than Hello Kitty. Sarah and I didn't make many friends. I did make one Japanese friend though, Koichi, a boy from another school. He had been an exchange student in the U.S. so he spoke a little English, was a bit more aware of the outside world and was thoughtful about social and political issues.

We were riding on a subway one day and a drunk man started hitting and kicking me. I kept trying to tell the man, in my broken Japanese, that if he wanted to join us, he could, just to please stop hitting me. I called him obnoxious in Japanese, "Urusai," since it was a word I knew in his language that seemed to fit. Finally, I'd had enough, so I stood up. I was taller than he was, as I was compared to most of the people in Japan. And then I backhanded him in the face. His glasses flew off down the train aisle and he seemed quite startled that a female would actually strike a man. He scrambled around on the floor, found his glasses and mumbled about how crazy I was. What was really disappointing was that not one man on that train looked up from his newspaper to help me. For that matter, neither did Koichi. I was so upset after all this that I started crying. Koichi asked, "Why are you crying, are you hurt?" I answered, "No, but I've never hit anyone before!"

Within a few months Sarah and I secretly got jobs teaching English at a surf bar. This bar on the beach was where people would come to take surfing lessons, have coffee, and engage in English-language conversation with me or Sarah. We'd sneak out of school, change out of our uniforms, go talk to people in the bar and get paid for it. I even got to try to surf with the owner, although the waves weren't very big and the water was awfully dirty. I wasn't taking drugs at the time since I couldn't find any, but we did drink a lot. What generally followed drinking for me was sex. I met a man at the surf bar and he took me to a "Love Motel." I swear to God, that's what they were called. You never saw anyone while you were there. You just drove up, went in, did your business, and left the money for the room on the table. They had revolving beds with mirrors on the ceiling and nice baths. It was fun, even if I couldn't remember the man's name.

What I learned was that most men in Japan, especially businessmen, had mistresses. A man's wife, usually from an arranged marriage, served to bear his children and take care of the house. The mistress was for fun. One night Sarah and I got so drunk we started exploring each other's bodies. I had never had sex with a girl before, but the truth was that I loved her, so it just felt right. We never talked about it, I guess, because it was a little scary and confusing for both of us.

Our entire school class took a high-speed bullet train south to Hiroshima for a week-long field trip. I wondered why the U.S. had never developed any of these trains. I assumed it was because we were addicted to big gas guzzling cars. The trains traveled at more than three hundred miles per hour and were clean and comfortable. I'd been worrying about going to Hiroshima as an American because I felt so ashamed of what my country had done, but I also realized it was important to never forget. I understood that, in war, people do terrible things. But dropping an atomic bomb was doubtless one of the worst.

The thing about war that made me angry is the grave injustice of it—that the people who decide to go to war are rarely on the front lines themselves. The men recruited are largely the young, the uneducated, and the poor. They serve as fodder in conflicts that they often don't really understand. And then, when all the killing is done, the leaders sit down and sign peace treaties and you wonder why they didn't just do that in the first place.

Looking back on the history of the world there are countless examples of enemies becoming allies and vice-versa. For example, there I was, an American exchange student visiting and studying in a country we had thoroughly bombed. I thought that maybe instead of war we could devise an international mandatory exchange program so all of us would be offered a chance to see that we are one people on one tiny interdependent planet. What impressed my seventeen-year-old self the most was that, at the end of the war, Japan signed an armistice and agreed to not have a standing army, and that the movie creature Godzilla was born to externalize the tremendous fear an atomic bomb can instill in a people for generations.

One of the things I remember most about Japan was the food. I had never liked fish and had a hard time in Japan finding food I could eat. There was one restaurant that my friends liked where you could point to the fish you wanted in a tank, and within moments it would arrive, still wiggling, on a plate. I put on a lot of weight living on rice and pork buns. The Japanese also ate dolphin and whale, which made me really angry. They argued that these majestic mammals were just fish. I would argue that you couldn't train a fish to jump through hoops or balance a ball or communicate with humans.

The inside of their homes tended to be clean, but walk out the door and you'd see an open sewage ditch running down the sides of the road. Frequently you'd see a man, and occasionally even a woman, peeing into it. The Japanese just didn't seem to appreciate nature much.

The only outdoor place I visited that wasn't overrun with trash and people, or hadn't been overly manicured, was Mount Fuji. Our school class climbed, slipping and sliding on the igneous rock, traversing switchbacks, until we arrived halfway up the volcano. We stayed overnight in long wooden bunk houses, where we unrolled our sleeping pads and ate our bento boxes for dinner. Before dawn we were awakened so we could witness the sunrise. Behind us was the snow-capped summit of the volcano and, for as far as we could see, there was a blanket of clouds below us. The sun broke through the clouds, suddenly turning them brilliant white with warm orange reflecting off our faces.

I had been unable to quit smoking, and my host family thought I was strange because I'd go for walks alone. When I was away smoking, I'd be in a nearly empty park relaxing and a family would come and sit right next to me. Granted, I was an oddity with my blonde hair and blue eyes, but I thought that the people were just so used to being jam-packed in next to each other that it made them uncomfortable not to be in close proximity to others. I sensed the Japanese didn't like to be alone.

At my school I would look out over the immense cemented sports area blanketed with a sea of identical black-haired heads, white shirts and blue shorts, all moving in precise unison. They were not big on individuality. However, with time I began to notice subtle details in hair texture, skin shading, and facial bone contours that I'd missed because I was accustomed to noticing the relatively obvious Western characteristics of diverse hair and eye color. I wondered if could ever find a true Japanese friend there because I'd never know if they wanted to be with me because of what I thought or felt, or because I just looked different and was an object of curiosity.

Within a few months my host family sent me to Tokyo for counseling. They thought I was crazy because they said I left too many shoes outside the front door. They were also upset because I threw away an empty container of chocolate cocoa instead of letting my host mother know it was running low. They said that this shamed her because she wasn't able to meet my need of having chocolate milk. I wondered who was actually crazy.

Every day for nearly two weeks I sat in a room with three female Japanese counselors trying to tell me what I'd done wrong, and trying to teach me how to be a good Japanese girl. I thought I'd left the same number of shoes outside the door as everyone else. I thought if a container was empty I should throw it away. It took a lot of energy to try to predict what might insult another person. I understood I needed to accept their culture and try to fit in, but it was just so alien to me and their logic seemed twisted. And it was part of my upbringing that I believed there weren't any behaviors or beliefs that could not be confronted and questioned.

When I wasn't being grilled and indoctrinated, I'd wander the halls of the office building, and there I met a young male English-speaking counselor, Takashi, who'd been an exchange student in the U.S. He was also a law student, spoke French, played the violin, and competed in ballroom dancing. He was tall by Japanese standards and had beautiful gray hair at his temples, even though he was not much older than I was. I felt rather unaccomplished around him, but he seemed to like me.

After a couple of weeks the counselors let me return to my host family. I didn't really feel changed, but then I couldn't make sense of why I'd been sent there in the first place. I decided to try harder, to lay low, and to do what was asked of me. And I learned how to lie really well.

It helped that I had a new obsession—Takashi. We stayed in touch by phone and letters for a few weeks, and then finally we got to meet. My stomach was so full of butterflies I thought I might fly away. I lied to my host family, saying that I was staying with Sarah, but instead I stayed overnight with Takashi in his friend's apartment. We had a lovely dinner and drank red wine. He was gentle and slow with me and I struggled not to come across as too lonely or desperate. Although I'd had a number of sexual experiences before coming to Japan, for the first time in my life I felt wholly connected to a man. After each lovemaking crescendo I thought that surely this time we'd be satisfied. But soon it would start again, with the searching in each other's eyes, the caressing of our cheeks with soft hands intermingled with deep breaths filling all our senses. Our slow rhythm would become nearly still and I could feel every detail so deep it seemed to connect with my heart. When we kissed I felt full and prayed he would swallow me so it would never end. In my past I'd always cry after sex because I felt lonely and ashamed. But this time I cried with joy, believing that perhaps two bodies really could melt into one, and for a brief moment each of us would not feel alone.

The time between our visits dragged on painfully, as Takashi was always so busy and I couldn't think of anything or anyone else. Even sleeping or eating brought no ease to the pounding of my heart and the aching in my belly. I visited him once at his home on the southern island of Shikoku. This time we told my host family he was a counselor for the exchange program and my trip was an educational one. But I don't remember seeing anything of the area because we never left his room. Another time we met in Tokyo for a lunch date and I felt so proud to walk the crowded streets hand in hand. He was six feet tall and had a commanding presence. But mostly for me this relationship consisted of incessant longing. This may have been the beginning of my propensity to crave only things I cannot have.

Then soon my year was over and it was time for me to go home. Takashi snuck me out of my final AFS gathering in Tokyo, where they were doing all the end-of-program speeches and paperwork. With a tight grip on each other's hands, we ran frantically through the subway train stiles, down the sidewalks, around buildings, gasping for breath with eyes darting anywhere but on each other, until finally we reached an apartment. I had no idea whose apartment it was he was taking me to or where we were or what I was feeling.

We were there to say good-bye. I broke the silence and blurted out, "I don't think I want to do this anymore." I'm not sure what I meant since I was leaving, so it was all going to end anyway. Takashi stopped, stared at me, then turned and went to a corner of the room, crumpled down onto the floor and put his head in his hands. His shoulders trembled as he started to softly cry. I'd never seen a Japanese man cry, but part of me wanted him to suffer as I had for the past months. I wanted to stop wanting something it seemed impossible to ever have. I wanted the aching in my heart, the sickness in my stomach, the spinning in my head, I just wanted it all to stop.

Then he handed me a letter, written in perfect penmanship, in near perfect English, on a piece of delicately thin rice paper. And with it he placed on my finger an equally delicate thin silver ring. The letter read:

> Urged
> by this mad butterfly in the stomach
> I'm offering you a little present
> Hope
> it be a reminder always nearest to you
> of a guy
> who
> is six foot tall
> who
> has an extraordinary way
> to pick up girls with whom
> you have to have good-byes
> at least three times

who
is very conceited
who thinks he is the safety driver
who
likes dry but rather sweet
red wine
who
could "make like"
who
has gray hair
and hairy nose
who
sometimes was good
at cutting you down
who
could not but be always honest
with you
who
at last
was not sure of his feelings
But
who
had never so much
wanted
to
fall in love
with
somebody
who
had fought through several fights
against the time and space
for the eternal mutual feelings
never to win
who
was weary of the fight
but
who
once again
stood up to face

against the time and space
dreaming of the time when
we could casually share
our everything
Fate
Like you told me you were going to buy some wine
in downtown that day
When I talked about wine, it lost a part of its fun when you said,
"Are you giving me an engagement ring as a friend?"
Never because you said that
I'm offering this to you
Yes,
it could be a ring "as a friend"
but
this ring
complies
sweeter, sadder
much more intense feelings
than
to a friend.

On the plane flying home I wondered what living in Japan for a year had meant to me. I loved learning the history but hated the sustained conservatism. I loved the pockets of natural beauty but hated the crowds and pollution. I loved the details of the various arts but hated people missing the big picture. I loved all the new experiences but hated how my being an outsider kept interaction superficial.

So what was Japan to me?

It was there that I loved.

Jamaica
1986

After returning from Japan I graduated from high school in North Carolina, then obtained a nursing degree from a university in Missouri. I was still there, working remotely on a second degree in psychology from a university in Massachusetts when I started dating a medical student named Bill. He and I made an impulsive decision to book a package deal to Jamaica.

We flew into Ocho Rios and were taken to a large gated resort that had its own private beach. Soon the cruise ships started docking and our cozy beach was overrun with tourists. The resort wouldn't allow the local Jamaicans to enter the property, which I found appalling. I asked myself, "Why would I come to a country and not get to know the people who lived there? Isn't that what I was there for?" I thought that if I only wanted to meet other people like myself then I might as well stay home. I doubted that offering guests a sterile rehearsed show or an Americanized buffet meal helped anyone experience a new culture. I didn't mind relaxing on a beach but it was not my main motivation for visiting a foreign country.

The situation bothered me so much that we rented a motorcycle and headed to Negril on the opposite side of the island. Bill didn't know how to drive a motorcycle so I drove with him on the back. Negril was much more to our liking because it was smaller, had fewer tourists and we were able to come in contact with locals. We could join the crowds that would spontaneously gather to eat from small food shacks and listen to reggae music on the beach. It was just as I had imagined Jamaica. We soon met a local man who offered to let us stay in his tiny shack on the beach in exchange for letting him use our rented motorcycle. This was probably not such a smart thing to do, but we drank enough rum that the idea seemed brilliant. The man disappeared. When he finally returned two days later the bike had a smashed headlight but still ran. We were able to drive it back to Ocho Rios, where the rental place responded to my "I'm so sorry" tears by not keeping all of our deposit.

Dunn's River Falls, two miles west of Ocho Rios, was the only touristy place we visited. It was a beautiful multi-layered waterfall that flowed over a slightly inclined cliff face and was shallow enough that we could swim and play in it. Otherwise we spent most of our time on the clean beaches. While we lazed in the sun locals would wander by and offer to hack open a coconut with their machetes, revealing the fresh clear juice and white meat. The Caribbean food was delicious, with beans, rice and plantains as the staples, mixed with spicy fried chicken or lamb.

The other popular thing to do in Jamaica was scuba dive. I had gotten my open water diver certification in the San Juan Islands in Washington State where the water was cold, dark, and had strong currents. Bill had never been diving but said he felt comfortable with my showing him what to do, and the tour guides didn't ask either of us for proof of our diving certifications. The water in Jamaica was warm and the visibility was phenomenal. I was able to dive wearing just my bathing suit—no wetsuit needed. I decided there and then that I would never go diving in cold water again. Bill did great and wasn't nervous at all. Perhaps the rum was again to blame for his sense of well-being.

I learned a few things on this trip besides never wanting to do cold water diving again. This trip set the stage for my future travels and my desire to find less touristed areas and more adventurous ways to see them. I knew I wanted to really see a place, meet the local people and learn about their joys and struggles. I wanted to learn how we were different, how we were the same and how we could learn from and help each other. I wanted to not be afraid to try new things even if they might seem slightly dangerous or irresponsible. I wanted to learn to trust myself and not feel ashamed of my mistakes.

Darwin

Cape Trib

Cairns

Great Barrier Reef

Mt. Isa

Magnetic Island

Townsville

Alice Springs

Whitsundays

Airlie

Jambin

Uluru

Australia

Brisbane

Surfers

Paradise

Coober Pedy

Lamington

Forster

Gilgandra

Manly

Barossa Valley

Sydney

Adelaide

Canberra

Mt. Kosciuszko

Melbourne

Tasmania

Australia
1988–1989

While I was in Massachusetts meeting with my advisor while earning my psychology degree, I visited my friends and went river rafting up in Maine. There I met Lars the Swede, a river rafting guide. He changed my life forever by simply telling me, "If you wait for the right man, the right time or the right amount of money, you'll never go anywhere." So I sent my advisor my video dissertation for my bachelor's degree in Massachusetts along with a letter that explained, "I will be in Australia by the time you get this. I hope it's good enough."

Sarah, my Australian friend with whom I had shared the difficult year in Japan as an exchange student, had then given me a small boomerang on which she'd written, "Come with this when it returns to me." And eight years later, I finally made it! Sarah worked for a bank in Sydney, where she actually used her Japanese language skills. She had lost a lot of weight, gotten married and had a son. A lot had changed. She seemed so serious and, even though I was now 26, I just felt like cutting loose.

We spent the first few days touring the fantastic city of Sydney, then headed a few hours inland to her family's beautiful property in Gilgandra. I had arrived in time to celebrate Christmas, which seemed so strange as it was ridiculously hot. We were all in shorts and wearing the delicate paper party hats that come out of their Christmas party poppers. Their property was like a resort with a pool and a tennis court. We hiked the Pincham trail, which had signs that served as good examples of the different English language expressions and names Australians used. There were words like Burbie Camp and Mount Wambelong in the Warrumbungles. The Australians used a wonderful combination of English mixed with words that came from the Australian aboriginals, along with many words they just made up. They also had different meanings to some of the slang terms both Australians and Americans used. For example, while Sarah, her sisters, and I were hiking, Sarah exclaimed, "Whew, I'm knocked up!" She meant she was feeling tired, not pregnant.

We saw lots of kangaroos, wallabies and sheep on our hikes and it amazed me how such cute animals like those, not to mention the koalas, could live in the same place as some of the most dangerous creatures in the world. Sarah pointed out that the taipan, a local venomous snake, could leap backwards and bite you, and that I was hiking last in line and so was the most likely to be bitten. They thought this was hilarious. I did not.

I came to find out that there were even more dangerous things in the water when Sarah's family took me up the coast to the Forster and Manly beaches. They were quite beautiful on the surface, but lurking underneath were sharks and deadly jellyfish. Stringer nets had been put in the ocean to protect the swimming areas. But the day I was there attempting to surf I got stung by several blue bottle jellyfish that were small enough to get through the net. There were tents set up on the beach for people to have their stings rinsed with vinegar. Because they offered these rinses, I assumed it would be okay to go back in the water, as that's what people were doing. But when I went back in and got stung again, I had an allergic reaction. I spent my second week in Australia on steroids and taking Epsom salt baths.

Since I bothered coming all the way to Australia, and spent all that money on airfare, I thought I might as well stay the maximum time allowed and see everything I could. I bought a year-long bus pass so I could go anywhere in Australia and stop wherever I wanted.

After a lovely time with Sarah and her family and having recuperated from my stings, I headed north, up the east coast, to Surfers Paradise. I discovered that there was an unofficial competition among backpackers to see who could find the cheapest place to stay. Well, I won when I found Arnold's for $3.00 a night. Granted, there was no hot water, the place stole electricity with an extension cord from the hostel next door, and we were crammed into dorm rooms with bunk beds. But the other travelers there were great and came from all over the world. On Australia Day, which celebrates the arrival of the first British fleets, we all went to an Iron Man contest. They did a lot of sports at these festivals, but mostly they drank. We ended the night at a pub which had live music and a manager who would rally the crowd to do silly things like seeing who could balance the most spoons on their face, and a contest to see who could blow up condoms the fastest by pulling them over their heads.

I continued going north up the coast by bus, stopping at Lamington National Park, a dense rainforest that was known for the Talangai Caves. The caves had been eroded by wind to form layers of ash sediment in stripes that swirled around like a kaleidoscope. Later I took a horseback riding camping trip in the Nimbin Valley, a green, lightly forested area southwest of Brisbane. I joined four girls and a guide, who was a seriously tough woman. She was loud and bossy and physically strong and she made us feel safe out in the wilderness. We made a campfire and cooked the typical damper and billy tea. Damper is bread dough stuck on the end of a stick and put over the fire. Billy tea is made by adding tea leaves to water boiled in a tin can that is then swung around and around over your head so the leaves sink to the bottom. Beautiful, brightly feathered birds, like lorikeets and cockatoos, could be seen almost everywhere. They were the kinds of birds you might see for sale in a pet store in the States, but in Australia they were as they should be—flying wild.

When I came on this trip, I knew I only had a limited amount of money and that I'd have to find work if I could. Being an American citizen I could not legally work in Australia, as someone from the United Kingdom or Canada could. A lot of young Australians would leave to work, usually in England, for a few years before starting university and settling down. So I knew I'd have to work illegally, which really wasn't that hard and was actually rather expected within the backpacker community.

I saw a newspaper ad for a jillaroo, the female equivalent of an Australian cowboy, a jackaroo. Some ranches preferred to hire women because, although they might not be as strong as men, they were believed to be more reliable since they tended not to drink as much. When I called about the job I was careful when asked, "Can you ride?" I answered, "I have ridden but am sure you could teach me a lot." This was because in Australia, if you said you could ride they'd make sure to put you on the wildest horse to humble you. I got the job and was picked up by my new employer. He drove me to his ranch, which they called a station, in Jambin, a few hours northwest of Brisbane.

It turned out I'd landed in the middle of nowhere. The owner of the expansive cattle station walked around barefoot and called himself "King Fly of Turd Island." His meek wife stayed in the house and cooked the five meals we ate daily, starting at about four in the morning. This station was run by me and another girl, who seemed to have been informally adopted by them. On the way back to the ranch after King Fly picked me up at a bus station, we stopped in the nearby town that consisted of a store and a small motel. The lady in the store snuck me her phone number and whispered, "If you need anything you call." I wondered what that was all about, but I didn't say anything.

The work on the ranch was hard but really fun. We mustered cattle by horseback and you really didn't have to steer the horses. You just had to stay on, as they could turn on a dime and knew what they were doing. One day we had about twenty-eight bulls in a pen and our job was to put their heads into a stock so we could cut the ends of their horns off. This was so they wouldn't hurt each other when they were loaded on a truck. There were arteries running through the horns, so after the tips were trimed the blood spurted out like a fountain. They didn't act like it hurt them too much. That was my hope anyway.

King Fly wanted me to "cut" the herd into fours so the bulls could be put in small groups onto the truck. He told me that the way a bull's eye views us, we seem bigger than we are, and I believed him and felt reasonably safe until one of the bulls charged me. I quickly climbed up the rails of the pen's fence, but the bull was able to smash it down and escape to the pasture. King Fly was so mad that the bull got away that he screamed at me to go get it on foot! Needless to say, I refused.

Things started to feel a little tense around the station. King Fly frequently hit the other girl with a stick, but he hadn't hit me yet, and I began to wonder how long it would be until he did. The other girl and I had to shower outside and I could never tell if he were watching. Then he started not to allow me to call home, even though I'd call collect so it would cost him nothing.

I snuck away one night and walked a few hours with my backpack all the way to the small town I knew was nearby. I was scared to death, but I was even more afraid to stay and have to deal with King Fly. I called the lady in the local store who had offered to help and I understood then why she had given me her number. It turned out that many girls had left like I had. I didn't have any money because I hadn't been paid. She let me sleep in her motel for free, then helped me get a bus the next day. This bus wasn't covered by my pass but the driver didn't charge me after he heard my story. I headed up the coast to Townsville, a college town, where I thought I might be able to find some work.

I met a great group of students who lived together and let me stay with them. They worked as clowns for parties or they busked, juggling and riding unicycles on the streets. The only other girl, Susie, was beautiful, sweet and ethereal, and was always drawing pictures of dolphins. One night we drank a bit too much and the gang thought it would be funny, and it was, if I drove a stick shift. They drove on the left in Australia, so finding the gear shift and the blinkers was a challenge, but the hardest part was trying to go around and not straight over the roundabouts.

I decided to take a boat out to Magnetic Island, just off the coast of Townsville, to see if I could find any work there, since I didn't make a very good clown. I could ride a horse though, and I quickly found a job on the island as a horse trail guide at the Sunset Lodge. An English girl, Karyn, and I lead tourists out through sandy paths to the beach where we would take the saddles off and let the clients ride the horses in the ocean waves. It was the first time I'd ever ridden a horse in the ocean and it felt so wild and free. We would also go for rides through the hills on full moon nights. The trails were narrow and rocky, and the ride taught me to trust that my horse knew its way and could find its footing.

All three of the horse trail guides were women and we lived in a basic cement building that didn't have a door, or any glass in the windows. Inside the house we all shared a room with two bunk beds. At night, when we'd get up to go to the bathroom, huge water bugs had collected on the ground and a loud crunching sound would be heard as we'd inevitably step on them. There was a piece of rubber hose sticking out of a wall which we used for a cold shower, and that wall was always covered with bright green frogs.

For fun we hung out at a nearby bar that held cane toad races. The toads, with numbers painted on their backs, were placed in the center of a large circle. People would bet on which toad would cross the edge of the circle first. Cane toads were an introduced and invasive species that had become a blight on the environment. The government had been trying to eradicate them without much luck. So, as Australians do, they turned a bad thing into a fun thing.

The races were run by the bigwig on the island, a nasty guy who'd often pop his fake tooth out with his tongue, making a disgusting slurping noise. He would especially do this while in conversation with the "Sheilas"—a uniquely Australian slang term for women. It dawned on me that most of the Australian men I'd met were rather rough. "Sports and grog" were all they thought about, and they were proud of it. I wondered if it was their criminal heritage shining through, since the first European settlement in Australia started as an English penal colony.

My jobs so far in Australia had only provided me with room and board, and perhaps a pittance for pocket change. After a month as a horse trail guide I got myself into a nicer situation, working as a hostess and cook on the Worripa, a large catamaran sailboat. I was still only getting room, board and a pittance, but the room was so much nicer.

I'd never been a cook before but it wasn't that hard throwing "shark on the barbie" and serving drinks. As we sailed, the tourists and I rode in the boom net which was strung between the two hulls of the catamaran and gave a hilarious bouncy ride as the net heaved up and down, in and out of the water. We'd also do what was called tunnel diving, where we'd jump out into the water in front of the boat as it was moving, then grab a rope that was strung between the hulls, and with this we could ride the waves. To get back on the boat we'd let go and were sucked through the middle between the hulls, where we'd hopefully grab the ladder hanging down into the water, and climb back on board. One Swedish girl missed the ladder and we had to circle around to get her, which took a while on a sailboat. Luckily the sharks didn't get her first.

Within a few weeks, I'd hooked up with the first mate, Peter, so I was sleeping with him and living on board. Rather quickly though he lost interest and moved on to another tourist, and for some reason this really upset me. I had a habit of becoming too attached to men, even when it was obvious that it would only be a temporary involvement. A part of me would know that my feeling of despair had little to do with the man, but was instead connected to my own insecurity. To contend with these thoughts and feelings, I'd tried drugs, alcohol, sex, spirituality, and adventure. All would provide only temporary relief. I told myself all the intellectual and psychological arguments as to why I should feel better, but the despair seemed physiological, a part of my body I couldn't rid myself of. I often wondered if it were genetic, hormonal, or chemical. I didn't know the answers, but I did realize that the attraction to Magnetic Island had been broken, and it was time to move on.

I caught the ferry back to Townsville, then caught a bus south down the coast to Airlie. I met some other travelers there and we celebrated my twenty-seventh birthday. One wild night I met an attractive man who was a paraplegic in a wheelchair. We got along great and headed back toward his apartment with me sitting on his lap screaming with laughter as the wheelchair seemed to fly down hills and around street corners.

His "parts" all worked. It was just that he needed to think of the one woman he loved, an old girlfriend, in order to rise to the occasion. I didn't mind at all that he had to think of someone else. In fact, it proved to me that the greatest sexual organ is the brain. We were able to comfort each other without expectations or judgment. We seemed to feel safe together in our melancholy.

As I was walking around a marina near Airlie I saw two tall sailing ships and I said to myself, "I'd like to work on one of those!" I talked to the captain of one of them, the Coral Trekker, and he hired me as a dishwasher for their trip through the Whitsunday Islands, just off Australia's Gold Coast. I was thrilled, as I could never have afforded such a luxury on my own.

It turned out that only a few passengers had signed up, so my dishwashing job was pretty easy. After meals I'd throw a bag over the side of the boat and pull up ocean water to use to wash the dishes. I also got to help the crew, climbing the tall masts to unfurl the sails, which was a little scary but very exciting. We stopped at many of the islands to explore. One of them was called Butterfly Island and, as its name implies, it had butterflies everywhere you looked, in various sizes and colors. As we walked on the island we were surrounded by clouds of them. They would land on our heads and noses while we were floating in the island ponds.

Some days we'd go windsurfing, but I wasn't very good at it. I could catch the wind to get out, but then I'd have to paddle back to the boat. It seemed like a metaphor for my life.

After the week on the boat ended, I headed up the east coast and did some touristy things—taking a train ride through the mountains, a bus tour to see giant termite hills, a boat to search for crocodiles in the Cape Trib rainforest, and a rubber raft to paddle madly down a raging river. Scuba diving the Great Barrier Reef was a highlight. I wasn't sure I'd be able to go because a hurricane was supposed to pass by, but luckily and rather amusingly, signs were posted that said the hurricane was "canceled." The surface of the water was rough but once you got down in it, it was incredible. The best part was seeing the giant clams, bigger than me, with their surreal dark blue edges glowing, as they seemed to breathe, opening or closing ever so slightly.

The east coast of Australia had been beautiful and full of adventure, laughter and heartbreak, but now I had reached the northernmost tip of the coastline. So I thought, "There's nowhere left to go but inland to the Outback." The interior of the continent is an immense, dry, flat, inhospitable, rugged desert that just isn't "user friendly," so most Australians live along the thin coastal edges. Getting to the Outback ended up taking a couple of days of bus rides and even a bit of hitchhiking. As always, I met other travelers and among them was Paul, an Englishman who I met in Mount Isa, and we were both heading north to Darwin.

Like any monochromatic scene, in time you're able to discern subtle variances in color, shading, texture, and hue, and you start to appreciate any movement such as the melancholy roll of a lone tumbleweed or the split-second scurry of a lizard under a stone. I also began to understand why every vehicle out in the desert had "roo bars," heavy metal pipes welded to the front bumper to protect them when they inevitably smashed into kangaroos.

We finally made it to Darwin, a city where I could strongly feel Australia's criminal roots. It was like an old Wild West gun slinging town and, not surprisingly, I ended up in a brothel.

It was lunchtime and a man we met on the street invited us to eat in a rather seedy bar. Inside were maybe thirty rather rough guys, and even some businessmen, eating and milling about. There was a bit of music playing and suddenly a young girl came out onto a stage in the middle of the bar. She was dressed in a young schoolgirl's uniform and she started stripping. "My God," I thought, "it's twelve o'clock in the afternoon!" The poor girl looked so vacant I couldn't imagine what drugs she must have been on. To add to the pre-pubescent theme, she had removed any hint of hair, except for the bleached blonde curls on her head. As if watching a tennis match, my head kept alternating between the stage and the faces in the audience as I tried to absorb the bizarre scene. Gradually I realized I was one of only three women in the place-me, the stripper, and a very large mean looking butch lady. The butch lady seemed interested in me, looking me up and down and trying to smile or smirk at me. That was when my new acquaintance thankfully decided it was time for us to leave.

While we were in the north, we visited Kakadu National Park to see the Nourlangie rock, with caves that had twenty thousand year old Aboriginal art. The Aboriginal people are the original inhabitants of Australia who lived there dozens of millennia before the English came to set up their penal colony. The English slaughtered or enslaved most of them for years. I didn't get to meet many Aboriginals, and the few I'd seen on the streets appeared quite poor or intoxicated and wore dirty tattered Western clothing. They were dark skinned with wide noses and soft brown curly hair. Sometimes their eyes would be light hazel or green, and their hair would be almost blonde from the genetic mixture with their European colonizers.

I was amazed to learn that the Aboriginals were the oldest continuous living culture on the planet. I would have liked to learn more about them, their lifestyle, and beliefs, like their Dreamtime stories that they use to explain nature, the planet, and the origins of people and animals. I would have liked to have heard more of the beautiful music of the didgeridoo, a long hollowed out tree trunk they play with circular breathing—in through the nose and out the mouth without stopping—so it vibrates low and deep to your very soul. I would have liked to have learned how they started a fire and then to have sat around it and maybe tasted a roasted witchetty grub, a delicacy they dig out of tree roots. But mostly I would have liked to learn how they survive a Walkabout—the spiritual journey they take alone with only a spear, wandering in that inhospitable land, finding water, sustenance, and perhaps a little peace of mind.

Paul and I viewed Kakadu from many angles—flying over it in a tiny plane, being on a lake in an airboat gliding by enormous lilies and crocodiles, and most beautifully, sitting in a canoe on the Katherine River, where we floated by red rock faces almost as tall as the Grand Canyon. As romantic as all this was, Paul and I never became physically intimate. It just never came up, and that was nice. We amicably parted ways due to different travel plans and I headed south down the middle of Australia to see the iconic Ayers Rock.

Out of the flat desert a massive oval sandstone fluke-of-nature abruptly rose nearly three thousand feet. It was two miles long and a mile-and-a half wide and had a circumference of nearly six miles. Uluru, it's Aboriginal name, was truly one of the most spectacular natural wonders I'd ever seen. Depending on the time of day, the stone changed color by reflecting and mingling with the light of the sun, the moon, the sky, the clouds, the shadows and the immense surrounding desert. It didn't matter when or how it presented itself; it was always mesmerizing. There was a chain affixed vertically to its exterior that you could use to climb to the top, and it was not easy. I felt like a wimp when an old man and a kid carrying his bicycle zipped right past me on their way up. With much panting and groaning, I did make it to the top, not realizing at the time that climbing Ayers Rock was disrespectful. I heard later that it's considered a sacred place for the Aboriginals, and if I'd known, I would have just admired it from its base.

I think my punishment for the climb took the form of flies—thousands of the most aggressive, persistent, up your nose, in your ears, in your eyes, drive you absolutely nuts, FLIES! There were some obviously experienced Australian tourists who had proper anti-fly gear like hats with nets that come down over your face, or hats with dangling corks to scare the flies away. From this inspiration I devised my own fly-thwarting gear. First, sunglasses, kept on at all times. Second, a bandana, pulled up over nose and ears. Third, unrolled shirt sleeves on, no matter how hot. And finally, a tent, for if and when all of the above failed and I just needed to hide and privately curse the creation of flies.

I traveled throughout Australia with camping gear which included a one person North Face Tadpole tent and a Marmot sleeping bag, the top half of which zips onto a Fat City pad, a covered egg crate mattress. I like this more open style of sleeping bag because I get too hot and claustrophobic in a cocoon style bag. Plus the pad is fantastically comfortable and can be used for a quick seating option on the ground in airports, on ferries, bus stations, and other venues. My backpack was from MEI (Mountain Equipment Inc.) and opened like a suitcase rather than the top loading kind, which I never liked because you have to take everything out to see what you have. All my equipment was guaranteed for life.

Whenever I could or had to, I'd camp. Otherwise I stayed in the many backpacker facilities that were abundant in Australia. I preferred backpacker accommodations to youth hostels because they didn't make you do chores or have a curfew and they were better than hotels because they were a lot cheaper. As a solo traveler I liked to start each travel segment at a backpacker place whenever possible in order to meet other travelers from all over the world and get ideas about work opportunities or places and routes I should not miss. The beauty of sleeping in your own tent rather than in an accommodation was that you got to sleep alone rather than being crammed into a usually raucous and questionably clean dorm room. After a few nights staying in a traditional lodging I tried as best I could to meet local people who were willing to either hire me in exchange for room and board or just put me up for a while. This way I felt like I got the best of both worlds.

Leaving Uluru, near the town of Alice Springs, I traveled by bus, heading south. My goal was to get to the highest peak in Australia, Mount Kosciuszko, in the state of New South Wales. I made periodic stops, getting on and off the bus and joining local tours to hike the Coupela Gorges and visit a rock sculpture garden. About 100 miles northeast of Adelaide I stopped to do some wine tasting in the Barossa Valley, the happening scene of Australia's burgeoning wine industry. I considered stopping at Coober Pedy, an opal mining town built underground to escape the heat. Although it sounded interesting, I am quite claustrophobic so this place did not appeal to me.

After the Barossa Valley I bypassed Adelaide and Melbourne and just cut straight across, heading east by bus toward Mount Kosciuszko National Park. The bus dropped me off in a tiny town and I wasn't even sure of its name. There were no buses going the direction I wanted to go so I waited for hours in a gas station parking lot, trying to catch a ride from anyone going toward Mount Kosciuszko. Eventually a man driving a milk truck, a huge eighteen-wheeler, offered to at least get me closer. Along the way we stopped at many farms and the driver would take a long flexible tube from the truck and put it in the farm's milk vats, then turn on the truck's vacuum mechanism to suck the milk out into the big silver tank on the truck.

The roads were winding and hilly and I had no idea where we were or where we were going. We'd been driving for a few hours and it was now completely dark. Eventually he pulled over to the side of the road and told me that was as far as he could go since his milk gathering route went a different direction. I looked out the window at the dark emptiness, swallowed hard and realized I had gotten in over my head. I didn't know what to do. He suggested I camp on the side of the road and pointed out a house nearby that he thought I could go to if I felt I was in any danger. He said, "Lawts a payple drive dis rawd ta de mountin durin de daey, mate, an yo'll probly kitch a roide." I thanked him, got out of the truck and found a flat place by the side of the road to set up my tent. As I snuggled into my sleeping bag, I tried to calm myself by thinking, "Well, at least I'm too big for a dingo to carry off."

The next morning I waited and waited and waited and it reminded me of something an old boyfriend used to say, "Life is like an amusement park. You spend most of your time waiting in line." Finally one car came by with a couple in it, and thankfully they gave me a ride to the next tiny village, which turned out to be on the outskirts of Mount Kosciuszko Park.

I'd gotten in the habit of asking someone where the most popular pub was when I first arrived in town. Then I'd go there straight away, all grubby with my backpack and gear. I'd get a beer and start talking to people about the cheapest lodging, possible work, or fun things to do and see. This time my strategy resulted in finding a free place to stay. I don't remember the name of the guy, but he was going to let me room with him and that was good enough for a very exhausted me.

While at his apartment he put on a porn video, and as strange as it may sound, I'd never seen porn before. I don't think the film was anything extraordinary. It didn't seem overly violent. It was just two heterosexuals having sex, grimacing and making a lot of noise. As a psychiatric nurse, I found this video to be an interesting sociological study in human nature. It was fascinating, and as I was watching I was making comments, laughing, asking questions and analyzing this social phenomenon that I was so unfamiliar with. And then I realized this guy was totally turned on. "Crap," I thought to myself. I felt partially responsible for having let things proceed this far, so I took care of the young man, albeit not quite as enthusiastically as the woman in the video.

The next day I was able to reach what was known as the highest mountain in Australia. From a distance it didn't look that high or majestic, perhaps because there wasn't any snow on it in the summer. Luckily the ski lift was still open and I was able to ride it up 7300 feet and take in the beautiful vista. I had to admit that it was the adventure of getting there that was memorable and the peak itself was rather anti-climactic.

Then came the challenge of getting out of the park, since there were no buses available. I was able to find a ride with a short golf caddy, but once again I faced the feeling of obligation to sleep with him when he let me crash at his house. In a way, I felt sorry for him and I was also feeling defeated in my attempts to convince myself that it was alright to accept the kindness of strangers without feeling I had to give something in return. And perhaps I was lonely too, and wanted to feel, even temporarily, some comfort and connection. I had been on the road alone for a long time.

I finally made it back to Sydney where I started. I never did make it over to Perth on the west coast. I was broke and seriously needed to find some work. I had met Phillip, an eighteen year old young Australian boy, when I'd been staying in Townsville and he'd been on vacation there. He lived with his family in Sydney and they said I could stay with them. Right down the road from them was a nursing home and I was able to get hired there as a nurse's aide. Even though I was a registered nurse, the nurse's aide job was better because it didn't require a nursing license, so I didn't have to transfer mine. They were so desperate for help that they didn't ask to see a work visa. I was able to get a tax ID number from the post office, which was like a social security number, so I could get a paycheck.

I met a couple of nice girls, co-workers at the nursing home, who told me about their plan to go out with sailors. Evidently, when the American Navy ships come into port, the sailors have a phone line to use to sign the boys up for dates. My co-workers said it was the best way because if the sailors misbehaved the girls could report them. I asked the girls if I could join them without having a date and they said that I could. I mostly just wanted to quietly tag along and observe an inter-cultural custom that I'd never heard of.

It seemed like hundreds and hundreds of sailors took over the city. The Australian girls liked them a lot. Compared to the Australian men I'd met, the American boys seemed clean, polite, romantic and, for the most part, honest. At the end of the evening, when the sailors were returning to their ships, there was a long line of sad boys on one side of a fence and the girls on the other, saying tearful good-byes. I later heard that after these visits, many of the boys went AWOL and never returned to their ships.

I was having boy trouble of my own, with Phillip. His mom pulled me aside one day and said he'd been asking her if he could take me camping. She wanted me to say no if he asked me, but really, he was a strapping eighteen year old virgin and she was only trying to dam the inevitable flow of a raging river.

Phillip was a natural lover. He was sweet and gentle and downright gorgeous. He talked to me about his dream to travel and his frustration with his family wanting to hold him back. They wanted him to start university immediately. I encouraged him to travel since he didn't know what he wanted to study and I thought perhaps he could find some clues out there in the world.

At times I'd regretted becoming a nurse. I'd gotten into it for the money and not out of a passion for the field. Luckily, it turned out I liked working with problem kids and I was good at it. But I'd dreamed of being a dancer, a marine biologist or an environmental lawyer, not a nurse. I wished all young people could take the time to see some of the world, try a few things, and really be able to find something they'd love to do for perhaps the rest of their lives.

Travel opens your mind. It puts issues that might seem so important to someone, especially the young, in perspective. It makes you not take the Western culture's everyday luxuries for granted. It makes you appreciate more what you have and maybe makes you realize you don't even need the things you thought you couldn't live without. Travel brings you in contact with diversity in language, food, the arts, religion, family and environment, which in turn makes you start to question many of the things you thought you knew. And this teaches you one of the most important attributes a person can have—critical thinking, the ability to question yourself and the world around you, and hopefully, the humility to know you might be wrong. And what a relief that could be.

I also wished that all young people got to have their first sexual encounter be like Phillip's was, with someone just a little older or more experienced, with someone who genuinely likes and respects them, someone they trust and can talk to, but not necessarily someone they are in love with. In fact, it seems romantic love can complicate things and can also become rather painful. I doubted that Phillip's mother would agree with me.

90 Mile Beach

Waiariki

Auckland

Waitomo

New Zealand

Mt.Egmont

Wellington

Nelson

Mt.Cook   Christchurch

Queenstown

New Zealand
1989

I'd been in Australia nearly seven months and felt it was a good time to move on to New Zealand. I thought that I had "done Australia" and Australia had "done" me. Not only did I feel like I'd seen a lot of the highlights—in its cities, on the coast, in the jungles and in the Outback, but I also interacted quite frequently with the locals, up close and personal.

In Australia I'd met a young man from New Zealand who'd invited me to stay with him and his family if I ever made it there. When I arrived in Wellington he picked me up at the airport and brought me home. We were not romantically involved so staying at his house was quite comfortable. His family was lovely, as was everyone I met in that country.

In 1985 Ronald Reagan became U.S. president for the second time and George H. W. Bush started his term in January of 1989. I wasn't happy with the direction the country was going, especially with trickle-down economics and all the deregulation that had happened under Reagan. So I decided I wanted to immigrate to New Zealand. My field of psychiatric nursing was on their preferred occupation list, which meant they wanted and needed people like me. I filed my paperwork and was told it would be at least three months before I would know if I'd be allowed to stay.

I had a feeling I would love New Zealand. The people were fantastic, the landscape was breathtaking, and the politics seemed right up my alley. They'd banned nuclear ships from docking in their ports and I respected their bravery in standing up to the United States. One evening on the news it was reported that a Swedish couple had gone missing in the mountains while hiking and the entire citizenry seemed to rise up to find them. I thought how that would probably never happen in the U.S., as we had gotten too big and too indifferent.

After staying a couple of weeks with Mark and his family, I took a ferry to the South Island and then hopped a bus to Christchurch. The South Island was more mountainous, rugged, and less populated than the North Island. I couldn't work as a nurse because my immigration paperwork was going to take so long. So while waiting in Christchurch I applied for a job with an English couple selling encyclopedias door to door. They hired travelers because potential customers were more likely to listen to the spiel of someone with a foreign accent. There were six of us—the lead couple, three guys and me. We drove everywhere in a van, up and down both islands, staying in dorm rooms in cheap hostels along the way.

When we weren't working we did a lot of tourist activities together. One of the best was a beautiful horseback riding trip alongside the ocean at Oneroa-a-Tōhē also known as Ninety Mile Beach, in the far north of the North Island. Another great stop near the beach was the Waiariki Hot Pools, where we soaked in their dark black mud pits.

Selling encyclopedias door to door was a fantastic way for me to not only see both islands, but to also make some money along the way. The group leaders, Janni and Simon, dropped each of us off in a different neighborhood, where we'd go door to door trying to set up an appointment for them to do the full presentation. I liked going to the Maori neighborhoods best of all. The Maori are the indigenous people of New Zealand and, as in so many countries, they'd been mistreated by their English colonizers. And, as also happens so frequently, these original inhabitants had a difficult time recovering from the years of oppression and often responded by falling victim to rampant poverty and the abuse of drugs and alcohol. That may have been the reason that they were more open to the idea of owning a set of encyclopedias, as they thought it might help improve the prospects for their children. Sometimes I'd start chatting with a family and they'd offer me a beer or snack. The next thing I knew the day had happily passed, regardless of whether I made a sale.

After about a month, Chester, one of the other sellers and I hooked up and decided to head back to the South Island. We'd saved a little money and felt like we were ready to explore on our own. He said his friend on the South Island had a car that we could use. We'd been taking buses and hitchhiking, heading south from the northernmost tip of the North Island. It felt safe in this country and the people were always so helpful and friendly.

At one of our stops along the way we stayed at a small motel where there was a shared shower outside the rooms. After bathing we realized that both of us had forgotten to bring our room key—and our clothes. We were the only guests staying at the motel. The owners had gone out to dinner, so wrapped only in our towels we tried to break into the motel office to try to find an extra key to our room. We were able to get into the office but were not able to find a key. Luckily the owners had told us the name of the restaurant they were going to so we could call to tell them what had happened. When they came back and let us into our rooms we all had a really good laugh.

The main sport being played all over New Zealand was rugby. We stopped to watch a few games and it is a rough sport. I wondered why Americans were so impressed by anyone who played football when these rugby players didn't wear any protective gear at all. A Maori war dance called the *Moke* is performed at their games to intimidate the opponent by yelling, stomping and grimacing.

We also stopped to see a beautiful cave called Waitomo, where we got in a small boat and rowed inside where it was completely dark except for the millions of blue glowing strands of worms dangling from the ceilings. It was truly a magical place.

As we neared Wellington, New Zealand's capital at the southern tip of the North Island, we stopped to climb Mount Egmont. We should have reconsidered when it kept raining and raining and raining and there was no one else out there. But we didn't. What was supposed to be a short hour or so hike turned out to be an intense obstacle course that seemed to never end. We stumbled over muddy trails, slippery boulders and raging rivers whose "bridges" were made up of three metal wires—one to walk on like a tight rope and the other two for handrails. It was terrifying knowing that with any wrong move we could fall in and be washed away. And if that weren't enough to concentrate on, we had the added distraction of swarms of gnats all over us. We finally made it, in the dark, to a little three sided hut to camp for the night, and were absolutely drenched to the bones. Of course, once safe and snug in our sleeping bags we could laugh and think how wonderful the adventure of getting there actually was.

By the time we finally made it to the South Island, I'd crossed back and forth between the two islands three times—twice by ferry and once by plane. We were near Christchurch and were staying with a friend of Chester's who loaned us his old car to use to tour around. The coolest thing about being on the road on the South Island was that it seemed we were the only ones out there. We would drive for miles and miles and miles without ever passing another car or seeing another human being. And the scenery was breathtaking.

We flew in a small plane over Lake Tekapo and Glentanner Park, with sparkling rivers and massive glaciers. The highlight was when we flew right next to Mount Cook. We camped on the rocky beaches around Queenstown and took a frightening jet-boat ride where the driver would race up next to a rock face, then at the last moment turn away. As much as I liked adrenalin rushes, I opted out of the popular bungee jump from one of the many bridges. I calculated it was too quick of a rush for the price.

After touring the island and while still waiting to hear about my work visa I was low on money and knew I needed to find a job again. I left Chester in Christchurch and headed up to Nelson, in the northwest corner of the South Island, where I found a job tying boysenberries up onto wires. I loved being out in the fields first thing in the morning with the crisp air and the sun coming up glistening off the dew on the vines. I'd be alone in my row and would experience a rare state for me, a quiet mind.

I was living in my tent at a campground and sleeping in all of my clothes since it had started to turn cold. The farmer I worked for felt sorry for me and gave me potatoes, carrots and cabbage to take back to my camp. I think I prepared those three vegetables in every manner possible in my old Girl Scout cooking kit—the small round aluminum set where the outside parts are the frying pan and bowl and inside there are utensils, a plate and a green plastic cup. The handle of the frying pan has a screw so it can move around to either close the kit or cook with it. It all fit inside a little green and red checkered bag with a long strap to carry over your shoulder. I'd had that thing nearly twenty years. I remembered with a sigh how I'd gotten kicked out of the scouts for sneaking over to the boys camp when I was ten.

As beautiful as New Zealand was, I was leading a cold and hungry life. I was tired, too, of waiting for the government to process my paperwork. The final blow that caused me to withdraw my immigration papers was when I found out that women had no reproductive rights there. I felt very strongly that women should have the right to make their own decisions about their bodies, and whether or not they felt ready to be a parent. Rather than return home though, I decided to continue my travels by flying to Hawaii.

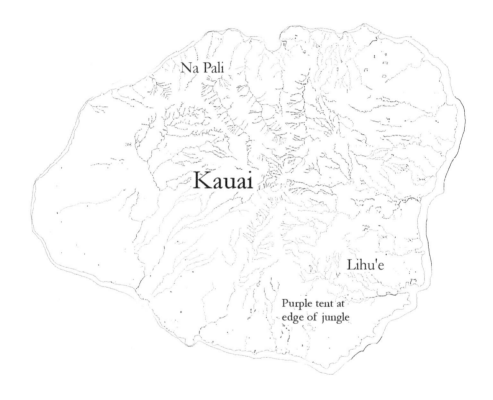

Na Pali

Kauai

Lihu'e

Purple tent at
edge of jungle

Kauai
1989

After landing in Hawaii my address for the next month or so was "purple tent at edge of jungle" on the island of Kauai. I was working in the middle of nowhere as an aide at a nursing home with all male patients. They charged rent for employee housing but they were willing to let me set up camp on the grounds for free. Since I'd gotten quite used to living in it, my tent felt like home. It amused me that North Face, the company that made my little purple tent, put a label inside that said, "not to be used as a permanent residence." Oops!

My nurse's aide job was to change diapers and sheets. I was the only staff on night shift and I'd hang out on the couch watching television and the geckos. I especially liked the squeaking big-eyed lizards which scurried around the walls and ceilings. I'd set my alarm in case I dozed off so that every hour I could make rounds to see if anyone had wet the bed or needed anything. The nursing home was simple, a bit run down, and none of the linens matched, but it was clean and cozy.

When I wasn't working I would go explore the island on the old beat-up bicycle the nursing home had loaned me. Kauai was a verdant paradise that had very few roads and no real mass transit. Luckily two of my co-workers were willing to drive me to sites that were too far for me to ride my bike to. One of those places was the Na Pali coast, where they filmed King Kong. With the lush dense green jungle I could see why the director envisioned the place with a giant gorilla in it.

One day I received a postcard from my grandmother telling me that my half-sister's half-sister lived in Kauai. It also included her phone number. My half-sister and I share the same mother. And she shares the same father with her half-sister, so we are not actually blood relatives. I called the number and left her a message briefly explaining our odd circumstance.

What I was beginning to appreciate about travel was how dramatically things could change in just one day. I practiced trying not to judge an experience as good or bad because you just never knew. Sometimes the best things came out of difficult situations and vice versa. My half-sister's half-sister called and said she'd pick me up, which she did, in one of her three Mercedes. It turned out that she and her husband had worked their way up to own a large chain of steakhouses on the East Coast of the U.S. mainland. They had retired in Kauai and lived in a large beautiful house.

Overnight my life changed from living in a tent to staying in a guest house that was nicer than any I'd ever called home.

Alaska
1989

I didn't want to overstay my welcome, so after a couple of weeks with my new found family I decided to continue my travels by flying to Anchorage, Alaska. I didn't really care for big cities, not that Anchorage was that big, but I preferred small towns or to be out in nature, and Alaska certainly had plenty of nature. I caught a bus heading south to Skagway, the northernmost town on the Inside Passage. Most towns along the passage could only be reached by boat or plane, but Skagway could be reached by bus. It was a long drive however that looped inland and passed through the Yukon in Canada.

Right outside Anchorage we passed close to the mountain that native Americans call Denali and the U.S. government calls Mount McKinley. I was fortunate to catch a glimpse of it during a break in the clouds. Alaska felt like the "final frontier," with wide open spaces, rugged mountains, caribou, bear, and eagles perched in trees by winding rivers. It was September and the bus driver said that this would be his last trip, as the freeze was heading down from the north. After a long day of driving we stopped to stay the night at Ida's Motel and Café in Beaver Creek, at the border crossing into the Yukon.

The bus headed out to Skagway early in the morning and when we arrived I fell in love with the Gold Rush town. The main road was lined with old wooden shops, restaurants, and bars. Every window held a glimpse into the past and a tribute to the idiosyncrasies of a brief but intense period of American history. The different names used to describe this exciting time were Klondike-Yukon Gold Rush, Alaska Gold Rush, Alaska-Yukon Gold Rush and finally The Last Great Gold Rush. The huge influx of prospectors and the rapid construction of communities to accommodate them all occurred in three short years between 1896 and 1899. What was most noticeable about these towns was what lay all around them—the grandeur of the mountains, trees, ocean, and sky—all which dwarfed the small speck of humanity.

In Skagway I communed with nature by hiking to Lower and Upper Dewey Lake. The hike wasn't difficult and I did it with two men I'd met at the hotel, "Papa Ecky" and "The Pope." "Ecky" was older and from Germany and "Pope" was in his thirties and from Switzerland. They had these nicknames because people like me couldn't pronounce their real names. As we hiked I thought of the expression, "You don't have to outrun a bear, just your hiking companions." We weren't lucky enough to see any bears but we did see spectacular scenery and lakes so pristine the clouds reflected in them looked as if they were on the ground.

My new found friends and I all purchased Alaska Marine Highway ferry passes to travel along the Inside Passage for $100 each. With the pass you could get off and on whenever you liked as you headed south toward Bellingham, Washington. Some people chose to stay in berths on the ferries but I preferred the cheaper and much better option of setting my tent up on the deck. This was where all the young travelers hung out and therefore where all the fun and action was happening. We all shared our stories and snacks, played guitar and cards, and kicked around a hacky sack—a small colorful bean bag popular with the hippie crowd—and all the while the most spectacular scenery drifted by and the whiskey flowed.

After Skagway the next stop was Juneau, the capital of Alaska. It seemed odd that the capital was way out here on the passage, only accessible by water or air, and nowhere near as large as Anchorage or Fairbanks. Here the main thing to do was visit and hike the Mendenhall glacier. Alaska is home to many incredible natural phenomena but the invisibly flowing rivers of ice that you can actually walk on are among the most spectacular.

I continued south on the ferry to Sitka, which turned out to be my favorite stop, perhaps because it was the most funky of the towns I'd seen, or more likely, because I didn't have to pay for a drink or a meal the entire time I was there. When I first arrived I walked into a dark hole-in-the-wall establishment which had a bear wearing a hat and a fish with antlers hanging over the bar, and I was immediately surrounded by at least six men. Back then the ratio of men to women in Alaska was about ten to one. The ladies there had a saying, "The odds are good, but the goods are odd." And that was the truth.

The men sitting around me in a booth were all from different backgrounds. One young man described himself as an "Aleut mix." The Aleuts were the indigenous people from a group of nearby Alaskan islands. But the "mix" part was what caused him problems and resulted in his being harassed and mistreated.

I was having a fine time when in walked Daryl, a "Marlboro Man," who maneuvered his way through the other men so he could stand right in front of me. His "right out of a movie" look started with an Indiana Jones hat covering long brown hair tied back in a ponytail and a forehead with one protruding vein. He wore a tattered flannel cowboy shirt with the sleeves rolled up which revealed a few tattoos I couldn't quite make out. A thick leather belt around sturdy hips looped through faded jeans that flowed down to abruptly tuck into rubber knee-high fishing boots. He reached toward his chest through a slightly opened shirt and pulled out a small leather talisman bag that hung around his neck. He spilled its contents out into his palm, then with rough calloused hands he gently pushed through the various small objects and told me the stories of where each had come from and why each was so special. The precious objects included a feather, a fish bone, and a shiny stone. He'd managed to get a seat next to me by now and as he spoke he'd look down at his hand then up to my eyes. It felt as though he was looking deep into my soul. As my attention was focused intently on Daryl, the rest of the men faded away into the background and the noisy bar grew quiet except for his deep gentle voice. We both knew in that instant that we'd be going home together.

Suffice it to say that this wild man did not disappoint. He was athletic, earthy, and animalistic. When things quieted down I made a request I'd often make, "Tell me a story." I'd gotten in the habit of asking this in the aftermath of passionate sex. This crazy man gently stroked my hair and proceeded to tell the story of how we met and what had happened between us. No one had ever done that before. And while my salty tears mixed softly with his skin, I knew he understood what I had asked.

The next day Daryl took me in his small fishing boat to a few of his special secret places. It was sweet, and heavy, and sentimental, seemingly for both of us, as we sensed we'd never see each other again despite making the obligatory promises to do so.

I left Daryl and continued by ferry down the Inside Passage, with stops at Ketchikan, Victoria on Vancouver Island, Canada, then finally Bellingham, Washington. I continued to superficially interact with the other travelers and tourists but I was starting to feel disconnected from the outside world and even a little from myself. It was as if I were a character in a story I was reading rather than the participant of my own nearly year-long journey. Like the trees in the crisp autumn air blowing down from the north, I felt the need to drop my leaves, pull in, and hibernate.

I was caught in an odd painful pull of being tired, oh so tired, and wanting to go home, while simultaneously consumed by the fear that if I did, I would get stuck there and never ever leave again. So I dragged out making any decision and instead hitched a ride with a guy I'd met on the ferry. He drove me from Bellingham to Idaho so I could see the changing leaves, soak naked in a secluded natural hot spring, and make love on the hood of a car on the side of a road while the sun set in all its red blazing glory.

Europe
1990–1991

A lengthy bus ride got me from Idaho to Missouri, where I just fell back into my old life of working as a psychiatric nurse. I was saving money to travel again, but I soon had to break up the monotony of my job in Missouri by going to North Carolina to work. I'd met a man while I was in Kauai and we'd stayed in touch. While I was working in Raleigh I lived with him and his two year old daughter. I helped him with parenting and became even more certain than ever before that being married with children was not the path for me.

During my free time I took dance classes in Raleigh with a man named Chuck Davis, the founder of a traveling show called Dance Africa. Throughout the years I had danced many different styles, but African had become my favorite. This style of dance had movements down towards the ground instead of up and away from it like ballet. It seemed to connect directly to the soul, and being overly concerned with counting the steps of the choreography was discouraged. Chuck would tell us, "Feel the movement," and let it flow from one step to the next.

After a few months of working I felt I had enough money to leave on another long trip, starting in Europe, to visit all the friends I'd made on my travels in Australia and New Zealand. After Europe I planned to continue to Morocco, Israel, Egypt, Kenya, Rwanda, India, Nepal, Thailand, Singapore, the Philippines, and then home. I prepared pages and pages of notes with all the prices of the planes, trains, ferries, and even motorcycles needed, and where and when to get visas or the next round of shots. I had lists of places to stay, including working on a kibbutz in Israel, which is a shared agricultural community. I probably didn't have enough money for this trip but the most expensive part was always the airfare and I at least had that. I hoped to stay with friends or in budget lodgings, travel mostly overland, and perhaps find a little work along the way. I was excited about getting out into the world again.

I flew to London and stayed with my friend Karyn, who I'd worked with as a horse trail guide in Australia. Her job was to deliver packages by motorcycle, so I would ride on the back. It was an exciting way to tour the city, seeing all the places I'd read about like Big Ben, Trafalgar Square, and Buckingham Palace with the changing of the guards, all while weaving in and out of the mad rush of traffic.

Karyn and I drove in her car to the southwest of England. We stopped by Stonehenge on the way, a surreal place that made us wonder if the earth had perhaps been visited by aliens. Our car got stuck in the mud of the flat marshy moors and brought up our fear of werewolves. We were lucky that a couple of hairy hippies helped us out. They reminded us of gnomes. We stayed in Karyn's father's small white stucco thatched roof cottage, which hadn't a single square corner. Just being there made us feel like hobbits. I could see why so many wonderfully magical stories had come out of England.

I said, "Cheerio" to Karyn and took a bus north to Middleborough to see Chester, the man I'd worked and traveled with in New Zealand. His family took me up the northeast coast to Whitby, an area known as Dracula country, as it was featured in Bram Stoker's novel. Everything was so old and with the foggy damp weather it was easy to fantasize that there were vampires around every corner. Chester and I drove up to Scotland to camp for old times' sake and I was pretty sure we saw the fabled lake serpent, the Loch Ness Monster. We certainly did see plenty of the long-haired Highland cows that looked like yaks and herds of sheep and goats grazing on the misty green rolling hills. It looked just like the postcards I'd seen. Inverness, one of the main cities in the Scottish highlands, was lovely, with narrow cobbled streets and the occasional local still wearing a kilt or practicing on a bagpipe.

From England I caught a ferry to Denmark to meet up with a young woman I'd met in Australia. She drove me around in her black Mini Cooper all the way to Grenen, where the Baltic and North Seas come together. When their differently colored waters met it looked like the Chinese yin-yang symbol. From Copenhagen I took a ferry to Sweden and was on a train to Stockholm when I met a man who lived in Norrköping. When I got off the train with him there I felt like I was walking through the pages of a fashion magazine. I did not see a single unattractive person. My new friend followed through on his promise to take me on a small sailboat for an afternoon over to a nearby Finnish island and back.

After my brief visit in Norrköping I continued by train to Stockholm. There my story seemed to come full circle, as I was able to again see the man who'd first infected me with the travel bug, Lars, the river raft guide I'd met in Maine. It was fantastic to see him again and to thank him in person for having inspired me to start the adventure not *of* a lifetime, but hopefully *for* a lifetime.

My whirlwind European catch-up-with-friends tour continued with my taking a ferry to Germany. I'd been at a festival in southern Sweden with another girlfriend I'd met in Australia. After drinking a bit too much I almost missed the train going to the coastal ferry port. At the port the train actually rolled onto tracks on the ferry and the passengers were allowed to leave the train and take advantage of the restaurants and showers available on the ferry—so I did.

When we were approaching Germany I got back on what I thought was my train and went to what I thought was my seat, but none of my stuff was there. I then saw another train on the ferry so I ran to it and still couldn't find my luggage. I continued running up and down the aisles of both trains searching while the other passengers cheered me on. I was starting to panic when a conductor stopped me and calmly explained that there actually weren't two trains. The one train had just been split into two parts in order for it to fit on the ferry. He reassured me we would find my train car and my luggage. It turned out that when I'd originally boarded the train I'd read my ticket wrong and had not been sitting in my assigned seat. When I finally sobered up, read my ticket, and returned to the train, I went to the right seat but my belongings were still on the other seat I'd chosen in a drunken stupor. I always kept my essential documents and money on my person so that even if I lost my backpack I could carry on. I felt like a total idiot but eventually I found all my things and all I lost was my pride.

In Germany I tried to find "Papa Ecky" who I'd met in Alaska, but he was out of the country at the time. I hopped back on the train and continued on to Aarau, Switzerland, where I hoped to visit "The Pope," the other man I'd met in Alaska. That was my nickname for him since I couldn't pronounce his real name, which did have some P's and O's in it. In Aarau I couldn't find the *Lonely Planet* guidebook's recommended hostel. An annoyingly helpful young man, who only spoke French, followed me around trying to help me find a place to stay, which he ultimately did. It was a disappointing stop except for the delicious food and the beautiful sixteenth century paintings underneath the eaves of the buildings. I was never able to find "The Pope."

The train ride through the Swiss Alps was spectacular and Geneva was beautiful, but Nyon was just plain weird. I went there because I'd worked as a psychiatric nurse for a corporation back home that happened to have a hospital in Nyon. The place was like a palace and finally all the corruption I had witnessed while working for them made sense. I concluded that this corporation was hiding all their money there and keeping the hospital as a cover, or at least as a nice vacation spot for the administrators. But even if they were corrupt, I thought maybe I could be hired in some capacity there—something simple like a janitor, since I didn't speak French. I met with the Director of Nursing who suggested that I apply instead for an *au pair* position, which is like a nanny, taking care of a family's children. She said she knew a family who might be able to use me and she'd let me know something in a few weeks.

While I was waiting I decided to head south to Mallorca, one of Spain's Balearic Islands in the Mediterranean Sea. "Not a rough way to pass the time," I thought. Friends of my family in Missouri owned a house in Mallorca and they'd told me that I could stay there if I passed through Spain. They were not going to be there but said that the housekeeper would let me in. On the ferry from Barcelona to Mallorca I met an Irish girl, Anya, and I invited her stay with me there. It was dark when we arrived in the island's capital, Palma de Mallorca, and neither of us spoke Spanish.

We were able to catch a taxi to the house, which we found apparently uninhabited and completely dark. We rang the doorbell over and over again but there was no answer. I decided I'd try to get in through an unlocked window. I don't know where I got these stupid ideas or, better yet, why I acted on them. But there I was with my head inside the house, with my chest on the sill and my legs dangling off the ground when a tiny fuzzy white dog started barking and the lights came on.

Suddenly I was face to face with a small toothless man staring at me aghast and yelling in Spanish all sorts of things I couldn't understand. He came out of the house in his bathrobe, screaming and waving his arms around. We tried to explain why we were there, with me speaking in English and Anya trying to communicate with the little bit of French she knew. When the toothless housekeeper heard the French, he went to get a neighbor who also spoke French. Finally, between Anya's few French words, the neighbor translating it to Spanish, and my gesticulating and repeating our family friend's name, he let us stay.

This little man was my first introduction to the Spanish flirt. In fact, he was so handsy that he could cop a feel before you could yell, "*¡Que pasa!*" The house was pretty but nothing worked in it and it was far from the city center and the beaches. Anya and I wanted just to catch the next ferry back to Barcelona only to discover that it didn't run every day. We decided to spend the night at a backpacker's hostel in Arenal, a beach resort south of Palma, and drown our sorrows in the readily available delicious cheap Spanish wine.

As we wandered around Arenal some cute young boys were in front of a disco yelling in English, "Forget the rest, Kiss is the best!" Kiss was the name of the disco and had nothing to do with the band. The boys said if we came back that night they would be giving away free T-shirts. I'd been traveling a while and knew I needed some fresh, clean, free clothes, so I was determined to come back.

Life on this Spanish resort island was lived on a completely different schedule than I was used to. People got up and started their day around eight or nine, then by noon there was the obligatory two hour siesta to eat and nap. Then businesses opened again in the early evening and people went back to work for a few more hours. Around this time the grandparents and children gathered in the square to walk, visit, play cards, drink beer or espresso, and snack on tapas—small plates of various things like fried peppers, mushrooms, or calamari. As the older and younger crowd headed home, the college and middle-aged worker crowd prepared for the next phase of the evening—eating dinner at about ten, then going dancing at the discos after that.

The discos stayed open until around four, and some even opened up after those closed for all the employees of the earlier discos. The next day it started all over again. I wasn't a disco person but Kiss was fun enough and I danced with a couple of American doctors and flirted with the bartender, who could balance bottles on his nose. As the night was winding down I asked myself, "What should I do on my last night in Mallorca? Should I go to a hotel with a boring white American doctor or go home with a sexy funny wild Spanish bartender?" The answer seemed clear to me.

The bartender, Federico Juan Carlos Pura Sanchez, Rico for short, took me to breakfast then home to his mother's house. She worked nights cleaning office buildings. Rico and I had a great time and ended up spending the next day together at the beach. Anya left on the ferry without me. Although I didn't speak Spanish and Rico didn't speak much English, we certainly communicated well with body language. Rico was about five feet eight inches tall, with caramel colored skin, black curly hair, an impish sparkle in his dark brown eyes, and big thick eyebrows that almost met in the middle over his slightly crooked nose. He wore tight cut off jean shorts that emphasized the thick muscular thighs he got from playing soccer. His feet were delicate and shapely and were nicely shown off in the typical brown leather Mallorcan sandals. He had a hairy chest and just a slight paunch. Rico was always in motion. He chewed his fingernails when his arms weren't moving and he bounced his leg when talking loudly and laughing.

The days began to run into each other and I never seemed to make it onto the ferry. Rico and I set up house with just a mattress on the roof of the disco overlooking the Mediterranean. On his days off as a bartender we toured the beautiful island, finding private crystal clear coves or exploring tiny villages. One of these villages was Deià, situated at the top of a serpentine stone roadway, and where the houses perched precariously on the cliff sides. The author George Sand and the composer Chopin had lived together in this solemn and peaceful area.

Another highlight of this island was the cathedral in Palma designed by Gaudí. He was able to create massive structures with organic designs inspired by nature. I hoped one day to see more of his work in Barcelona.

Some days we'd head out to sightsee but end up stopping along the way at a village bar. We'd end up visiting with the locals and never make it any further. I liked this culture because they didn't insist on cleaning up all the "work" you'd done in a day—the pile of cans, bottles, overflowing ashtrays, bread and sausage crumbs, all stayed on the table, giving you a sense of accomplishment.

Rico was known around the island for being somewhat of a soccer star. He was also impulsive, spontaneous, and just plain charming. Everyone seemed to know and love him. One day he had just gotten paid so we went out to see a Flamenco dance show at a small club nearby. I'd never seen this style of dance before and I instantly loved it. Flamenco and Sevillanas are complicated, passionate, and rhythmic styles of dance with a lot of stomping and clapping. At one point in the show a little old man came limping slowly out on stage, and with a pained grimace opened his mouth and started singing. I couldn't understand a word he said, but I could feel the emotion and started crying. Rico bought champagne for everyone in the bar, spending his entire paycheck in one go. We stayed through the night, and after the customers left the band and dancers all gathered around the table with us, talking, laughing, and bursting into song. I fell in love that night, with Spain.

Rico and I moved from the roof of the disco to a small apartment in Arenal. The disco life was wearing us down with its exhausting schedule. Rico would leave for work at 10 p.m. and I'd continue sleeping. I'd set the alarm for 4 a.m. to go meet him at the disco, then we'd party all morning, eat breakfast, go to the beach, then back home to sleep a bit before it all started again.

Eventually Rico quit working at the disco and we moved into my family friend's house I'd first stayed in when I initially arrived in Mallorca. The plumbing still wasn't working so we'd shower on the balcony with a hose, pee into a vase and poop into a plastic trash bag. There was also no electricity so we'd have to cook outside over a fire. The handsy housekeeper seemed thrilled to have the company. The place was free and it was home.

Rico had gotten a job making neon signs and I'd given up waiting for the au pair position in Nyon to come through. Instead I'd been hired to work at a nursing home for English expatriates in Mallorca. My plans to travel next to the Middle East were now foiled, as the Gulf War had started in Kuwait, Israel was fighting again with Palestine, and it had worsening tensions with Egypt. Even the Philippines had become a mess and the U.S. was pulling out its Peace Corps workers. With most of the places I'd planned to go suddenly immersed in war and chaos, I figured I might as well just hunker down, work in Mallorca, save some money, and wait for things to calm down.

My job at the nursing home wasn't supposed to start for a couple of months and I still had some time left on my Eurail Pass. Andrea, an Argentinian woman who worked at the disco and who was a friend of Rico's, decided to go with me on a short trip. We briefly stopped in Vienna to visit a friend and have lunch along the Danube.

Andrea and I then headed south to Venice, which I believe to be one of the most beautiful cities in the world. It was such a romantic place I only wished Rico were there with me instead of Andrea. Venice was magical with the muted colors of the old stone buildings that seemed to be floating on the maze of canals. The intricately carved facades and wrought iron work, the soft light from street lamps reflecting on the narrow cobbled streets and alleys, the arched bridges gracefully bending over the water as gondolas glided by, poled by men with iconic striped shirts and ribboned straw hats—I loved it all. I'd also love to rave about the food, but as odd as it may seem, we ate one of the worst pizzas I'd ever had. Traveling on a budget in Venice limited our food choices.

From Venice we took a train to Brindisi in southeastern Italy to catch a ferry to Greece. I thought it would be cool to get a haircut in Italy, so right before we left I did. The small shopkeepers were so excited to have me there that all the ladies were jabbering and giving their input to the process, which ended up with some drastically lopped off bangs. On the twenty-two hour long ferry ride we met a young Australian named Justin. It was going to be his twenty-sixth birthday when we got to Greece so we all planned to celebrate together.

When we arrived in Patras, on the west coast of Greece, it was dark. We were told that most of the country's workers were on strike, so we weren't too surprised when our run down hotel had no water or electricity. But we had a birthday to celebrate, so we wouldn't let that stop us. I was getting pretty good at miming what I needed. By pulling out my pockets to say I had no money, and putting my hand to my mouth to say I wanted to eat, we were directed to a cheap restaurant, the desired outcome of my miming. Trying to get there in the dark was a challenge though because the streets seemed like a post-apocalyptic war zone, with potholes, mounds of rocks, and other hidden obstacles. We did finally make it to George's place, and it was indeed a find. His name wasn't really George of course, but that name was what we could all pronounce. His cozy restaurant was lit up with candles, had good food, and a happy vibe. He kept bringing over dishes for us to try, and every time he opened a bottle of beer he'd fling the bottle cap out the back door. At that moment I was thankful there was no electricity so I couldn't see the details, just the nice warm glow of new friends around the candle's flame.

Since everything, and I mean everything, was on strike, there were no buses or trains to Athens. So our small group decided to hire a taxi to take us there. It was a bit pricey, but we didn't have much choice. In Athens I bought one of those postcards that was solid black and the joke read, "The Parthenon at night", except that, for me, it wasn't a joke. I was afraid the airlines would go on strike next, so I camped on the lawn at the airport with hundreds of other people waiting to get on a plane. Andrea and I had now given up on seeing Greece and were going back to Mallorca.

Upon my return Rico and I just picked up where we'd left off. I was to start work in Mallorca soon and still had hopes of someday continuing my world tour, maybe even with Rico. Unfortunately we'd started arguing more and I had started asking myself if I should leave the relationship and, if so, how? And then I got a call telling me that my grandmother was in the hospital with pneumonia and lung cancer. I immediately flew home to Missouri to be with her.

I'd been overly dependent on my grandmother throughout my life. I thought of her more as a mother and she was one of the few voices of reason I had in my family. I used to write poetry to her and beg her to never die before me. And I used to have nightmares that she did.

Over the next seven months my grandmother went in and out of the hospital. Every time she was out and getting better I'd fly back to Spain to see Rico. My family thought I'd lost my mind and would say, "You only want him because he has an accent!" I couldn't verbalize it at the time, but I was so distraught over my grandmother's illness, at the thought of losing the one stable person in my life, that I needed a dramatic distraction from it all. And that, without a doubt, was Rico.

The first time I went back he wasn't there to pick me up at the airport. It took me two days to find him and when I did he cried and begged my forgiveness. He explained that he'd not come to the airport because he thought it could never work between us—that it was just too complicated. But after much discussion, and against all odds, we decided we were going to try to stay together. We packed a small bag, which held all his worldly possessions, and took the ferry to Barcelona. There the U.S. consulate refused to give him a tourist visa to come to the U.S. because he couldn't show enough assets to convince them he'd ever return to Spain. We were frantic, wanting to be together, but also knowing that I was going to have to be in the U.S. to take care of my grandmother. We asked the consular staff what our alternatives were and they suggested a fiancé visa. And that was how Rico "proposed."

We returned to Mallorca and started the mountain of paperwork needed to get the visa. While all of this was going on, I'd fly home to Missouri to check on my grandmother. Every time I flew to Spain or home via New York City and got in a cab with a driver from say, Pakistan, I'd inquire, "How the hell did you get a visa?"—with no disrespect, just sincere curiosity and utter amazement.

After seven months and six trips to and from Spain, I was finally able to bring Rico into the U.S. I was twenty-nine and he was twenty-eight. I can't even say if we were in love with each other or if we had just fallen in love with the challenge. What I can say is that he was the most expensive souvenir I ever brought home.

South America
1994

On Friday, the 13th of September 1991, Rico and I were married in Columbia, Missouri. The ceremony was held in a dance studio with everyone in Latin style costumes. A few family and friends were there, along with some of the dance studio students that we'd been taking classes with. Poor Rico danced a waltz with me in front of all those strangers, and recited his vows in a language he barely understood.

Rico fed and bathed my grandmother as she slowly died of lung cancer, and I went to work as a nurse to support us. He once declared, "I wouldn't even do this for my own mother!" I know it was hard for him. My grandmother passed away in May 1992.

In 1993 we lost our car in a flood and with the insurance money we bought a restaurant. This had been Rico's lifelong dream. We called it Café Olé, and for the small town of Columbia, Missouri a Spanish restaurant was an enigma. People would come in wondering where the tacos were and why the coffee cups were so small. Instead we were serving paella, tapas, and sangria. We put on shows with visiting flamenco dance troupes. We taught customers salsa and merengue dancing and were some of the first people in the country doing the Macarena. It was a unique place.

Prior to opening the restaurant I begged Rico to travel with me for a few years, promising him I'd then be able to settle down happily. But we went ahead with the restaurant instead. The following year I finally convinced Rico to leave the restaurant in the care of our business partners and go to South America with me for seven weeks. To some that sounded like a long time, but I was used to traveling for months at a time, so this seemed like nothing. Still, I was so happy to be going at all.

We flew into Manaus on the Amazon River, in northern Brazil. The accommodation was a bit rough and the town a little seedy. The first thing we did was to organize passage on a boat that started in Manaus and ended in Brazil's far east coastal town, Belém. We then bought two colorfully woven cotton hammocks to use to sleep on the boat. These boats were used as local transport and held two hundred people. The men were supposed to sleep on one side and the women on the other. But because Rico and I were a foreign couple, we were allowed to stay together on the men's side. They grouped us with the only other foreigners, four Argentinians and three Israelis. The hammocks were strewn in long rows up and down the inside of the boat. They were surprisingly comfortable and when you were lying down in them, the sides would come up, providing a bit of privacy while you slept.

Meal times were totally chaotic. There was one picnic table that seated ten, so two hundred people gathered around it and waited while ten people shoveled food into their mouths. The ten then passed the plates back to the head of the table for dunking in what I was sure was river water. The plates were then refilled and slung down the table for the next group of ten. The food was unidentifiable—some sort of meat and grain, sprinkled with the ever present farina. There were only three toilets on board, but after everyone ate what we did, it was evident that we needed more. Since the boat was the local transport, it made many stops for people to get off and on. At each stop there were crowds of vendors selling food and drinks, which was lucky for us, as this way we could at least find some fruit.

We really enjoyed meeting the people on the boat. Mostly we interacted with the Argentinians since they spoke Spanish. The Portuguese dialect spoken in the north of Brazil was extremely difficult for us to understand. We spent most of our time up on the top deck trying to get a glimpse of the rainforest, but since the Amazon river was so wide in that part, we really couldn't see much.

Every now and then we'd see some shacks on the riverbanks, usually built on stilts. They rarely had doors, but many did have a satellite dish and we could see the glow of the TV inside. As we neared Belém the river narrowed and the people from the villages along the banks would paddle out in dugout canoes to collect bags of gifts the boat passengers tossed overboard to them.

After four days on the Amazon river, the boat finally reached the Atlantic ocean in Belém. Once there, the first and the most important thing to do was to find some caipirinhas. This is the typical Brazilian drink made from a sugar cane liquor called cachaça, with a touch of sugar and lime juice.

After Belém our next stop was to be Jericoacoara, mentioned briefly in the *Lonely Planet* guidebook as, "a beautiful place to go." We had read that the best way to get there was to head south past Jericoacoara and then catch local transport back north since there were no roads going there directly. I never like to backtrack so I wanted to try to get there from the north, despite the warnings. I soon realized we should have followed the directions.

From Belém we started by catching a local bus heading south to São Luis. We arrived there late at night and soon caught another local bus in order to continue driving south toward Parnaíba. The roads were horrendous, with potholes big enough to swallow us. We tried to sit in the front for a better view but that was sometimes just too frightening. After riding all night long, we caught yet another bus in Parnaíba going to Camocim.

Once in Camocim we wandered around the village trying to find the next bus we were supposed to catch. We found it with its hood up and swarming with mechanics in the process of getting repaired. The workers loaded us on while waving and nodding to reassure us that this was indeed the bus we were supposed to take. We sat on hard metal seats, shooing flies away and waiting for it to depart. Little by little people boarded, weighed down by enormous bundles, boxes and even a chicken or two. Finally the bus started its engine and pulled out onto the road, only to stop every few blocks to pick someone up. As we started to leave the village, we realized we were going back the way we came.

Soon we stopped in some teeny tiny town and the driver got off the bus and we saw him just standing around talking to some locals. By now Rico and I were a little crazy from lack of sleep and the total confusion about where we were, so Rico got off and started screaming at the driver. While this was happening I went to talk to some taxi drivers nearby, trying to find someone to take us to Jericoacoara. All the taxis refused, for any amount of money. Our driver finally found a man who spoke some Spanish and by now we seemed to have the entire town gathered around to witness the spectacle. The man explained that this was the rainy season when the roads washed out and routes changed so frequently that only this particular bus driver knew the way to Jericoacoara. We accepted this with a deep sigh, got back on the bus, then realized in the fray that we'd lost our seats. So now, after having not slept in nearly forty eight hours, we found ourselves standing.

The nightmare went on and on and on. The roads, if you could call them that, were made of sand, and indeed were often washed out to the point that the entire busload of passengers would have to get off and push the bus out of a ditch. At times the bus would break down and the driver would crawl underneath with a piece of wire, tape or gum. At one point I felt so overwhelmed I looked at Rico and was about to start crying. With furrowed brow and gritted teeth, he intensely whispered, "Don't you dare!"

We were sure that there was a bus-wide conspiracy to kidnap, rob and kill us. I kept thinking of the video camera that Rico had convinced me to bring that, if sold, could probably feed all these people for a year. We couldn't understand anything anyone said, and everyone seemed to be glaring at us suspiciously. We were so unreasonably paranoid that we briefly considered using our ridiculously small Swiss army knives to demand the driver take us directly to Jericoacoara. At this point we were starting to think it didn't even exist. Finally we stopped at just a slightly wider sandy part of the road, where the driver told us to get off. We looked incredulously at him and asked, "Jericoacoara?" He nodded yes.

There was nothing there but two beat up trucks. We asked one of the truck drivers, "Jericoacoara?" and he nodded affirmatively. We climbed in the bed of his truck expecting to get a ride into town. Soon many people from the bus joined us and we all just sat there, and sat there, and sat there. Finally Rico went over to the other truck with its bed full of propane tanks and asked if the driver were going to Jericoacoara. But this time Rico added the question, "NOW?" That man said yes, so we moved to that truck and everyone from the first truck followed us. This driver started his engine and pulled away with at least six of us piled in the back along with the propane tanks, various boxes, bags and belongings, and our two huge backpacks.

The sun was starting to set and we were heading off into what appeared to be sand dunes, along absolutely no road whatsoever. Now and then we'd catch a glimpse in the headlights of glowing eyes that revealed themselves to be those of donkeys. Then, up on the horizon, I saw the shadow of a carcass hanging from a tree. It was the body of a cow. We pulled up right beside it and were told that this was Jericoacoara.

Suddenly we were bombarded with people trying to get us to stay in their accommodation, but we just kept repeating the name of the pousada, what they call a hostel, where we wanted to stay. After wandering dark sandy streets teeming with pigs and chickens we reached our destination and were greeted by a blonde angel of a man saying, "Welcome, my name is Urs."

Urs was Swiss and was married to a Brazilian woman, Tatiana, and they had an adorable little boy. We liked them and we absolutely loved their hostel. The rooms were sparse but clean, and there were generators so we had a bit of electricity at night. We were surrounded by enormous brilliant white sand dunes and the turquoise sea. We were indeed in paradise. The days melted into each other as we wandered the beach or the sandy streets, or rode on makeshift cardboard sleds down the dunes. Every evening as the sun began its descent to the western horizon people left their dwellings and fell into step on the trails converging at the base of the largest dune. Together we helped each other struggle in the sand to the peak of the dune to reverently witness another rotation of the earth.

As a nurse I started helping the locals by treating cuts and allergic reactions and administering other basic first aid that they seemed to know nothing about. I assisted the local shaman one night with a man who had gotten the fluid of a poisonous plant in his eye and was in a lot of pain. She chanted and put leaves of something over his eyes and then dabbed them with breast milk. I gave him codeine. Between the two of us, he was healed.

We were so mesmerized by this place that we felt we never wanted to leave. We decided to buy property in town and open a medical clinic. Towards that end, we drove by dune buggy to the closest administrative town, Acaraú.

We did all the paperwork, got all the notary stamps, and paid the "owner" for his little slice of heaven. We learned that the Brazilian government actually owned all the land but allowed people to buy and sell the pieces they had been assigned, knowing full well that if the government wanted the land back, they could take it. We tried to overlook the risk for the moment, but by the time we got back to Jeri we were told that the "authorities" had changed the demarcation of where we could build. That meant they heard an American was buying land and they all wanted to be paid off.

Urs told us all we had to do was go out one night and build a small structure and the officials weren't allowed to tear it down. We weren't sure we wanted to get into all that, on our vacation no less. We found the guy we'd bought it from and got our money back, even though he'd already spent some of the proceeds on booze. Luckily he was nice about it. Having come to our senses, we continued south down the coast to Aracati for Carnival. We'd thought we'd be in Recife by this time, but in Jericoacoara it had been easy to lose track of time.

Carne Vale, "farewell to the flesh," is the big party celebrated every year before lent, and there is no better place to experience it than in Brazil. We were actually quite happy to be in a small village to celebrate Carnival the more common local way. The problem was that we didn't have any money on us and all the banks were closed. After asking around however, we found a man in a back alley black market willing to change a traveler's check.

On the beach the people gathered to drink, dance, and perform capoeira, a slow-moving non-contact martial art with lots of kicking and acrobatics. It was developed by slaves for self-defense, but was disguised as dance to hide it from the slave owners.

After Carnival we continued down the coast, stopping along the way to swim with wild dolphins in Pipas, soak in silt at the Blue Lagoon, and take horse carriage rides down the beaches. All of our adventures had been fabulous, but the time had come to head inland to start the long leg of the journey across Brazil to Iguazu Falls on the border with Argentina.

This necessitated a series of difficult bus rides. We found ourselves on buses for over twenty-four hours at a time and all too often we'd be assigned the bumpy seats right over the wheel axles, which finally resulted in my becoming grossly ill. On one of the buses the bathroom door got stuck and wouldn't open. Rico demanded the driver stop so he could climb in through the window from the outside in order to use it and then open it for the rest of us. Rico was the hero of the bus.

Finally we arrived at Iguazu Falls, and they were, without a doubt, worth the arduous journey to reach them. The walkways passed so close to the falls that we could feel the spray. They were over two hundred feet high and there seemed to be miles of them all around you. We visited the falls from both the Brazilian and Argentinian sides, and I was able to find a reasonably quiet place where we could swim. Along the paths surrounding the falls were many birds, butterflies, and coatimundis, small mammals that looked like a mix between a raccoon and a monkey.

From Iguazu we continued north by bus to Asunción, the capital of Paraguay, in order to get a plane to La Paz, the capital of Bolivia. When we arrived we noticed there were many guards carrying heavy weaponry. We soon discovered that this was due to some political problems that had also affected the local airlines, which meant we were unable to obtain plane tickets to depart right away. We didn't let this bother us however, and we ended up having a wonderful time over the three days we were stuck there.

The highlight was a beer garden with a fantastic barbecue and entertainment. There was a young harp player who could strum so fast in a way I'd never heard, accompanied by a man who'd whistle really loudly, sounding like a screeching bird. There was also traditional dancing being performed while the audience ate and drank. One of the worst experiences was going to a zoo where all the animals were kept in tiny cages. The gorillas were obviously angry and spit or threw their feces at the visitors. I didn't blame them one bit.

We were finally allowed on what we were told was the last plane out of Asunción before the airline was evidently going to shut down. I was intimately searched by a rather large woman behind a curtain and just hoped Rico wouldn't say anything to make the situation worse. On the plane to La Paz they served us coca tea to help with any potential altitude sickness. At over 13,000 feet La Paz has one of the highest airports in the world.

Bolivia turned out to be one of my all-time favorite countries. It was like stepping back in time. The people, especially the women, were so colorfully dressed, wearing bright skirts with petticoats, and carrying their babies, vegetables, or wares strapped on their backs with beautifully patterned woven fabrics. The women wore small bowler hats, a remnant from the 1920s when British railway workers were there.

We continued north by bus, which they actually loaded onto a small barge to cross Lake Titicaca and enter Peru. Once in Peru we continued by bus to Puno, where we caught a small panga boat out to the floating islands of Uros. The Uros were a pre-Incan people who made their islands, houses, and boats, all out of the indigenous totora reed. Some of the boats were shaped like miniature Viking ships and the women on the islands still pounded their grain with stones.

We continued by bus north across Peru to Cuzco, a beautiful Spanish colonial town and the gateway to Machu Picchu, a fifteenth century Inca site situated nearly eight thousand feet above sea level. In Cuzco we bought almost everything that there was to buy because it was all so beautiful and cheap. We purchased anything made of llama fur, including gloves, hats, and sweaters. We also bought pan pipes, jewelry, wall hangings, rugs, music CD's, slippers, backpacks, and even some hanging strands of garlic to decorate our restaurant back home. We had to buy two beautifully hand tooled leather suitcases for all of it to fit in.

Since Rico spoke Spanish he became the official bargainer for all the tourists on the train from Cuzco to Machu Picchu. He helped whenever we stopped and goods were being wildly bought and sold through the windows. Eventually the train left the small towns behind and meandered alongside the sparkling Urubamba River, past grassy knolls that were silhouetted against the backdrop of a sharp blue sky dotted with fluffy white clouds. The final ascent to Machu Picchu was by bus, on a treacherous winding road that caused our arrival to this ancient wonder to be all the more exciting.

I didn't know what amazed me more about this place—that it was hidden nearly eight thousand feet up between sheer verdant mountain peaks, or the construction of the site itself. Each huge stone was cut perfectly to fit with the next one. The mysterious history of the site itself, and what the stones were used for, weighed heavy on my imagination. Some theories were that it was a spiritual retreat for emperors, and that could have involved sacrifices, perhaps even those of children. It was hauntingly quiet, and the few tourists here spoke in reverent hushed tones. We explored the site completely mesmerized, caught between the past and the present.

Machu Picchu was the perfect note on which to end our South American adventure. The ever-present pan flute bands played the "El Condor Pasa," which was originally a Peruvian song before Simon and Garfunkel added lyrics and made it famous. I was in sync with the words as I hummed along, "Away, I'd rather sail away, like a swan that's here and gone."

Yucatán
1995

Rico and I purchased a package deal to Cancun, Mexico, for Valentine's Day. After arriving in Cancun I realized, as I had on a package deal in Jamaica, that the resort life was not for me. Package deals that include airfare and lodging can often be cheaper than buying plane tickets and hotel rooms separately, and sometimes they can even be cheaper than just getting the airfare. But with the hotel included, we at least had an airport transfer and a place to go right after disembarking and a place to stay before departing. The rest of the time we chose not to stay at the resort. Instead we paid for budget accommodation as we traveled without a set itinerary.

We stayed a night or two on the nearby island of Isla Mujeres, which was then much more tranquil than Cancun. I went scuba diving while Rico sat in the small boat and watched. He was never interested in learning how to dive. There were only four of us on the boat: the two of us, the dive master, and the boat driver. Other dives I've been on always had many more passengers.

We then returned to Cancun to catch a bus to see the Mayan ruins of Chichén Itzá. We climbed the steep narrow stairs up to the top of the El Castillo, using our hands to help us reach the top. This pyramid-style building was constructed between 600 and 900 AD and, even with hundreds of tourists clambering over it, you could still appreciate its historic significance and imagine what life must have been like way back then.

Then we continued going southeast by bus to Xcaret, a coastal park where I'd read that they had facilities to swim with dolphins. In order not to stress the dolphins they only allowed a small number of people to swim with them a few times a week, and only once a day. So when we got to the park we ran to the ticket office because we wanted to be sure to get in. We waited in line and saw a man in front of us buy a group of tickets. He said he was buying them for a wealthy family that sent him so they wouldn't have to wait in line. Then the ticket office told us that we couldn't go because the limit had been reached. I was so upset I was crying with disappointment. Rico marched right up to the ticket counter and told them how unfair this was and convinced them to let us in. I loved how bold he was in my defense.

An American female marine biologist who worked in the park told us that these dolphins were actually wild and were allowed to swim out to the open ocean if they wanted, but that they chose to stay because the staff fed them. In retrospect, I doubt this was true, but the dolphin encounter was staged in a large penned-in area of the ocean. At least the animals weren't kept in a swimming pool. They'd swim with us and push us through the water by putting their noses on our feet and they also let us hug and pet them. I could only hope that they could sense how happy and honored I felt to be near them. For the grand finale the dolphins swam under us, then jumped over our heads.

Rico and I also found a bullfight near Cancun. As much as I love animals and abhor cruelty to them, I loved the spectacle of the bullfight. Once the bull was killed, we saw that the meat was given to the poor. The bulls for the fights have been pampered and raised specifically for their aggression. If a bull fights particularly well, the crowd will wave handkerchiefs to convince the judges to save its life so it can produce more brave bulls.

After the bullfight we found a Spanish tapas bar near the arena. Tapas are small dishes of food such as fried mushrooms, meatballs, peppers, or calamari. We had octopus cooked in its ink, and it was delicious. It made Rico happy to see his country so well represented in Mexico.

This was a short trip, but it was packed full of adventure and variety.

And I learned again that it's really possible to travel cheaply if you're willing to get off the beaten path, take local transport, and sacrifice a little bit of luxury. In fact it seemed the less money I spent, the better I was able to get to know the local people and their culture.

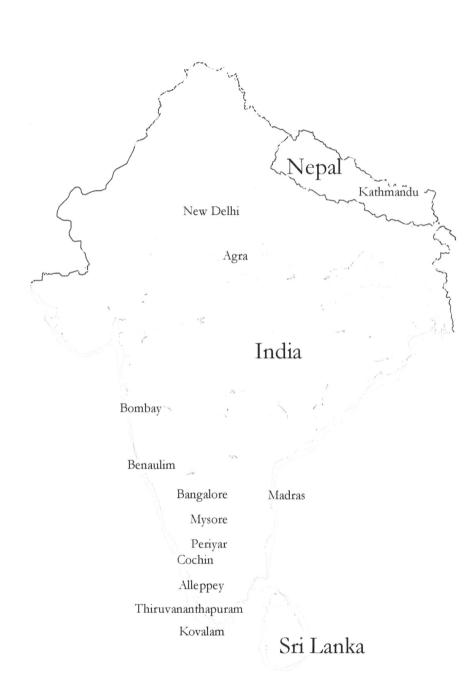

Nepal | India
1995

Rico and I drove two hours from Columbia, Missouri to the St. Louis airport, flew three hours to New York, had a three hour layover in Amsterdam, then flew nineteen hours to Singapore, where we missed our connecting flight to Nepal by just minutes. The airline gave us a free hotel room and we were able to explore Singapore for a day.

Singapore was a clean, well-organized island that appeared to have practitioners of every possible religion co-existing harmoniously. We never saw a beggar, and anyone disabled looked like they were on their way to school or work. The trains had no workers—it was all automated. Chewing gum was illegal because the government got sick of cleaning up after irresponsible slobs. We heard that if you were caught taking drugs they would provide rehabilitation services, then set you up with a job and housing. However, if you ever relapsed, you'd be executed, and that would be the end of that. Anyone bringing drugs into the country received an automatic death sentence.

I had to admit that, on some level, I appreciated this country's approach. It seemed that the U.S. floundered somewhere in between the total freedom and progressiveness of Amsterdam and the unforgiving control of Singapore.

For the flight from Singapore to Kathmandu the airline bumped us up to first class. First class was nice. I didn't believe in or like the class system—I just wished everyone could fly like that, all the time.

I had butterflies in my stomach, tears in my eyes, and Cat Stevens lyrics about this "strange bewildering place" running through my brain as we descended into the green, terraced, and temple-filled Kathmandu valley. Once off the plane the immediate impression was that it was crowded and filthy but nonetheless amazing.

Our hotel was a modest place located down a muddy back alley. It had a great view of the city from the roof. When we looked down to the street we could see shacks with no doors and families living with their livestock in the eerie glow of a TV. Everyone we met was lovely, friendly, and helpful. This was especially true of Krishna, the bicycle rickshaw driver we hired to tour us around the city.

Krishna was incredible. Not only was he strong, but he was able to weave in and around mud, potholes, cattle, pigs, and people, all the while whistling loudly and abruptly to clear a path through the traffic. We visited a few public squares and temples replete with barefoot near-naked dreadlocked yogis with their painted bodies encircled by the thick smoke of their pipes. There were hundreds of monkeys everywhere climbing through intricately carved buildings, and the sacred Brahmin cows ambled peacefully through the streets. The gentle half-closed eyes of Buddha, painted on every temple, peeked through hundreds of colorful prayer flags, sending hope out on the breeze, and reminding us to look inward.

The serenity I was experiencing was briefly disrupted when we stumbled upon students protesting the current ruling Communist Party. We'd also heard there were problems with Maoist bandits demanding money at gunpoint from hikers in the Himalayas. I really didn't understand Maoists. Hadn't they read about, or maybe even experienced for themselves, just how cruel Mao had been? This news did help us feel a little less disappointed that we hadn't time to visit the mountains. Instead, we had to catch our plane to India.

We arrived at the New Delhi airport at night and were welcomed by a blackout. We wondered if this was a portent of things to come. My first question was, "How could India be so geographically close and yet so different from Nepal?" Things seemed dirtier, more crowded and the people were more pushy. The taxi ride into town was downright frightening.

It was monsoon season and our driver warned us that the roads from the airport to the city were flooded. We pushed on, literally at times, getting out to help the taxi get through a particularly deep section of water. As we neared Delhi we joined a sea of cars with seemingly no lanes, no lights, and no sense to it at all. But we made it to our hotel, which we got for $20 a night. The hotel happened to be located next to a fairly nice one, which prompted one of my new tricks—to sleep in the cheap place, but then hang out in the nice place to eat, drink, and use their bathrooms.

We toured around Delhi a little, the highlight being Gandhi's resting place. I really didn't have many heroes, but Mahatma Gandhi was one of them, along with Nelson Mandela and Martin Luther King, Jr.

We went to the Indian Airlines office to initiate our Indian Airlines AirPass. First they said they'd have to charge us more because the prices had gone up, even though we'd already paid well before we arrived in India. Then they told us all the flights were overbooked to all the places we wanted to go, so we'd be stuck in New Delhi for a week. This was when we were introduced to the famous Indian head wobble, always done with a big smile. It didn't seem to mean either yes or no, but rather, "I wish I could tell you what you want to hear but I can't, so you're screwed." While considering our options, we took a bus southeast to Agra to see the Taj Mahal.

The roads were overrun with a menagerie of pigs, camels, elephants, entire families piled on mopeds, and crazy truck drivers. And, God forbid there should be a sacred cow in the road; all traffic stops and waits for it to decide to move. And they do not wait quietly—the cacophony of sounds was deafening. We saw one lone traffic director in a uniform standing on a pedestal in the middle of the road, meekly trying to get anyone's attention with his two white gloved hands and a tiny whistle. The two-lane roads were the most terrifying because no one really stayed in his lane, and they'd pass within a hair's breadth of each other. At night the drivers would turn off their headlights, explaining that was to, "save the bulbs."

The Taj Mahal, however, was well worth the harrowing trip. Breathtakingly beautiful, it was built by emperor Shah Jahan in memory of his wife Mumtaz Mahal. She had died in childbirth bearing her fourteenth child, and the Taj Mahal is actually her tomb. After fourteen children it brought a whole new meaning to the phrase, "rest in peace." The most scenic views occurred as its white marble changed color depending on the time of day and the weather, and then was reflected in the long pool that lay in the foreground. It was doubtless most deserving of its UNESCO World Heritage Site status.

Since we couldn't get flights to Jaipur, Udaipur or Aurangabad we asked, "Where on our list CAN we go?" The answer was to go to India's smallest state, Goa. We flew to the beach town of Benaulim, which had brightly painted houses reminiscent of its Portuguese colonial days. We set up house in a lovely bungalow looking out over miles of beautiful beaches and palm tree forests.

The process of getting anywhere in India was usually more exciting than the destination. And the destination was rarely what we expected. Taking crowded local buses, we made it to Margao to go to the bank. The first bank we tried said that they hadn't received the exchange rates, so they couldn't change our money yet. At the second one the line extended around the block. The third try was the charm and we were able to change our money.

Buses were always ridiculously crowded, so whenever possible we would take an auto-rickshaw. These were three-wheeled closed-in motorized scooters with a roof and plastic windows that were usually rolled up to let in the not so fresh air. We were never quite sure where we were going, given that we didn't speak the language, nor were we able to read their letters. We tended to get lost or miss transfers, which was exactly what we did on the way back to Benaulim. Our rickshaw driver was a wizened old man who took thirty minutes to go three miles from the bus stop to our bungalow. As we passed ever so slowly by trees swaying in the breeze, by the cows and chickens in the fields, by the rice paddies and the songbirds, we were again reminded that the joy in travel was often in the journey—not the destination.

There were a lot of Indians vacationing in Goa. The people we saw didn't have any coolers or umbrellas and no one was laughing or playing. It seemed odd to us that the women would just sit in the water fully dressed in their saris and the men would roll up their pants in order to wade in the water. Some men would gather around the tourists in their bathing suits and just stare at them. Indian culture considered a person in a bathing suit to be nearly naked, which in actuality, they really were.

We headed south by bus and entered the state of Kerala on India's southwest tip. We stopped and toured around the port cities of Cochin and Ernakulum, where we took a small boat ride through the canals and around the islands lined with colorful fishing villages. You'd see small fishing boats everywhere draped with enormous nets looking like a sea monster's wings.

One day we were strolling by a church and a wedding party was having their photos taken. They invited us to join them and explained that the predominant religion in this area was Christian rather than India's most common religion, Hinduism.

One of my favorite things we saw in this area was the Kathakali dance show. We went early and were allowed to watch the dancers apply their face makeup, which takes hours to do. The makeup is thick green, red, black, yellow and white paint that completely transforms the dancers into bizarre mythical creatures and characters. There were only male dancers and they'd play both the male and female roles. The stories they enacted were mostly Sanskrit tales from the Mahabharata, a lengthy epic historical poem. The dancers took the time to break down the dance and show the audience what each intricate hand, finger, mouth, eye or eyebrow movement meant.

Rico and I got tired of being on the coast so decided to head east to Periyar Wildlife Sanctuary for a change of scenery. We passed through the Ghat mountains and through lovely tea and rubber tree plantations. At the sanctuary we went on a boat ride where we spotted deer, monkeys, otters, pigs, and elephants. During one of our hikes Rico and I stumbled upon two elephants with their keepers. They let us help them wash the elephants in the lake, and then climb up on their necks, with our legs tucked behind their ears, and wander through the jungle.

Leaving the Periyar sanctuary we headed by bus back through terrifying mountain passes toward Kerala and the beach city of Alleppey. Along the way we stopped in Kottayam, where we encountered a bunch of kids dressed like one of Hinduism's most important Gods, Krishna, dancing and singing in the streets for a festival called Onam. Hinduism has thousands of Gods, and there seemed to be some sort of festival happening nearly every week to celebrate one God or another.

Back on the coast in Alleppey we took a small wooden boat to Quilon via backwaters surrounded by rice paddies, fishing boats and people bathing or slapping their laundry on rocks.

Getting anywhere in India seemed to carry with it the same travel options: board a packed bus and hope it doesn't smash into oncoming traffic, take a crazy taxi ride with a driver who turns off his lights at night to save his bulbs, or catch an auto-rickshaw and assume you'll be lost a few times. So it was with some relief that we finally were able to use our Indian Airlines AirPass and fly to Thiruvananthapuram. From there we still had to get back on a bus in order to reach our final destination, the secluded beach town of Kovalam. There were no roads, only sandy trails lined with tiny shacks on the beach, one of which was ours, and all were lit up with wire strands of bare light bulbs and rows of flickering candles.

The days started to run into one another. "Vacation brain" we called it, where we'd kill flies, discuss our tans and make big plans for the day like "mail a postcard." One afternoon on the beach a group of beautiful tribal women came by and braided my hair. They looked like gypsies and had old rough-hewn handmade silver hoops dangling from their noses. They were draped in dirty, worn, thin, colorful scarves. I believed they'd made their way to Kovalam from Orissa, which was far away on India's east coast, in order to sell their wares in this slightly more touristed area.

In Kovalam we got full body Ayurvedic massages, side by side, overlooking the ocean, for a whopping six dollars an hour. Ayurvedic medicine is an ancient Hindu form of treatment that focuses on promoting health to avoid illness, rather than treating disease. It was a gentle massage and the setting was what was special about the experience more than the massage itself.

We again used our AirPasses to fly from Thiruvananthapuram northeast to Mysore, and then on to Bangalore. Both were big, dirty, crowded cities, which I'm sure had hidden treasures if only we'd had the energy to seek them out. We'd been traveling for a while by now and were feeling saturated with the Indian experience. We did go to an area in Mysore that had many shops that sold gold. In India the gold was 22 karat instead of the usual 10 or 14 karat. We saw many poor women covered in gold—on their hands and feet, wrists and ankles, ears and noses. Evidently gold worked like a bank savings and checking account: Save it, cash it out when needed, then buy more if and when there is surplus cash.

In India people seemed to live on the edge—very close to life, death, and with their daily functions often performed in public. We saw people brushing their teeth with sticks, bathing in the streets with a hose, or relieving themselves in some of the most horrendous pit toilets I'd ever seen or smelled. We also passed women working on the roads making gravel, unbelievably, by hand. Sitting on the side of the road, under a single palm frond for shade, they hammered large rocks into smaller and smaller pieces. We were told that they were protected by unions and therefore larger machinery to do this severe manual labor wasn't allowed, as it would take away even the small pittance they earned.

By the time we got to Madras I was overwhelmed and worn out. I didn't even want to leave our hotel and the only food I wanted to eat was white rice, toast, or a simple fried egg. I loved the rich spicy heavy Indian food, but eating it every day, all day, for six weeks had done a serious number on my guts. Not to mention that it just got boring.

I'd heard you either loved or hated India. Not only was it a huge country, but it was a complicated one. All the major religions were practiced there, and the Indians had a painful history, especially with British colonization and partition. The society was further divided by its oppressive caste system and burdened with crushing overpopulation. But they were a hardworking, friendly, fascinating people with myriad gods, festivals, architecture, dance, music, art, and good food, all set in a vast and diverse landscape. I needed to get home to be able to evaluate my reaction to India. It had certainly piqued my curiosity, but all I wanted at the moment were a burger and fries.

Senegal | The Gambia
1996

We had been back home in Columbia, Missouri for a while, had weathered the death of my grandmother, and I felt it was time for a change. I'd always wanted to live in the country and have horses again, so I told Rico, "Hell, we should just buy a farmhouse!"

We picked up a newspaper, scanned the real estate section and drove around checking out prospective properties. By the end of the afternoon we'd put a deposit down on a two acre lot in the country, with a brand new house on it. This was how life was with Rico—everything happened really fast. I liked our impulsiveness for the most part. It was exciting. The main problem was that I did most of the work.

Within a few months we'd not only moved into the house, but we'd gotten a puppy, two kittens and a horse. Even with all of that "domestic bliss" I couldn't stave off the urge to travel. For the first time in our five year marriage, I decided to go on a trip without Rico.

I'd always wanted to study African dance more in-depth with Chuck Davis, who I'd trained with briefly in North Carolina, back in 1990. He led a yearly group trip to western Africa, visiting various tribes. So I signed up and took off, knowing Rico wouldn't be interested in a trip like this. I hoped he could manage the new home, animals, rental properties, and restaurant. It really was amazing that, in a mere five years, we'd put together our little empire. In addition, I'd been working a full-time job as the program director of a behavioral treatment center for adolescent kids.

I started the trip by briefly visiting friends and family in New York before going to the airport to meet the other fourteen members of the tour. Most of the participants were African-American dancers and I was the only non-artist. After landing in Dakar, Senegal, we visited Gorée island, which had been a holding area for slaves before they were shipped off to various countries. It made me very sad to think that we, as a species, are able treat each other that way.

We also got to see a fantastic dance performance that served as an introduction to the style of dance we'd be learning. It was incredible to me the way the dancers moved their bodies with such rhythm and power.

The first night at the hotel in Senegal I met a local businessman who bought me a couple of drinks. Within a short time I felt drugged and was having a difficult time walking and talking. One of the women in the group kept an eye on me and made sure I made it to my room safely and alone. I'd never had that happen before and made the decision not to drink again during the trip.

The next day we drove south down the coast of Senegal toward The Gambia, a tiny strip of a country that cuts an east-west horizontal line through Senegal, and consists only of the small sliver of land on the banks of the Gambia River. We boarded a long boat in order to cross the river to the capital Banjul, situated where the river flows into the ocean. We were based in a simple but nice hotel right on the water for the next three weeks. Every morning we met on the beach to do intensive dance warm-up exercises, then we'd have some sort of language or history or drumming class. In the afternoons we'd drive with a caravan of Jeeps to visit different tribes to learn their styles of dance. It was a grueling but exhilarating schedule.

I'd spoken with Rico on the phone a few times and things seemed okay for the most part. I was exhausted but was really loving this trip. I especially enjoyed my fellow tour members, Rennie and Clyde, who were with the Pure Movement dance group that Rennie had founded in Pittsburgh. They were a Hip Hop group with amazing dancers. At one village the two of them showed the locals their Hip Hop, in the sand, within a circle of tribal people clapping and slapping and stomping. It was interesting to see how similar some of the Hip Hop dance movements were to the African dance styles we'd been learning. Everyone had a laugh as the locals, with a great sense of humor, tried and failed to mimic some of the moves Rennie and Clyde were doing.

Jean, an artist from Miami, was working on an exotic foods cookbook while on the trip. Her room was full of souvenirs and it looked like she'd been there for months instead of days. She was one of the most amazing people I'd ever met. Long ago she and her daughter were riding bicycles in New York City when a cement truck careened out of control. As Jean leapt to push her daughter out of the way, one of her legs was run over by the truck. Her leg was now mostly just skin and bone, with little muscle remaining, but she certainly wasn't handicapped by it and it seemed that nothing could stop her.

One day we were taken to see a marabout, a psychic of sorts. He'd meet with each of us individually and have us blow into a fountain pen while we thought of what we wanted in life. Then he'd tell us our fortunes. I'd always wondered what I should be doing as a career, and he answered that I should keep doing what I was doing, and that I was good at it. It was true that, even though I'd gotten into nursing by accident, I'd enjoyed working with problem teens because I'd been one myself. He also said I should get married. I guess he didn't notice the wedding ring on my finger. When I mentioned I was already married he said if I gave him two packs of cigarettes, some candles, and a chicken, he would make my husband love me more. For some reason, in that moment, I didn't want Rico to love me more, and I wondered if I even cared if he loved me at all.

We were then asked to participate in a naming ceremony for one of our local guide's newborn baby boy. Most of the men in this Muslim country had more than one wife and we heard from many women that, in general, they didn't mind since there was so much work to do. Most families lived in a compound with a courtyard in the middle. Our group of women joined the wives and helped with the shopping and cooking while the men in our group joined the tribal men in preparing a goat for slaughter. I watched as the goat's neck was cut and its blood spilled onto the cement of the courtyard. In its eyes you could see the life leave its body. It was sad but I felt that, to be fair, if you were going to eat it, you should be willing to watch it die. It all ended up in large black wrought iron pots hung over the fires in the courtyard.

While the food was cooking we were entertained by a griot, one of the tribe's storytellers, who danced and put thin chains through his nose that he then pulled out of his mouth. After the griot performed the marabout snipped a bit of hair from the baby's head, said some prayers, and whispered a name into the baby's ear. He named the baby Chuck Davis Joof, in honor of our trip leader.

I'd been trying to be careful about what I was eating, since everyone sits in a circle around the bowls of food and eats communally with their hands. I'd had two bouts with intestinal parasites in the past, so instead of eating, I took pictures. I tended to lose weight when traveling because, although I consider myself an adventurous person, I am not an adventurous eater, and my digestive system seems to be prone to tummy bugs.

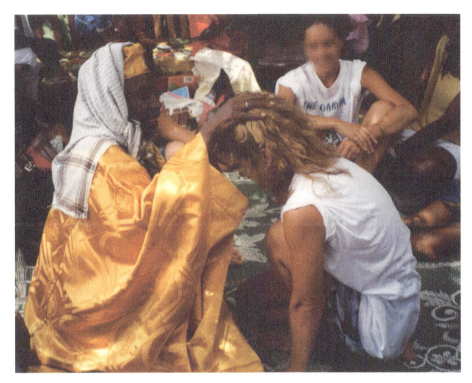

While visiting another tribe a marabout performed a ceremony to name each and every one of us in the group. I was given the name "Fatou," which means beloved by all. Getting an African name didn't make me African, or loved by all for that matter. Some of the African Americans in our group expressed that they expected coming to Africa to feel like returning to their ancestral home, perhaps to be received as long lost family. They were visibly disappointed to find that they were treated no differently than any other rich American tourist. We were all treated very well, mind you, but it was obvious that no matter the color of our skin, all of our money was green.

While on the tour we were all given the opportunity to visit local schools and medical clinics. Female genital mutilation was still being done in the area but there was a governmental movement to try to educate the people to stop this horrible practice. In the schools Muslims had separate classes from the Catholics, and the girls had separate classes from the boys.

I got to visit a psychiatric hospital and it was wonderful. There were no locked doors and it felt like a home, albeit with dirt floors. They had

British doctors and used Western medications. Abortion was not a problem in this country and that turned out to be a good thing since my roommate discovered she was pregnant by a boyfriend back home and didn't want to wait to return to the U.S. to deal with it. We went to a clinic that barely had windows, had floors with holes in the old linoleum, and only had a thin curtain for patient privacy. But the doctor was a fantastic African woman who was kind and efficient. They gave my roommate drugs that knocked her out and they performed the procedure quickly. We then moved her to another cot in the same room so they could start helping the next woman. Evidently there was no moral guilt tripping going on around there. These local women were down to earth and if a woman didn't think she could manage having another child, then so be it. As it was we saw that almost every woman had a child holding her hand, another strapped to her back, one on her breast, and she was likely to be pregnant, too.

I talked on the phone to some of our restaurant workers in Missouri who said I shouldn't have left, that Rico had gone off the deep end—drinking and not showing up at the restaurant for days. We'd had some problems in the past when he wouldn't come home, but he always had a good excuse that I chose to believe, and he always swore that he wasn't seeing someone else.

The big sport in The Gambia was wrestling. There was a large round stadium, and the contestants, who were all big men, wore tiny loincloths. They strutted around and circled the inside of the stadium with their entourage, collecting bets on who would win. The actual wrestling match went quickly. They would face each other, lunge, and after a few moments of sweaty oily bodies intensely hugging each other, one of them would end up in the dirt on the ground with the other on top of him. That signaled the end of the match.

The day before we were scheduled to leave an African-American woman in our group announced that she was marrying one of our drivers to become his second wife. I wasn't sure what was motivating her—perhaps it was to feel in some way more African. As for the driver, I suspected he was hoping he could come to the U.S.

In a way, I wanted to feel more African, too, just as I had wanted to feel more Spanish when I married Rico. I had to admit that I hadn't married him only to distract me from the pain of my grandmother's illness, but rather there had been a degree of vanity involved—I liked having someone exotic to show off as my husband. I'd also hoped I could someday live legally in Spain. It didn't seem fair that the moment he first got off the plane in the U.S. he had a green card, but the same didn't happen for me in Spain. So far, he hadn't even registered me there.

I loved the trip to Africa, and I'd made friends that I would have for years to come. I was now convinced that I actually had a half-African, half-Spanish soul trapped in what I'd always thought was a rather boring white body.

Mexico | Guatemala | Belize
1998–1999

I was now on my way to take a class in Puerto Vallarta to become a teacher of English as a foreign language (TEFL). My plan was to be able to travel and work around the world. Unfortunately I'd allowed myself to get easily sidetracked by relationships, thinking that perhaps I could have both things I cared the most about—travel *and* love.

Within eight months after my return from Africa, Rico and I divorced and I'd hit an all-time low. A friend said that she was worried about me. It probably saved my life that I listened and joined Alcoholics Anonymous. It was good for me to work the Twelve Steps of AA and to finally give myself a chance to grow up. It also helped me process a lot of my anger and sadness and taught me more constructive ways to deal with my anxiety. I felt calmer and more confident.

I'd now been riding on a bus for an immeasurably long time. My mother had driven me from Missouri down to Texas, and from there I'd taken a bus to the border with Mexico and crossed over to Nuevo Laredo. From there I took another bus heading south, stayed overnight in Saltillo, then continued on to the town of Aguascalientes in the center of the country. I didn't really have any set plans, and was just stopping when I was tired of being on the bus, or heard from someone about an interesting place.

The bus would occasionally be stopped at night by armed policemen who were camped on the side of a road sitting around a small fire. They'd board the bus, check everyone's IDs, maybe take a couple of people off, and we'd carry on. I was the only foreigner and they never bothered me.

There wasn't much to do in Aguascalientes. The hot spring baths were really run down and so was the ranch where they raised bulls for the bullfights. It wasn't much but at least I got to go to an AA meeting and had time to organize my backpack. It needed that fairly often since I'd be living out of it for a few months. I stayed only one night then continued south by bus toward San Miguel de Allende.

On the way I ended up stopping over in Guanajuato, and what a lovely surprise that was. It was nestled in the mountains, had brightly painted houses on the slopes, and fabulous architecture. The museum of the mummies was weird; evidently, some mineral in the ground preserves dead bodies. The family of the deceased could inter their loved one at the cemetery for five years for free. After that, if the family couldn't pay to continue having the body buried there, it would be exhumed and they'd have to figure out something else to do with the remains.

San Miguel de Allende was essentially an American artist enclave. It was lovely, but because of all the expats there, it was expensive. Luckily the aunt of a friend from Missouri lived there, so I had someone to stay with for a couple of days. She recommended that I go to Xilitla in the Sierra Madre jungle, which was a two-hour bus ride away.

Near Xilitla I stayed at a beautiful hotel called El Castillo that was built by Edward James, an eccentric English artist who ended up in Mexico and created an eighty acre sculpture garden in the jungle called Las Pozas.

Each room in the hotel was different. Mine had a high ceiling with a metal light fixture in the shape of an enormous butterfly and a huge bathtub surrounded by windows that looked out over the mountains. The sculpture garden had a small river running through it that had been shaped to have pools in it. As I wandered around the property I'd encounter cement spiral staircases that lead nowhere, tall thin cement bamboo trees that actually moved in the breeze, and huge painted cement flowers and bugs. It was magical. It was also really quiet out there, which was something to say in Mexico, where there always seemed to be blaring music at any time of day or night.

I continued by bus, headed south for Ixmiquilpan. Because of the rutted and extremely curvy roads the bus was filled with vomiting children. I arrived too late to catch the bus to my final destination so I had to hitch a ride in the back of a really old truck with a really old man who kept snorting and spitting out the window, and the spray would splatter on my face. We headed northwest on a dusty winding road that seemed to head out into nowhere. It began to feel like the Mexico of my imagination—dry and sparse, dotted with the silhouettes of cactus, and over-burdened burros struggling up the mountainsides. The old man ground the gears and the truck strained as we climbed higher and higher and our road became merely a dirt path with turns so tight I thought for sure we'd go over the edge.

Finally we descended to Grutas Tolantongo, where there was a thermal river coming out of the mountain. People were camped alongside it, of course playing loud music on their crappy boom boxes. I was able to find a tiny room with one lightbulb for $8 a night and felt grateful since everything else was sold out, and I hadn't brought my tent on this trip. Despite the noise, it was fairly peaceful, and I spent my days soaking in the thermal baths, or staring at a sky so full there couldn't possibly be room for more stars.

Las Grutas was Spanish for the grottos where the thermal waters began. Because the sun didn't reach there, it was lush and green with moss and ferns. A short hike past the grottos there was a natural hot spring called La Gloria, where the water was both hot and cold depending on where you were sitting. As I continued climbing I passed through a crack in the mountain where I came upon a bright turquoise pool with a waterfall raining down into it.

My leaving this paradise went something like this: I got up at 7 a.m. to catch a bus, which arrived an hour late. Its undercarriage was already full of luggage so I had to sit for an hour-and-a-half with my feet on my large backpack on the floor in front of me and my knees up to my chin all the way to Ixmiquilpan. I certainly missed my old man with his spit and his truck. In Ixmiquilpan they told me I couldn't get the bus to Pachuca because the road was closed so I'd have to go out of the way to Mexico City, another three-and-a-half hour bus ride, and the one place I absolutely did not want to go.

In Mexico City I waited in a long line, only to find out the bus to Xalapa was full. So I went to Puebla instead, another two hours, in order to get a bus to Xalapa. At the Puebla bus station I almost slugged a lady who jumped the line. At that moment I was just plain fed up with all the noise, pushing and spitting, and after three-and-a-half more hours on a bus, I didn't really feel like talking to anyone. But after I offered a Kleenex to the man sitting near me we started chatting and it turned out he'd worked all over the world, plus he liked to scuba and sky dive. He filled me in on all the great things to do in Xalapa, and he and his friends knew of a really cheap and absolutely gorgeous hotel.

This was what I call "the great cycle of travel"—from feeling discouraged and doubting my decisions one moment, to discovering a wonderful person or place and realizing it had all worked out even better than I'd imagined. I reminded myself that, since it was a cycle, fate surely would continue back around, so I might as well just try to enjoy it all.

I managed to find a wonderful AA meeting where they asked me to speak, which was a challenge with my broken Spanish. I cried as I always did in meetings because I felt at home and safe in those rooms with people just like me. A family I met at the meeting invited me to their home for Christmas, to join in the celebration of placing the baby Christ figure in his manger. It was great to have an "adopted" family for the holidays, replete with food and piñatas. Originally piñatas had seven cones that represented the seven deadly sins, and the idea was to try to break the cones until you got the sweet reward inside.

The next day I spent sixteen hours on buses, through Villahermosa to Misol-Ha to see the beautiful turquoise waters of Agua Azul and its many waterfalls. These are near the Mayan ruins of Palenque and were beautiful even though they were packed with tourists. I hadn't met anyone from the U.S. yet, and didn't mind at all.

I was, however, road weary. I'd been riding on local buses and staying in cheap accommodation for quite a while. One day, while trying to decide where to go to next, I found myself standing in the rain with all my gear on my back at a pay phone calling my mother collect. I was crying and expressing to her how miserable I was feeling that day when she suggested I try staying in a nice hotel. I was stunned—the idea had never occurred to me. I spent twenty dollars to be alone in a nice room, sleep in a large comfortable bed, take a private hot shower, and order meals from room service. It was worth every penny.

After resting up I decided to head to Guatemala. I bought a ticket with the Viajes Tomanin tour company and joined a van full of ten tourists who hailed from Belgium, Germany, Canada, and Italy. The driver seemed a bit dodgy and we were all on our guard. We finally arrived at a river, the Rio Usumacinta, where the van driver passed us off to the men who drove the long thin wooden boats we boarded. They rode very low on the water, had thatched roofs, and would be taking us to the border with Guatemala. One of our group members had misplaced his entrance paper to Mexico and we were all concerned about that since we assumed it would be needed at the exit border.

We were stopped alongside the river by two uniformed soldiers with big guns who checked our passports. They didn't ask for the entrance papers and didn't give any of us Mexican exit stamps. So we all worried again about what might happen next since we were now seriously in the middle of nowhere. Our boat drivers didn't speak English or seem to know what was going on and none of us spoke Spanish very well. We re-boarded the boats and kept floating down the river towards Betel, where we saw a dirt road and a couple of cement buildings, one of which turned out to be Mexican immigration. This surprised us because we all thought we had just gone through immigration when we were checked by the soldiers.

We said good-bye to our boat drivers and entered one of the small cement buildings. I'd read that the exit fee for Mexico was $10 so I wasn't surprised when I was asked for it by a man seated at an old wooden desk. The rest of the group paid their $10 but complained because they'd read it should only have been $5. I really didn't care about five lousy dollars at this point and was more concerned about the guns in the hands of all the men who worked there. But one of the Belgian girls haggled relentlessly until she got back all the money we had all overpaid.

We then boarded an old bus crammed to the gills with people and their ducks, boxes, and bags. We had to stand in the aisle for the long, dusty ride to Flores, Guatemala, where we all found rooms at the hotel Dona Goya.

Flores was a base from which to explore the abandoned Mayan city of Tikal, which was mystical, magical and just unbelievable. Our little group had bonded well at this point and we all decided to sleep outdoors in hammocks provided by the Tikal National Park campground.

In the middle of the night we heard a horrifying screaming, as if jaguars were ripping the throats out of some poor small animals. We huddled around, hoping we would not be next. The following morning we were embarrassed to discover that the sounds were the normal night calls of the howler monkeys.

We all hiked to the top of Tikal's "temple number four"—a climb of a little over two hundred feet up steep narrow stone stairs—to watch the sunrise. It was wonderful for us that there were no rules and you were allowed to go anywhere. There were no fancy walkways or signs or lights or guides. We were on our own. I did worry though that this lack of oversight could cause these amazing ruins to decay all the faster. In silence, with flashlights, visitors climbed and sat and waited for the sunrise. As it burst over the horizon the rays caught the mist rising from the jungle and the peaks of temples one, two, and three reached up and out of the carpet of trees. The toucans and bright green parrots began their day and a deep sigh was shared by all. I spent a quiet New Year's Eve with my new friends, welcomed in 1999 sober, and was ready to head to Belize.

I traveled by bus from Tikal in Guatemala to San Ignacio, Belize. In San Ignacio I found the eco-tourism resort that had been built by Max, a friend of my sister, and was being managed by Max's father. This resort would normally have been way too expensive for me, but he let me stay for $10 a night in the bunk house. He also fed me and even let me use his kayak to float the river for free. I felt bad about being so dependent on him, but we were so far from town I didn't have much choice.

The resort was full of loud partying Americans and Belize seemed to have a different rhythm to what I'd been experiencing. There was a generator for occasional electricity and cold running water for showers. I also had to shake huge black scorpions off the outside of my mosquito net every night after I'd walked down the long dark path to my room. Along the path tarantulas ducked back in their holes in the tiny beam of my flashlight. And then there were the pumas and snakes. I wondered, "Have I landed in Hell?"

I took a little excursion through Barton Creek cave, where you had to lie back in your canoe and propel yourself along by going hand-over-hand on the roof of the cave. There were skulls and pots placed there to show how the cave might have been used in the past by Mayan royalty. They reportedly thought this cave was the Underworld with all the roots, stalactites, and dripping waterfalls. Apparently they thought they were in Hell too.

I decided to leave the resort and head west to Dangriga to take a boat to Tobacco Cay, where I planned to go scuba diving. I waited alone for hours for the water taxi since the tide was out, but I did finally make it. Tobacco Cay was a small island of sand that you could see from one end to the other. The only other people there just happened to be a couple I'd met earlier on the *Lonely Planet*'s tourist route. The *Lonely Planet* guidebooks were the "backpacker's Bible" and you frequently ran into the same travelers over and over again at the places it mentions. It usually worked out okay because everyone could share their useful notes and experiences with each other.

It rained and rained and rained and the wind blew like a hurricane. I wondered if we shouldn't be evacuating. The weather made it too dangerous to go scuba diving and I was feeling like Belize was just not working out for me. I missed Guatemala so I headed back to Dangriga and continued south by bus toward Livingston, a small beach town in Guatemala at the mouth of the Rio Dulce.

As we neared Guatemala the roads and the buses became rougher and more worn down. I smiled and sighed with relief because Guatemala just had a more laid back, more authentic, less touristy feel to it. Livingston proved fascinating with a diverse native population, the Garifuna people being the most interesting to me. They were dark skinned, with an African and Caribbean ancestry. I liked this place and ended up in a hole-in-the-wall bar where a Garifuna transvestite in tight bright pink spandex danced to some amazing tribal drumming.

From there I took a boat down the Rio Dulce, then a bus to Antigua, a beautiful old colonial town with stone streets and colorful buildings. On the day I arrived there was a huge market with absolutely everything you could imagine for sale. There I met Mark, a kayak instructor from the U.S., and he was the first man I'd met in a while who I was attracted to. We decided to catch a bus to Lake Atitlán, where we caught a ferry to the island of San Pedro. At the hotel where we stayed they grew coffee and the beans were spread all around on tarps to dry. The smell of coffee in the air was divine.

We rented a kayak and paddled to San Marcos, a nearby village on the lake that was famous for the "pyramid people." These were hippies who traveled the world seeking out "energy vortexes" that were supposed to be "highly charged spiritual centers." They built pyramids out of metal poles, stones, or glass, and believed the shape of the pyramids intensified the healing energy from the vortex. Most of the hippie gringos we met at the pyramid village smoked a lot of marijuana.

One day we rode horses up to a dormant volcano and, as nice as that was, we realized we'd rather go up an active one. So Mark and I went back to Antigua to climb Volcán Pacaya. This involved a ferry ride across the lake, an hour-and-a-half bus ride, and a two hour hike. It was tough hiking, with three steps up then two back due to the sliding and sinking into the fine pebbles of igneous rock. At times we literally crawled on our hands and knees. We did see actual lava in some fissures, glowing and pulsing in the fading daylight. It was like watching the heartbeat of the planet just waiting to explode. Then we had the painful hike down in the dark.

Soon Mark and I went our separate ways. I left Guatemala by bus and continued up the west coast of Mexico until I stopped at Puerto Escondido. I'd debated whether or not to go there or to San Cristobal de las Casas in the Chiapas highlands. I felt I needed a bit of clean easy living, and the fresh healing salt water breeze helped me not regret my decision. San Cristobal was where the Zapatista reportedly congregated. Zapatistas are a leftist political group which frequently cause trouble for the Mexican government because they want to earn fair wages for their work and produce. I didn't blame them and would have liked to investigate firsthand what was happening there. But I was road-weary and needed a break, so I chose Puerto Escondido.

I had a nice room where I could hear the waves, go to AA meetings nearby, and the Australian women's surf team was there for a photo shoot. There was plenty to do.

After a few days of rest and relaxation I took a bus the rest of the way up the coast to Puerto Vallarta where I would begin my TEFL certificate training. New World Teachers, based in San Francisco, had three campuses around the world where they trained and certified their students to be Teachers of English as a Foreign Language. I'd signed up and paid for their course and had chosen the Puerto Vallarta campus so I could improve my Spanish. I'd learned quite a bit of Spanish while married to Rico, but I really wanted to learn more. My month long trip through Mexico, Guatemala, and Belize was just a round-about way to get me to Puerto Vallarta to start the course. It was to last a month and we were to learn and practice by actually teaching the local children. The technique utilized total immersion where only English was spoken, and the kids would learn by association, the same way we all learn a language when we are young. I was excited about the program and was ready to start.

There were about twenty TEFL certificate students and we all stayed at a hotel near the classrooms we used to practice our teaching skills. We spent our days either in classes learning new English teaching techniques or teaching with the new techniques we'd just learned in front of a class of local Mexican children. Our evenings were spent in a hotel break room frantically preparing our lesson plans, which were always really fun and creative. We'd each take turns teaching about twenty students whose ages ranged from ten to fourteen. The techniques encouraged us to use props and to get the students to engage with each other with set scenarios such as shopping for dinner or catching a bus. On balance I think we learned more than our students. About once a week we'd get a day off to go watch a sunset, snorkel or scuba dive. And I would try to cram in an AA meeting as often as possible.

On one of our evenings off we all went out dancing and I met Luis. He was a great dancer and he didn't drink alcohol, so we hit it off right away. He also played guitar, sang, and had the most beautiful smile nestled in his chiseled Mayan features. Luis didn't speak English so it was an opportunity for me to practice speaking Spanish, and for the both of us together to improve our body language.

After school let out we loaded up his car with two of his friends and one of my classmates for a road trip. We covered a lot of territory. We drove down to Malaque to hang out on the beach, then up a mountain to camp under the stars by a river and waterfall, then to Guadalajara, Patzquaro and Morelia. All the while Luis played guitar and sang, and anywhere we could, we danced. Little by little our travel companions returned home, which left just the two of us for our final adventure—seeing the breeding grounds of the monarch butterflies in Michoacán.

It can take up to three generations for a monarch butterfly to migrate between Canada and Mexico, which means a newborn butterfly flies somewhere it's never been before. By the time the butterflies meet up in Mexico there can be as many as three hundred million of them there to breed over the winter. At the Santuario de la Mariposa Monarca (Monarch Butterfly Sanctuary) in Michoacán the butterflies were flying in swarms so thick we couldn't move without touching them. They hung from the trees in enormous clumps so dense we couldn't even see the branches. We had to walk slowly and gently so that we didn't crush them as they mated on the ground.

In their brief existence these delicate creatures had the power to evoke great joy in anyone seeing them. I felt blessed and grateful to have witnessed this unusual phenomenon of nature. And perhaps, after nearly three months on the road, I was sharing their internal genetic compass, and realized that I too was ready to migrate home.

Calama
Antofagasta
Chuquicamata

Atacama Desert
Copiapo
La Serena
Pisco de Elqui
Valparaiso
Mendoza
Santiago
Pichelimu   Argentina

Chile
Huerquehue

Puyehue
Puerto Montt

Chiloe

Torres del Paine

Gray & Serrano Glaciers

Puerto Natales

Tierra del Fuego

Chile
1999–2000

I took a long bus ride home from Mexico to California, then drove to Missouri with my sister, then drove alone to Miami where I was going to sell my car so I could afford my airfare to Chile. I sold the car in Miami, but the same day the transmission went out so I did the right thing and gave the people their money back, fixed the transmission, then sold it again. This meant I started out in Chile with a lot less money than I'd anticipated.

Most people who want to work overseas teaching English sign a two year contract with a school before they leave home. But as I didn't like long-term commitments, and two years seemed like long-term to me, I just showed up and hoped for the best.

First things first. I went to an AA meeting. From there things started to fall into place, as someone at the meeting referred me to a small agency that hired English teachers. The agency acted as a broker and would send me all over the city to teach, with one of my clients being a large international insurance company. The downside was that the students were all adults and I preferred teaching children. My class had only five students, which wasn't enough for me to be able to use all the fun techniques I'd just learned in Mexico.

After having spent so much time in other loud, fun, and colorful Latin countries, Chile seemed really boring. The men and women all wore dark business suits and the train stations played classical music. I rarely saw anyone laughing or smiling. They called themselves the "English of South America." I called them the Japanese since they were way more conservative than any English I'd met. Some of this may have had to do with Chile's history of oppression and violence during the Pinochet dictatorship years. In fact a woman I'd hired to practice my Spanish with told me her husband was beheaded by Pinochet's police thugs. The conservatism may also have had to do with the isolation Chile garners by its geography. To the north there is the brutal Atacama desert, to the south lies rugged Patagonia, to the east, the Andes, and to the west, the Pacific ocean.

I did see young people being more expressive than their elders, at least with kissing in public. And I'm not talking about a simple peck on the cheek. No, this was deep tongue to throat slurping. It was, "How can you breathe—please get a room!" kissing. And that was the problem. There were no rooms. Most young people lived with their families, so the only place to make out was in public.

Here people were very involved in politics. Businesses closed on election days, and everyone was required to vote, or they'd be fined. I thought that was a great idea and wished we did that in the U.S. The young people also engaged in political protest. I witnessed a few demonstrations with people marching and yelling, cars burning, and police in riot gear calmly lining the sidewalks.

When winter arrived Santiago became a miserable place. Since the city lay in a valley surrounded by the Andes, the smog just sat for days and days. You couldn't see the mountains in the winter, but you could go up onto them and ski. I went a few times to Cajon de Maipo and hiked, skied, and even took a snowboarding class, which almost killed me. I'd met an athletic man, Roberto, who played rugby and took me with him on all these activities. He was a really nice guy, and I adored his mother. These were the first real friends I'd made since arriving.

I made a big mistake and chose to live about an hour out of town so I could see a tree now and then. In my life and travels I had done this a few times, forgetting that when I'm by myself, and it's difficult to get to town, it's easy to feel isolated. I should have taken an apartment in the city. For a few days during a transportation strike I had to ride my bike or hitchhike to work and back. I had rented a room from a California man who taught English and who also failed in his attempt to have an international relationship. He had bought a house with a local girl, and then she dumped him. Relationships are hard, even with someone who speaks your language and comes from the same country and background.

I chose this country in order to practice my Spanish and because it was one of the more stable economies in South America. I may not have been making much money but my Spanish was coming along nicely. Unfortunately that did me little good because the slang Chileans spoke made it impossible for me to understand them. They even had a book titled *Surviving the Chilean Jungle,* which translated the slang words into normal Castilian Spanish.

On one short jaunt I joined a few female English teachers going to Valparaiso, on the coast, to see the house of the Nobel Peace Prize winning poet Pablo Neruda. The house was as colorful, eccentric and expressive as his poetry. There was a festival going on which had military parades plus dances and parties we could participate in. It was my first introduction to Cueca, the national dance of Chile. It reminded me of square dancing, with the puffy skirts, the waving of handkerchiefs, and dancers circling around each other with little bouncy steps. It was certainly not reminiscent of any of the sensuous Latin dances I knew like salsa, merengue, or tango.

This dance was not from the native Mapuche tradition. I never witnessed one of their dances and only ever saw them selling jewelry or textiles at museums or markets. Like all indigenous peoples around the world, they had been brutalized, marginalized and nearly driven to extinction by Chile's colonizers—in this case, the Spanish.

On another short trip, this one by myself, I ventured further north and inland to the town of Pisco de Elqui. This was where the traditional brandy, Pisco, was made from eight varieties of both red and white grapes. Being in AA, I never tried it. Elqui was a lovely village, surrounded by dry mountains, but with a creek that ran through the town which nurtured a few green trees.

The nearby town of Vicuña had the huge Mamalluca observatory and telescope. This area was great for stargazing and reportedly had clear skies three hundred days a year. My trip north continued past Copiapó, past Antofagasta, then inland to the driest place on earth, the Atacama desert. I camped in San Pedro, a funky village in the middle of a vast emptiness, and strangely, there I found the best coffee I'd had in Chile. There was a desert with sand dunes and dust devils in the Valle de Luna, but then you'd stumble upon geysers, hot springs, and flamingos. At night I'd look up and there were so many stars I felt like I was on the inside of a speckled marble.

Near Colama I came upon the biggest open pit copper mine in the world, Chuquiquamata. I wasn't sure why I wanted to see this place, as it was just a deep scar on the skin of the planet. Everything there was built to a huge scale, even the tires on the machines that dug up the soil were twice my height.

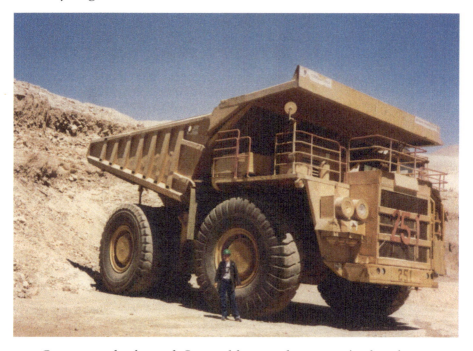

On my way back south I was able to make some nice beach stops at Bahía Iglesia and La Serena. I noticed that as much as I liked to travel alone and feel free, there were times when I would get lonely. When I was too tired to think of fun or interesting activities or destinations, I would have liked someone else to come up with something, or at least to bounce ideas off of. Sometimes I just wanted someone to talk to or listen to so that I wouldn't get lost in my own thoughts, which weren't always so pleasant. And sometimes it would have been nice to share that special place with that special someone and not even have to talk about it, to just know that they were also noticing how very special it all was. But honestly, on the practical side, I would have liked someone to watch my bags for me while I went to the bathroom.

I was in that place of wanting to share my travels when I met Cristofo

Marinar Vespuche at a Narcotics Anonymous meeting, where he was dealing with his history of cocaine abuse. In Chile the electrical outlets had three holes in a vertical row. When we made love he said it was as if, for him, the three had all been plugged in—the mind, the heart and the groin.

Cris was married but had been separated from his wife for nearly seven years. Since Chile was a Catholic country it was against the law to divorce. He had two young daughters from this marriage and two sons from a previous relationship.

Our relationship progressed slowly with all the verbiage and game playing that seems to occur with most couples, in or out of Twelve Step programs. I fell for him pretty hard and struggled with obsessing over wanting to see him all the time. Cris had little money so he couldn't travel with me. He sold large mining equipment but the economy had slowed, and so had his business. Little by little he let me into his life and I met his children, his sister, and his friends. But he liked to limit our time together, saying that it was good for us to be apart. I didn't agree of course and it felt like it would nearly kill me to be away from him. But given my history in relationships and how difficult it was for me to function without him, I wanted to give him the benefit of the doubt and try to be more independent. So I'd go off on trips to try and prove to both of us that I was okay without him.

I preferred the south of Chile to the north because it was greener, more mountainous, had lakes and volcanoes and ultimately Patagonia. On my way south I stopped in a little beach town called Pichelimu, where I visited another man I'd met in the Narcotics Anonymous program. Sadly he was schizophrenic and had been off his medication. He started drinking, acting strangely, getting more and more paranoid, and really downright scary. I ended up having to move across the street from his lovely cottage on the beach to a small old rickety wooden shed that was full of junk. As cramped, dirty and open to the elements as that shed was, I felt safer there.

As I continued south by bus the landscape got more and more beautiful. I stopped at Puyehue and Huerquehue to see the lakes and volcanoes and to do a little hiking. As frequently happens to me, I got lost, twice. The first time I thought the path I was hiking continued and was just not well maintained, so I was beating back tree branches and bushes and just kept going. Finally I heard some people talking, so I ran through the forest to find them. They were shocked to see me. Evidently I had hiked to the complete opposite side of the mountain. Fortunately they drove me back to the park where I was camping.

The next time I was on a gorgeous hike to a mountain lake and came upon a sign that had an arrow pointing down toward the ground. I'd never seen this before and thought it was directing me to go straight. As I kept walking, for what seemed like hours, it dawned on me that I was the only one on this rather rough trail. This time I started screaming and running back the way I came until I found the sign again. No one heard me, and that was probably a good thing since I would have been horribly embarrassed to have anyone learn that I didn't know that an arrow pointing down meant to go in the opposite direction. The screaming felt good though.

I continued my Chilean journey heading south, stopping at Aguas Calientes for some much needed time in the hot springs, then on to Puerto Varas, Puerto Montt and Chíloé. All these places along Chile's narrow coastline were filled with old Spanish colonial architecture in muted shades of yellow, red, blue, and orange, and had small marinas with fishing boats, with paint peeling off their hulls. The scene was made all the more dramatic by the surrounding snowcapped volcanoes.

Getting to Conchi required a ferry ride. The town turned out to be a tiny rustic fishing village where the cottages were built on stilts. All along the way I was tent camping and cooking over an open fire, all by myself. Cris couldn't come with me, but before I left, he snuck a tiny plastic Hercules from a cereal box into my backpack for protection. Gestures like that just made me want to be with him even more.

Ultimately, in this long thin strip of a country, to go south is to end up in Patagonia, the southernmost region of South America. From Puerto Natales I'd joined a small tour group which traveled by van to Torres del Paine, then hiked to the edge of the waterfalls. It was breathtaking. I loved the misty weather, the wind and chill, and the snowcapped gray rocky pinnacles that jutted up like earth's scraggly teeth. The guanacos, smaller relatives of llamas, alpacas and vicuñas, grazed on the surrounding plains. Their fur is the softest and most prized of all.

The tour continued on a boat that let us off to hike alongside the Serrano and Gray glaciers. Up close I could get an idea of the immensity of these ever-so-slowly flowing rivers of ice, and I could lose myself in their ethereal blue color. The best part was standing beside a mountain lake so clear and smooth that it held mirror images of the surrounding mountains. That was until one of the tourists threw a rock into the lake.

After the tour I continued on alone to Punta Arenas and stayed in a hundred year old hotel. There I visited their expansive cemetery, which reminded me of similar places in New Orleans, with large carved stone mausoleums. On the day I was there I was fortunate to witness families visiting and cleaning the graves of their loved ones. You could tell which graves were those of children by the size of the tiny brightly painted wrought iron fences surrounding the sad spaces. When I travel, I like to see how a culture passes through the cycle of life—from birth to schooling, puberty, marriage, and death.

I caught a ferry to Por Venir in Tierra del Fuego, Chile's southernmost town. As evidence I was near Antarctica, and as a reward for the journey, I got to see penguins, which are some of my favorite creatures.

Upon my return to Santiago I learned that my California roommate was going to sell his house, so I needed to find a new place to live. I ended up moving in with a woman I'd met in Alcoholics Anonymous who lived in a beautiful hilly area called La Barnachea on the outskirts of Santiago. Unfortunately this place was even farther away from the city center, and all of my students, than my current house.

The woman I was living with was on a two-year contract as an art teacher. She taught at an expatriate American school which had kids from all over the world whose parents were working and living in Santiago. I still didn't like the idea of committing to two-year contracts, so I'd just roll with the punches, work when I wanted, and keep my freedom. The upside of having a contract was that she didn't have to leave the country in order to renew her visa.

I, on the other hand, was working illegally. My tourist visa had to be renewed every three months, which couldn't be done within Chile. I'd have to leave the country and then return in order to get a new stamp in my passport, which would then be good for another three months. The closest border to Santiago was with Argentina, in a town called Mendoza on the other side of the Andes. I'd been to Mendoza twice, once by plane and once by bus. Both were spectacular trips but Mendoza itself was a rather boring place. You could tell the travelers on visa runs from the locals or tourists because we looked bored sitting in a café for hours, we only had small daypacks, and we didn't stay overnight. It seemed it should be fairly obvious what was going on to the customs authorities, but they overlooked it.

During one of my teaching breaks, Cris and I went to Cartagena, Colombia for an international Narcotics Anonymous convention. It seemed ironic considering all the news regarding drugs coming out of that country. When we arrived President Clinton happened to be visiting, so there were police stationed on every corner.

Cartagena was a beautiful beachside city that certainly felt safe, and the convention was interesting. Everyone had headsets on so we could hear the speeches translated into our native languages. During breaks between speakers we could visit various booths selling Twelve Step paraphernalia such as books or T-shirts, or we could walk around the convention center enjoying the view from the enormous sea walls. I later found that this was the least well attended international Narcotics Anonymous convention ever held because a lot of people couldn't afford to fly there, or they thought it would be unsafe. But there were still a few thousand of us.

Upon our return to Santiago Cris continued to try to limit the time we spent together. He said everything was going too fast and was too intense. With this, and the fact that I wasn't making any real money in Chile, I decided to return home to the U.S. to work as a nurse. Cris and I needed a break anyway, and as a gift to myself, I flew home on Valentine's Day.

While apart we stayed in touch through e-mails and phone calls, and soon we decided to try again, but this time, I would live with him. For a while after I moved in things went well and Cris seemed happy I was there. I cooked and cleaned and brought some life to his place. I planted flowers in the window boxes, put a grill and table on the balcony, and rescued a tiny abandoned kitten that we named Pookie La Gritona Malone because she had the loudest meow coming out of the tiniest body. We settled into a bit of a normal life. We'd go to meetings, cook, entertain now and then, and take his daughters skiing or bike riding.

It was nice and I was bored stiff. I wanted to work so I could get out of the house, meet people and have something more interesting to do. I was offered a job editing the small English language newspaper there, but the pay was horrible and Cris wanted me home, so I didn't take it. Although he supported me as far as room and board went, we couldn't really afford to do much on the money we had.

One night he was in the bathtub and said, "So where do you want to go?" Then he picked up a National Geographic. He giggled and said, "See, you can travel by just opening this magazine." And then it sunk in and hit me hard. He was never going to go anywhere.

I wasn't sure if I agreed with the lyric "love is all you need" as there were many logistical issues in life and in maintaining a relationship. There were the legal requirements of staying in a foreign country plus the language and cultural differences. Then there were the complications of family, work and finances, and the creative and emotional desires of the individuals involved. I loved Cris. There was no doubt in my mind about that. Up to that point I would have called him "the love of my life." But in Chile I learned a painful but critical life lesson—that I needed more than love. Love was not enough and probably never would be. I now knew with all certainty that I needed to travel.

Africa
2001

I left Chile and Cris, returned to the U.S., and went back to work as a nurse. I was saving money for the next trip and planned to travel through Africa for at least six months starting in Cape Town.

My flight to South Africa was long, with a half day's layover at Schiphol airport. But it just so happened that I knew someone in Amsterdam— my friend Joan, an American who I'd met in Peru, so I decided to visit her while I was there. Joan had married a Dutchman and was living on a beautiful houseboat on one of Amsterdam's many canals. I liked this city with all the waterways lined with boats, streets full of bicycles, and world famous art museums. Since I was still clean and sober I didn't visit any of the legal marijuana shops. Joan told me that mostly tourists smoked pot, not the locals.

Once I got to Cape Town I stayed briefly with my English friend Karyn, who I'd met in Australia. Karyn's house was very small however, so I soon moved to a hostel. One of the more interesting things to do in Cape Town was to climb or take the sky tram up Table Mountain for fantastic views. The rocks strewn around the mountainside were home to hyraxes, small furry animals that the locals called "dassies." They resemble guinea pigs, but these tiny creatures are the closest living relative to elephants.

After my visit with Karyn I joined the Baz Bus, a van full of young backpackers that would make beach stops along the South African coast. Many of the passengers were surfers who traveled with their surfboards loaded on the roof of the van. The farther away from the city I went the more it looked like the Africa I'd imagined, with fewer Caucasians, cars and construction, and more open space with thatched huts and farms.

Apartheid had ended in 1994 but I could still see some evidence of the fighting, with the occasional burned out vehicle left abandoned along the roadside. My first stop was a coastal town called Wilderness, where I'd hoped to see the famous dolphin migration, but sadly, there weren't any passing nearby that day. The beach, waterfalls, and hike through Nature's Valley were pretty, but I quickly moved on to Jeffreys Bay for a surf lesson.

The waves were small for my lesson so I was actually able to stand up a few times. In the surfing community and in all of these beach towns there was a lot of partying going on. I always traveled with an international directory of Alcoholics Anonymous meetings and contacts, and I was able to find one in the nearby city of Port Elizabeth. At the meeting I met a counselor who offered me a job at the local drug and alcohol treatment center, but I felt I hadn't traveled enough yet, so I decided to keep the job offer in my back pocket just in case I changed my mind in the future.

When I first planned this trip to Africa I'd thought I might seek out work in an AIDS orphanage. But while traveling I was reading a book about a European non-governmental organization (NGO) that spent lots of time and money developing a fish hatchery, not realizing that the people they were trying to help were herdsmen and would have preferred a project related to cattle. One of the problems with trying to assuage our white guilt in Africa was that we tended not to ask the Africans what they wanted or needed.

At the Alcoholics Anonymous meeting I also met a couple who invited me to speak at a Narcotics Anonymous conference in Namibia. I loved the fact that AA was all over the world and that with my international directory I could always find a meeting where I could meet local people who made me feel at home.

I continued on up the coast where, in Coffee Bay, I met a couple of salesmen for the Cadbury chocolate company. They offered to let me ride along with them through the Transkei, a small area that was set aside by the South African government for the Xhosa tribe in 1959. It became a controversial area because people who chose to live in the Transkei lost their South African citizenship and many felt that the existence of it just supported apartheid. This area was even less developed than any I'd seen so far, with thatched roofs atop mud huts, surrounded by cattle, pigs, and goats being herded by women with large bundles balanced on their heads. The people smeared mud on their faces to protect themselves from the sun. We passed the humble childhood home of Nelson Mandela, who I consider an inspiration and a hero.

After returning to Coffee Bay I traveled to a little coastal village called Hole in the Wall. It was named after the massive geological rock formation just off the coast. In the center of the rock wall an archway had formed which created a large hole that the ocean could pass through. If you stood on a stone ledge half way up the arch and leapt into the water at just the right time the tide and waves would suck you back through the hole like soda in a straw. With encouragement from the owner of the hostel where I was staying, I took that terrifying first leap and bodysurfed the wave up to the shore. It turned out I was the only guest at his hostel, so I had the large bunk room all to myself. With no electricity around for miles the full moon seemed to take up the sky and there was plenty of light for me to get around the hostel grounds.

I joined a small van tour headed to Lesotho through the Sani Pass. The country of Lesotho gained its independence from the British in 1966 and was still an independent country despite its being totally surrounded by South Africa. The pass was breathtaking, with scary hairpin curves and miles of misty mountains dotted with herds of reeboks and elands. There were also many small rodents called ice rats that could actually live under the ice. Our small group visited some of the local people in their huts, and everyone was so welcoming and friendly. The official language was Sesotho, but many spoke a little English.

After the tour I caught a local bus and headed inland to Hluhluwe to stay at a wonderfully rustic hostel called Isinkwe, where each room was shaped like a Zulu beehive hut. I hadn't brought my camping gear on this trip and ended up regretting that since I had to sleep in co-ed bunk rooms. I liked to have a choice to be social or not, and generally preferred to sleep alone in my cozy purple tent.

I was in Hluhluwe to take my first African safari. In just one day we saw zebras, giraffes, impalas, nyalas, wildebeests, water buffalos, porcupines, warthogs, and a white rhino with a nursing baby. An elephant appeared just a few feet in front of our Jeep and flapped its ears, meaning it was feeling threatened and might charge, so we slowly and quietly backed away.

I then looped back to the coast and continued north to Sodwana Bay to scuba dive. It was a nice easy dive, which I did alone with the dive master in warm clear water, surrounded by every color of fish and coral. While at a local restaurant I met a man named Steve who offered to take me camping in Kruger National Park for a few days.

In Kruger Park we saw even more zebras, giraffes, buffalos, warthogs and elephants. But here we added gnus and hippos to the list. A leopard crossed the road right in front of us as we passed a lion eating a freshly killed giraffe. All of this wildlife was congregating near scenic rivers and ponds, surrounded by beautiful trees filled with exotic birds. The trees were what I imagined when I thought of Africa—the baobabs that looked like they'd been stuck in the ground upside down, and the acacias whose delicate trunks came up and branched out gracefully overhead, providing much needed shade. Steve and I spent three days camped under some of those trees which, I suppose, should have been scary considering all the wildlife, but mostly it was exhilarating.

From Kruger Steve drove me to his home in Johannesburg so I could regroup and do some laundry. During this time a total solar eclipse was happening north of us in Zambia and from where we were we could see three quarters of the sun darken, and that was plenty of magic for me.

I thanked Steve profusely for an amazing experience and boarded a bus for the long haul heading west to Namibia. It took a good day and a half on the bus to make it to Keetmanshoop in southern Namibia. I ran into some folks I'd met in South Africa and we hiked together around the Fish River Canyon. It was the second largest canyon in the world after the Grand Canyon in size and majesty and was a beautiful introduction to this part of Africa. I carried on to Windhoek, Namibia's capital, to join up with a tour group, Krazy Kudu, since the local transport didn't go where I wanted to go. There were nine women and two men in our group. One man was part of a couple and the other was the guide. I could see trouble brewing because I was the only one who didn't party, which was what young people tended to do on group tours. I'd heard too that young single women would throw themselves at male tour guides. Perhaps it was something about the guides being in a position of authority. I could see that our guide was going to end up with at least one of the women on the trip. I was just glad it wasn't going to be me participating in that cliché.

Our Jeep passed through Etosha National Park, where we saw giraffes, zebras, kudus, oryxes, springboks, impalas, warthogs, and jackals, but only one elephant. It was funny how within the first hour of the safari we'd get so excited over seeing an impala, but so quickly our expectations would increase and we'd be disappointed if we didn't find a lion at a fresh kill.

In Abu Huab we saw the petrified forest and some bushmen drawings scratched into the side of large boulders. Both were fairly interesting but our campsite turned out to be next to a donkey watering hole so I don't think any of us got much sleep. The next day, with everyone exhausted, fate would have it that we had three flat tires in the middle of the desert. Our tour leader arranged for us to overnight in a hotel in Swakopmund so he could have the Jeep fixed. I didn't really mind since that meant we all got a break from camping and from being crammed in a vehicle together. I'd just about had it with watching the not-quite-covert white elephant of a relationship between the guide and the Italian girl. We were all aware of their sneaking around and the noises emanating from their tent while feigning ignorance and dealing with the subsequent tension that everyone felt. This was probably the beginning of my serious aversion to traveling with large groups.

The next day the tour was redeemed, however, when we arrived to the incredibly vast glowing orange sand dunes of Namibia. In the stark atmosphere there was so much detail to notice—cascades of sand sliding down the slopes as people walked the sharp peak angles, the shadows shifting as the sun moved, and intricately artful patterns of dung beetle footprints on the sand. We camped here and had time to really absorb the beauty of this place.

After the tour ended I needed to decide where to go next. Botswana sat just east of Namibia but was expensive to visit since most accommodations were in safari parks. High-end tourists went there as well as stupid people who paid a lot of money to go hunting to kill some of the most beautiful and endangered animals on the planet. It was also a lot more difficult to find transportation there since most people were part of a tour group.

I decided instead that I wanted to go overland to see Victoria Falls, on the border between Zambia and Zimbabwe. To do so I had to join a caravan of trucks and buses. I was on a public bus and we were accompanied by a military escort in order to pass through the Caprivi Strip. The Strip was a narrow piece of Namibian land that ran eastwards between Botswana to the south and Angola and Zambia to the north. There had been violent political discord between Namibia and Botswana over ownership of this strip. And to complicate things even more, some people living in the strip wanted to form their own independent country.

As our trucks lumbered slowly along this dangerous desolate border we passed young boys in tattered clothes dancing beside the bus windows as a way to beg for money, and little girls with matted hair carrying babies on their backs, their small hands outstretched, but their eyes without a glimmer of hope. Security guards with AK-47s wandered the streets and every house was surrounded by a wall topped with chunks of glass or barbed wire.

The route I was on took us from Namibia through border crossings into and out of Botswana, then a border crossing into Zambia to the town of Livingstone, then across the border with Zimbabwe before finally reaching the town of Victoria Falls. Border crossings seemed to take forever, due in part to seemingly shady characters on both sides of the desk—the customs officer AND the African "businessman." The poor government employee probably wanted to be paid off and the even poorer local just wanted to sneak through with something to sell. At some of these places I wondered if the employees could even read or if they were just staring at my passport because they were trying to look official.

The town of Victoria Falls in Zambia was surprisingly undeveloped for such a world-renowned attraction. There were no street lights when I walked down the dusty avenues as people and animals went about their business in and out of the shadows. The lights from the shops fell softly out onto the streets where people would gather to eat, drink and visit with friends and family. I always held out the hope of finding pizza, and here again, I was not disappointed.

I'd read that Arnold Schwarzenegger was six feet two, but when I saw him at Victoria Falls, surrounded by his entourage, he looked really short. At least I thought I saw him and I thought the group he was with must be a visiting professional wrestling team since they were all so huge. Later that evening when I was watching the news they confirmed that he was in fact visiting. "Darn it," I thought, "I hadn't said, 'Hello.'" And I didn't think "he'd be back."

Victoria Falls is one of the most impressive falls in the world. They are 355 feet high, much higher than Niagara Falls, and more than a mile wide. They are known as the widest falling sheet of water in the world. The place was swarming with tourists and they all seemed to be doing some crazy activity like bungee jumping from the bridge or zip lining across the gorge. I chose to do the death defying peaceful solo walk, where I was chased by baboons. I did end up rafting the Zambezi, the river that feeds the falls. This was my first rafting trip on a class five river, which has the most difficult rapids, and we were turned over and dumped so many times I thought I'd surely drown.

Another backpacker I met convinced me that I mustn't miss a place called Jungle Junction, so I signed up at their main office in Victoria Falls for a week's stay. I was driven from Victoria Falls to Jungle Junction Island on a truck loaded with supplies to be delivered there. We drove through open spaces, over potholed dirt roads, past villages with mud huts and thatched roofs before finally arriving at a tributary to the Zambezi. The driver unloaded the truck and put me and the supplies on dugout canoes called mokoros. Men with long poles stood in the back of the canoes to propel us along the river, rowing through reeds and over gentle currents, each of which had cone shaped fishing baskets strung across them.

When we reached the island we were greeted with whoops and whistles, as the local staff was celebrating a Christmas party in July. The island was small but had dense vegetation, including palms trees, thick underbrush, reeds, vines and primitive ferns. A maze of sandy paths crisscrossed the island. There were fifteen tourist huts of varying sizes scattered on the island's periphery. The huts were three sided, open to the air on the fourth side, and had cushions on the reed floor covered with a mosquito net hanging from the thatched roof.

The toilets and showers were in separate huts open to the sky. To heat the shower water there was a gas powered pump that drew water from the river through pipes into a huge wrought iron pot hanging over a fire. Using pulleys, ropes and weights, buckets were filled from the iron pot to hang over the shower huts. The buckets had holes in the bottom which, when suspended, provided a nice hot shower. There was also a "hammock land" hidden in the forest, a rope bridge over a creek, and a tree swing with a perch. The "resort" had been designed by two Englishmen and had been open for a few years. It was indeed a Robinson Crusoe sort of place.

The Christmas party was in full swing, with everyone drinking the homemade beer, Chibuku, except me. It was a thick beige porridge-like substance made from maize or sorghum. A cow head rested on a bench, appearing to wistfully watch its body being spun and marinated on a spit over a fire.

Getting to my tiny hut was a challenge in the dark, as there was no electricity and no lights on the paths. I got a fairly good sized gash on my shin when I tripped over a root in the path and my oil lantern smashed and went out in a burst of flame. Because there were so few tourists I was then given a better hut for the same price I'd been paying. It was easier to get to, had a cot instead of a pad on the ground, and had a view of the river.

We were warned never to get near a hippo, as they were Africa's most dangerous animal. My only wildlife encounter during my stay was the daily visit from the monkeys, who'd ravage my belongings looking for something yummy. I'd lie quietly on my cot and watch their bright turquoise testicles as they bent over my backpack. It was a funny way to wake up and I figured I could always get more Chapstick, which seemed to be their favorite snack. A Jennet cat, that looked like a half-spotted and half-striped raccoon-mongoose, also visited my hut just to check me out as it perched in a nearby tree.

It was easy to lose track of the days on this island. I went on sunrise and sunset mokoro dugout canoe rides on the river and visited a village market, which consisted of just a few women squatting on the sand by the river. They cooked biscuits by burying them in the ground with coals like an oven, and they were delicious. The locals were friendly. They'd lightly clap their hands, smile and say, "Muesli hula." I wasn't sure what language they spoke since there are so many in Africa. What I did know was that I was covered with bug bites and scratches, and I was fighting a fever.

After about a week at Jungle Junction I moved on to Livingstone, a bigger city near Victoria Falls. All I really wanted to do here was go to a church to meet with Father Joe, who I'd heard about from a local. He had fourteen years of sobriety. It isn't that he told me anything I'd never heard before or didn't know, it was just nice to be reminded that I wasn't alone in enduring life's never ending struggles.

From Livingstone I endured riding seven hours to Chipata in an overcrowded bus. From there the passengers who were continuing on were asked to cram into taxis that sat for hours at the border with Malawi, waiting to be processed by the customs officials. Once over the border I was crammed into another bus to head down to Llillongwe, the capital of Malawi. It was much poorer there. The roads were covered with trash and dirt, packed with old rusted vehicles and lined with dilapidated tin and wood stalls. Everything was being sold, from household goods to animal carcasses covered with flies. There I waited over an hour for a bus to Mzuzu and again withstood the pushing and shoving to board the bus, only to stand shoulder to shoulder for another eight hours. The aisles were packed not just with people but also with any belongings that hadn't been piled high on the roof of the bus. The seats, if any were available, were made of hard wood and were shared by more than the number of passengers that should fit there. I felt grateful to even have that. At night the stops were chaotic, scary and dark, lit only by candles or the glow of small fryers cooking chicken skewers to sell to the passengers. There were no bathrooms on these buses of course. Bathroom stops were made on the side of the road, where we'd go behind a bush, or use a hole in the ground inside a small shack. I preferred to be outside even if the color of my skin drew attention as more of it was bared.

After Hell, I found myself in Heaven, sitting on the deck of a lovely quaint hostel on a hill, overlooking a Lake Malawi sunrise. A light cool breeze blew off the lake and it was quiet. I'd made it from Mzuzu to Nkata Bay, then by boat to Njaya, a backpacker's paradise. It was a great place to regroup. I went for a scuba dive in the lake to see the cichlids, a fish that builds large circular arenas in the sand on the bottom of the lake where they perform their mating displays.

What also lived in the water was bilharzia, a parasitic blood fluke. There were many creepy things you could catch in Africa, the most common being malaria. Preventive anti-malarial pills could be quite expensive if purchased in the U.S. and were supposed to be started a week or so before you began your trip, then taken during and a few weeks after you completed your trip. There were many types of malaria and doctors often recommended different medications depending on where you'd be in Africa. I chose to buy my friend Karyn's old medication that she had left over from a trip she'd taken a few years prior to mine. These had surpassed their expiration date, but I knew medicines were often still effective after those dates had passed. Whether due to the medications, bug spray, mosquito net or dumb luck, I didn't catch malaria.

After a week at Nkata Bay I decided it was time to move onto Tanzania, so I headed into town to find transportation. I'd met an English couple at the lake who were also heading out so we decided to go to Mzuzu together, which was a hub of sorts for people to catch buses onward. We found a van, the common form of local transport, and the three of us crammed in with the other passengers. We asked the driver if he were sure he had enough gas to get us to Mzuzu and he said, "Yes," which turned out to be a lie. Halfway there we drove backwards up a hill because the driver thought the gas fumes would blow forward to the engine and keep it running. They didn't. So we all sat by the side of the road waiting, while one of the drivers hitchhiked to go get gas and come back. I was glad I was traveling with the English couple I'd met since they'd been all over the world and had what was necessary to face the challenges of travel—a great sense of humor.

In Mzuzu we went our separate ways and I bought my bus ticket to Tanzania. This time I paid the premium price for a "luxury" bus so that I might actually get a seat. I waited and waited and waited and finally at 2 a.m. the bus pulled up. The driver was shouting and shoving what looked like two hundred people onto the bus. I showed him my "luxury" ticket, but he was unimpressed and just pushed me on. As I was standing in the aisle being crushed I snapped and grabbed the overhead rails in order to lift my feet over all the heads in the aisle so I could get out of the bus. I started screaming at the bus driver about my first class ticket, waving and pointing at it, but he just glanced at me, nodded, and shoved me back on. At that point I'd even lost my space in the aisle, so I spent the rest of the trip sitting on the engine hump next to the driver with my head on the dashboard. This actually might have been one of the better "seats."

Mzuzu, Malawi to Mbeya, Tanzania was about 250 miles and should have taken about five hours. But once you figured in traffic, stops for picking up and dropping off passengers, and the time it took them to unload all of their belongings from the top of the bus, it turned out to be so much longer. Added to that were the ever inefficient time consuming border crossings. The trip took all day, and that was not the end of it. The next leg entailed a train ride from Mbeya to Dar Es Salaam, which was about a 530 mile trip going east toward the coast. I was sharing a questionably titled "sleeping compartment" with a couple of young girls from England. The seats we were supposed to sleep on were unpadded hard wood and, with the window open to cool it down, the compartment filled with exhaust from the train's coal fired engine. This trip took over twenty-four hours, and during that time, miraculously, we slept.

The countryside looked even more desolate, drier and with fewer villages. Amongst the few people we did see, there were more that were disfigured, missing limbs, or with severe handicaps. And the begging became more desperate. At the frequent stops the train made we started seeing members of the Masai tribe out the window. In the midst of all the filth, poverty and despair, these people walked with an aura of dignity. They were tall, thin, graceful, and draped in their iconic red checkered woven kikois, a type of sarong. They were also adorned with layers of colorful beaded jewelry and often carried a wooden staff, the symbol of the herdsman.

When I finally reached Dar Es Salaam I took care of the usual chores and errands of travel: doing laundry in the sink and hanging it up around the room to dry, shopping for food that was cheap and easy to transport like bread, cheese and tomatoes, locating an internet café to let my friends and family know I was still alive, even if just barely so, and lastly, buying a ticket for the next leg of the journey—in this instance, a ferry ticket to the island of Zanzibar.

Zanzibar was also known as the Spice Island and was used by the Persians as a base for trade between India and Africa as early as the 1600s. It had cocoa, pepper, cardamom, cloves, starfruit, breadfruit, cassava—the list goes on and on. This was the place to be to eat well. Every night dining tables were lined up outside on the beach in long rows. Fabulous seafood dishes were cooked in braziers, then sold to the visitors to eat as they wandered to the next table of delicacies.

Zanzibar City had an old Moorish feel, with architectural elements like heavy carved wooden doors with protruding metal spikes. I learned the spikes had been used to keep elephants from ramming the door. I liked it on this island so I decided to stay longer and explore it more in depth.

I took a dalla-dalla, the local transport, over to the eastern part of the island. Dalla-dallas were small trucks, with benches installed in their truck beds for the passengers to sit on. The beaches on the eastern side of the island were a little dirty, but the water was a beautiful turquoise, and the accommodation was basic but cheap. It had cold showers that sputtered, no electricity, music or TV, no activities offered, no one selling anything, no development of any kind—just a few bungalows and swaying palm trees. I spent my days walking the beaches, reading, riding a borrowed bike to nearby villages, and one day I joined a spice tour. It was all very relaxing.

After leaving the beach I experienced what I call a travel blur. That happened to me sometimes when all that was going on was getting from point A to point B. I took the island's local transport back to the ferry, which took me back to the mainland, and then after hours on a bus, I awoke from my blur in Arusha, Tanzania.

The call to prayer emanating from the mosques would rouse me from my clean hotel room early, and in an eerie but mystical way. I decided I couldn't afford to climb nearby Mount Kilimanjaro because it cost $100 a day and took five days. I could travel for a month on that. So it had to suffice to sit at its base in a café and enjoy the view from my Coca-Cola inscribed table, sheltered by my Coca-Cola emblazoned umbrella, with the Coca-Cola ashtrays, under the Coca-Cola clock, and ponder how it was that this cola drink took over the world. I can't begin to recount how many times I've been hiking in various far off places when I've stumbled upon a dilapidated shack with no electricity, and therefore no refrigeration, but they'd have a hand painted Coca-Cola logo on the side of the shack, and they'd sell warm bottles of that stuff. And I'd feel grateful.

While in Arusha I joined a group for a safari to the Ngorongoro crater, which turned out to be, without a doubt, the BEST safari I'd ever taken. The crater was formed when a massive volcano exploded and collapsed in on itself, creating an immense caldera, or valley, a hundred square miles in area. We camped on an escarpment at the crater's edge so we could get an early morning start. From the get-go it was like a choreographed wildlife documentary, except of course it was live and that was so much better. The backdrop was an amazing orange, purple, red and yellow sky emerging from the starry night. We were in the first Land Rover to enter the crater that morning and immediately we saw a pack of hyenas on a fresh zebra kill. Right after that there were three lions feeding on another freshly killed zebra, so fresh the steam from its body was rising into the crisp morning air. The animal show just kept going, with thick herds of wildebeest and water buffalo, hippos, flamingos, pelicans, more lions, baby jackals, elephants, rhinos, and a cheetah with two cubs. And just when I thought it couldn't possibly get any more incredible, a lioness jumped on the hood of our vehicle. The funniest thing was the look on the faces of the other tourists in our Land Rover who had cameras with two-foot-long lenses, when they turned around as I said, "Excuse me," and snapped a photo with my little plastic Kodak. Given the simplicity of my camera, my close-ups of animals can only remind me how very close I really was.

I carried on to Nairobi, Kenya, also known as "Nairobbery." It is definitely not the city you'd want to arrive in at night, and I'll be damned if that isn't exactly what I did. The poor van driver was getting frustrated with me as we drove around Nairobi from hostel to hostel and I wouldn't get out of the van because the places looked just too run down, dirty, dark and scary. Finally we came to one that seemed doable and I waved to the guard at the front door to come over and get my backpack, then come back and get me. The guards had rubber clubs to beat off the kids and riffraff. I got into the hostel all right, but on my way up the creaky stairs I ran into a tall drunk blindingly white young Englishman. Slurring his words he told me never to go out alone, to actually pay the guard to go with me to eat, and never to wear any jewelry. So I followed his advice and I paid the guard to go across the street with me for dinner, and I bought him food as well.

Between the street noise and the cockroaches and rats scurrying about, I didn't sleep well. By the next morning I was a bit freaked out and went to the English guy's room since he'd told me I could if I needed any help. I knocked and knocked and knocked and finally he answered the door. He had obviously slept in his clothes and there were empty whiskey bottles on the floor and an ashtray heaped and overflowing. He let me in, turned around and sat down on the edge of his bed. He sighed, hung his head in his hands and pulled his beautiful long pale fingers through his lovely lank blonde hair—and I knew I was hooked.

I'd been clean and sober for nearly four years and was learning that you could rid your body of the drugs and alcohol, but the attraction to another addict was not so easy to get rid of. His name was Gene and we packed up and left the hostel together. On our way out he jokingly told the desk clerk, "We're off to be married!" What we did do was more like the honeymoon without the wedding.

We shared the cost of the top floor suite in one of the best hotels in town and rarely left the room for the next ten days. He'd driven a Jeep from England to Ethiopia, then sold it to a man from Nairobi. There had been some problem with the sale, so he was in Nairobi to get it straightened out. I was there to obtain a visa for Uganda. My passport pages were full of stamps, so the U.S. embassy had to add pages before I could get a Ugandan visa. I was going to be in Nairobi for a while.

The city was neither pretty nor friendly, so when we went out it was usually to conduct business or shop for food that we ate in our room. We talked a lot. And while he was drinking and smoking he'd tell me in his lovely lilting accent about his idea for writing a book that would, as he put it, change the world.

I finally got my passport back including my visa for Uganda, so we said our tearful good-byes and I boarded a bus. I sat next to a priest who was able to get a free room for me at a retreat for nuns in Uganda's capital, Kampala. And just to balance my peaceful moods with my adrenalin rushes, I rafted another class five river, the Nile.

The Nile begins at Lake Victoria and courses through Uganda on its way north to Egypt, where it becomes wide and calm. The part of the river I was on was nothing short of terrifying. Like on the Zambezi, we were dumped out of the raft more times than I could count. One time I was in the water under the raft and could see one of the young fellow rafters in the churning water and I briefly thought to myself, "What a shame, he is too young to die!" But there was no way I could rescue him. Then both of us remembered the pre-trip instructions we'd been given, to "ball up" and the river would spit us out. And it did.

Another memorable moment came when we went over at least an eight foot waterfall and got stuck in the turbulence at its base. My fellow rafters and I dropped our paddles and were scrambling around the bottom of the raft yelling for help when suddenly we realized that the guide was doing this on purpose. We could put our hands into the falls behind us.

It was amazing the control that young man had of the raft. These river-rafting guides traveled the world doing nothing but working these wild rivers, a fascinating sub-culture to say the least.

I had come to Uganda to see the gorillas. Most people signed up for this years in advance because the few available spaces sold out quickly. I put my name on a waiting list at the office for the Bwindi National Park in Kampala to see if there might be a cancellation so I could join a group to see the gorillas. This was yet another example of when it was a plus to travel alone. After a few days of making daily visits to the office I was told there'd been a cancellation but I'd have to wait about a week for my visit. I decided I'd rather wait in the park than in Kampala.

It took a full day of travel on a local bus to go the three hundred miles from Kampala to the park. As always, the bus was packed to the gills. Somehow I fell asleep at times, only to wake up with piles of puking kids on me. The locals believed you shouldn't open the bus windows because that would cause motion sickness. They even covered the kids' heads with scarves. In reality the exact opposite is true—fresh air and keeping your eyes on the horizon helps.

I'd catch myself hoping that if the bus went over one of the precarious high curves and flipped over or landed on its side, that my window would end up on top, because otherwise I'd be hopelessly crushed. The bus made a few bathroom stops, but I'd trained my bladder to hold pee for hours since the pit toilets were so disgusting, and because mine was the only white butt out there in the hinterland, shining like a beacon.

Inside the park the only accommodation was a cement building with no electricity or running water. The owner was so sweet. He'd boil water for me over a fire, then pour it into a bucket with small holes. I'd then get naked in a tiny thatched hut and he'd climb up a ladder and discreetly hold the bucket out over me, hung on a big stick, so I could get a little shower.

He took me on a walk through the jungle one day, and he showed me how they made banana beer in dug out logs. It was a fascinating process and the brewers were so resourceful. On the walk he kept saying to me, "Big building fall down, big building fall down." I had no idea what he was talking about.

Later that day I heard voices coming from a shortwave radio and tracked down the source to another room belonging to an American scientist in the park who was studying the gorillas. I asked her if something were going on in the world that I should know about. She burst into tears and said, "The Twin Towers in New York have been hit by terrorists in hijacked airplanes." I stood there, shocked. Then I sighed, exhaled, shook my head and wondered, "What have we done to cause people to hate us that much?" The date was September 11, 2001.

I had to wait two more days to see the gorillas and luckily they were close to our camp so our small group of six didn't have to hike far. We had armed guards with us because in 1999 some tourists had been killed by Rwandan rebels. There were only a few gorilla families left and the government was trying to get the locals to realize they could make a living with tourism, so it was worth saving the forest and not eating the wildlife, or selling their paws as ashtrays.

Our small group sat on the ground, staying still and quiet, just a few feet away from the gorilla family. They were so beautiful. There were several gorillas including a mother with a newborn baby and the huge silverback male standing guard. The family gently groomed each other as they munched on delicate leaves. Their big dark eyes looked so wise and sad, as if they knew and shared the pain their human descendants inflicted upon each other and the earth. I cried, feeling a strong mix of emotions, from the magic of the moment with the gorillas, to the horror of what had happened in New York. I knew that the world had changed forever.

As quickly as I could I caught a bus to Kampala in order to find an Internet connection so I could check on my family in Manhattan.

On all my bus rides from then on perfect strangers approached me to express how sorry they were about what had happened. In Nairobi the airlines were making every effort to get Americans back home as quickly as possible. I'd been in Africa for four months and had originally intended to stay six. But with the events that had transpired in the U.S., I felt it was better to get home and regroup with my family. And I wasn't sure what the repercussions of the attack were going to be.

Nearly a week after September 11, 2001, as I flew into New York, the sky was still black with the smoke billowing up from what was now being called "ground zero." The skyline looked so eerie and misshapen.

My family and I joined in a candlelight vigil in Manhattan for the fire department near my niece and nephew's school, which had lost at least half of its members in the terrorist attack. We walked in a long procession to their station and the men who were left alive were standing outside it facing us while we sang *Amazing Grace*. I was sobbing so hard I could barely get the words out. And those men, those strong brave men who devoted their lives to serving and protecting us, those men who we could never repay, those men thanked us.

Cuba | Haiti | The Dominican Republic
2002–2003

It had now been nearly a year since the events of September 11th, 2001. During that year Gene, whom I'd met in Nairobi, came to stay with me in Missouri for three months over Christmas and through my fortieth birthday in March 2002. While in Missouri he worked on his book, which he said, "Would change the world." But what he mostly did was drink and, after he was arrested for assaulting a policeman by throwing his shoe at him, we decided it was best that he return home to England.

I'd kept in touch with Jean, who I'd met in The Gambia, and she arranged a Cultural Exchange Visa for us to go to Cuba to participate in their film festival. She and her husband, Patton, had entered a short film in the festival called, "Welcome to Miami" about how the Cubans in Florida negatively treated any visiting Cuban artists. It was a complicated issue: During the time Castro was taking over the country many of the wealthier and more educated Cubans left and came to Miami because he was confiscating all their property. Even after all these years, many were still very angry and resentful. Their children, born in the U.S., often inherited their parents' negative attitudes about Castro and communism. These Cuban Americans would throw things and physically attack the visiting Cuban artists.

My drive from Missouri to Miami, and the flight from there to Cuba were both uneventful. Upon arriving in Cuba I noticed that the capital city, Havana, looked like a Monet painting, with its rather blurry muted pastel colors from the dilapidated buildings losing the luster of their facades from years of neglect. It was like stepping back in time, with the old American cars from the 1950s that they somehow kept running. We stepped back even further to the 1930s and the Great Depression when we went into an old Woolworth's store where there was a glass display case that had only one pair of underwear and a bowl of beans in it. Right next to that was a shelf full of some off-brand soap and a few bottles of oil, evidence of an obscure shipment that made it through the embargo. The U.S. initiated an embargo against Cuba because of Castro's nationalization of the properties that had been owned by American businesses, but the only thing that the embargo had really accomplished was to keep the Cuban people hungry, families apart, and scattered the ocean with dead bodies of Cubans trying to reach our shores.

Because Cuba is a communist country the people are given a certain amount of the basic foods like cheese, milk, and rice, that they pick up at government run stores. The people I met didn't have much, but they seemed happy, with lives full of dance and wonderful music. Everyone we met had at least two jobs, for instance, being a doctor by day and a dance instructor by night. Evidence of the religion Santería, a mix of Christianity and old African customs, could be seen in the images of saints painted with local sensibilities such as black faces and bright colors, or religious fetishes like dolls or small jars of shells, beads, buttons, mysterious fluids, or a marble resembling an eyeball.

Not surprisingly there was an overabundance of political propaganda, with signs everywhere declaring how wonderful Fidel Castro, Che Guevara, and the Communist Party were. Che, of course, was their martyred hero. I realized that he'd started the revolution because he wanted to improve the lives of the poor. But as so often happens, once leaders become powerful they frequently turn into dictators. Che was brutal to his young enthusiastic recruits; He shot them if they changed their minds and didn't want to fight for the revolution anymore.

The film festival was fantastic, and Jean's film was well received. We met many interesting people, including a couple of celebrities, Danny Glover and Harry Belafonte, who were political activists and helped to spread the word regarding the plight of the Cuban people.

Jean, Patton and I rented a car and drove southwest from Havana through the countryside, stopping by El Rincon, where the festival of San Lazaro was in full swing. People were crawling down the long road, or prostrating themselves every few steps as they made their way to the church where they'd light candles, leave flowers, and pray. We continued our road trip to Viñales, and the Cueva de los Portales, an enormous cave where Che Guevara hid during the Cuban missile crisis of 1962.

We drove from town to town, through Santa Lucia, Mantua and Guane, searching for a place to get a room for the night. Finally in Guane we met a dirty sweaty gap-toothed man who leeringly said we could stay in his home if he could, "Have the blonde," meaning me. We all laughed, but I think he might have been serious. We did stay at his house, the three of us in one room. Fortunately the man did not try to collect his "fee."

Restaurants were few and far between and, when we did find one, the food was always the same—beans, rice and a scrawny chicken that moments before was running for its life.

The roads were nearly empty and we were often the only car for miles and miles so we'd pick up any Cuban hitchhikers we saw. This was a wonderful way to get to know the locals. At various times we picked up a pharmacist, a veterinarian, and a teacher who was carrying a large seed sack full of ancient rifles. At one point we had a tire go flat and it was almost no time at all before someone came walking by and was more than willing to help. Their stories were always the same—the embargo made it difficult for the people, but they were proud to have stood up to the bullying of the United States. Mostly, they missed their family members who had fled.

I met an old friend of Jean's named Robért Miramar, pronounced with a French accent. He was half Cuban and half Haitian. His mother had been a famous singer from Haiti who'd immigrated to Cuba to escape the brutal Duvalier dictatorship. Robért was tall and dark, with fine features and snow white hair. He invited me to come visit him in Haiti, where he ran a foundation to help young girls with health care and education.

After returning to Miami I drove home to Missouri, loaded my car with a few belongings, and drove back to Miami Beach to live with Jean and Patton. I was now so taken with the film world that I wanted to learn more, and they offered to let me join them in making documentaries. We worked on projects intended to help raise funds for the Florida Immigrant Advocacy Center (FIAC). The center helped defend illegal immigrants who'd been arrested and thrown into U.S. Immigration and Naturalization Service (INS) prisons without a defined release date. There was no habeas corpus for these prisoners, which is the right to be brought before a judge if incarcerated. Even mothers with their children were locked up.

At one of the rallies to support these people I was fortunate to meet Jonathan Demme, the director of the movie *Silence of the Lambs*. He was politically active and had made a documentary film called *The Agronomist* about the Haitian radio journalist and activist Jean Dominique. The fundraising films we made consisted of interviews with prisoners who'd been released thanks to FIAC.

During a break between films I decided to take Robért up on his offer to visit him in Haiti. Robért lived in Cuba most of the time, but periodically he came to Haiti to check on his foundation for young Haitian girls. Teachers at the foundation taught the girls Spanish and basic health care. Even though Haitians spoke Creole, which is a French based language, the surrounding countries spoke Spanish, so it was useful to speak both languages. Robért spoke very little English, so Spanish was what we used to communicate.

When I arrived in Haiti's capital, Port-au-Prince, I immediately noticed that it had a dark smoky run-down feel to it. Robért's foundation was in his home, a two story white stucco house surrounded by walls and barbed wire. Inside there were locked gates in front of every door and on the stairwells from floor to floor. There was a wall where all the keys for the locks hung and were labeled, but I still worried that if there were a fire, I wouldn't know how to get out of there. The electricity shut off at 7 p.m. throughout the city and there was absolutely nothing to do but drink and smoke and talk. I decided to start smoking again since I didn't feel ready to drink again.

It had been nearly six years since I'd smoked a cigarette, had a drink or taken any drug whatsoever, unless you count sex, "the drug of love," to which I was apparently still addicted. I decided smoking would do for the moment, as I was resisting Robért's desire to give me some of his personal stash of "love." He was thirteen years older than I was, but was in wonderful shape. He was a musician, knew everyone in the community, and I found him extremely sexy. He said he had been separated from his wife for quite some time.

The foundation kept a housekeeper, a cook, and a driver, so I was quite spoiled. Robért wouldn't let me go out and explore on my own because he said it was too dangerous. We always drove with a gun in the glove compartment. The streets were alive and packed with people, cars, and intricately painted busses called "tap-taps." Tiny storefronts lined the streets where all sorts of things from household items and food to clothes and artwork were sold. The artwork was called naive because it was simple and not necessarily lifelike, but it was colorful and happy. The local artists made beautiful wall hangings or toys from old metal cans, or they'd cover bottles with layers of bead work. Robért took me to a Voodoo ceremony where they sacrificed a chicken and poured a splash of rum onto the ground for the gods. The Haitian people really got into these ceremonies, where they'd become "possessed" by one of the gods and start flailing and screaming to "channel the spirits."

On the flight to Haiti from Miami I flew over Hispaniola, the island Haiti shares with the Dominican Republic. From the air I could see the difference in the colors between the two countries. Haiti was bare and charred from all the trees having been cut down and burned to make charcoal, whereas the Dominican Republic was a rich fertile green.

I found it odd that the Dominican Republic, having been colonized by the Spanish, was doing well economically, whereas Haiti, which had been colonized by the French, was an abysmal failure. I realized of course that Haiti had endured an unfortunate and complicated history and that the American involvement in Haiti had not always been helpful. For example, the U.S. government hadn't supported the popularly elected leader, Jean-Bertrand Aristide. Instead, we'd assisted in ousting him. The U.S. had a history of supporting pro-American business regimes even when that was to the detriment of the country's native people.

I took a nice tour bus from Port-au-Prince across the border and to Samana on the northeast coast of the Dominican Republic. Humpback whales migrate to this area during the winter to breed and there could be over a thousand of them there during those months. I took several whale watching trips and it was breathtaking to see, everywhere I looked, whales breaching, blowing, and slapping the surface of the water with their tails and their enormous white pectoral fins.

After seeing the whales I headed back to Port-au-Prince where I finally succumbed to Robért's advances. I discovered the stereotype about a black man in bed was well founded. He was an attentive and creative lover and I believe we tried out most of the surfaces in the house.

I returned to Miami to learn that my biological father had been murdered. I barely knew him because he had been a violent alcoholic who'd brutalized my mother and she had left him when I was two years old. When I heard he'd been murdered I wasn't surprised. He was stabbed to death and then hammered repeatedly by a roommate who'd had no previous history of violence.

A few months later I returned to Haiti to visit Robért a second time. I had started smoking on the last visit. This time I started drinking again. I thought I'd just gotten bored with the AA program. I didn't make the connection at the time between my alcoholic father's murder and my choosing to drink again. But AA had worked well for me and I'd matured so much, and I knew that if I ever needed the program again, it would be there for me.

Robért and I just picked up where we'd left off, but this time it felt different. I noticed that he had a wedding ring on that he hadn't worn the last time. He said that he and his wife had gotten back together but that this fact didn't need to affect our time together. I said that it did and flew immediately back to Miami. I had always known that there was no future for us as a couple, so it was just as well that it ended. I wished him well with his marriage and hoped we could continue to be friends.

So now I was back again in Miami with Jean and Patton. Jean had been a teacher and a spiritual guide for me. She'd introduced me to the world of storytelling and advocacy through film. She'd also introduced me to a seriously strenuous form of yoga called "Ashtanga," which was designed for young men. There I was, a woman now over forty, taking it on with a passion. I worked my body so hard that my mind had to shut up. We went to yoga classes together a few times a week and I was getting really strong.

I moved out of Jean and Patton's house and was living down the road from them in a subsidized housing complex where I was the only one paying full rent. I had a pool overlooking the water where I could sit and watch the dolphins in Biscayne Bay.

I'd noticed that, as a psychiatric nurse, people tended to tell me deeply personal things, even when I wasn't working. My new neighbor was a woman with dwarfism who had two sons, one was normal size, the other not. She drove a car with big wooden blocks on the pedals so her feet could reach, and she ran into my car one morning. While she was crying and apologizing she blurted out that she'd been sleeping with her brother for years.

There was very little that could shock me anymore. I had to pause and wonder if perhaps, just maybe, I could learn to apply the acceptance I always seemed to give others, to myself.

Russia

Terkhiin Tsagaan Nuur   Ulaanbaatar

Tsetserleg Karakorum

. - Mongolia

Gobi Desert

China

Mongolia
2005

In 2004 everything changed. After getting back from Haiti I spent about half a year migrating from Miami to North Carolina, to New York, to Spain, to Missouri, and finally to Santa Cruz, California, to live near my sister.

Within three months I met Carson, my neighbor, and we hit it off right away—and not necessarily in a romantic way. From day one we were like an old married couple. We cooked and watched movies together and talked and talked and talked. He was a little overweight, wore glasses, was calm and quiet and reserved, and was really, really smart. He was not my type at all. When I asked him, "So what do you love about me—my frizzy hair, cellulite, and wrinkles, or my cynical pessimistic negative personality?" without missing a beat he replied, "both."

I had learned that if I had butterflies in my stomach over a man then that relationship was probably doomed. I would respond to the feelings that I thought of as "love," but which were really rooted in insecurity, by sabotaging things just to be able to break my own obsession. So rather than reacting to my lack of a gut reaction, with Carson I kept telling myself, "This time don't think with your glands. For once, use your brain!"

A year later we decided to move in together. For the first time in my life I could travel without the internal pressure to hook up with someone. I also didn't have to worry about leaving home only to come back to a relationship in ruins since now I had a stable, loyal, responsible man waiting for me back home.

Nestled between China and Russia lies Mongolia, one of the planet's final frontiers and the old stomping ground of Genghis Khan. Of the mere four million Mongolians, a million lived in the capital, Ulaanbaatar, a modern bustling city. My flights took me from San Francisco to Los Angeles to Seoul, Korea, finally arriving in Mongolia seventeen hours later. With the sixteen hour time change I arrived at 11 p.m. Instead of using the popular *Lonely Planet* guidebook, I'd found a guesthouse online called Mongolian Steppes, and they'd agreed to pick me up at the airport for $5. It was such a relief to see someone holding up my roughly handwritten name on a piece of cardboard amid the sea of unfamiliar faces.

Most guesthouses were former apartments that had been crammed full of beds in dreary square Russian cold war era cement buildings. How had the Russians gone from building gorgeous onion domed churches to erecting these ugly things? The addresses were nearly impossible to find. Everything was written in Cyrillic script and the addresses went something like this: "Building behind statue around corner on left, third door, blue, number 7, up three flights, MS on door." Turning your apartment into a guesthouse was the new booming business.

Iggy, our hostess, was a real sweetheart who spoke English well. Of course that wasn't her real Mongolian name. Apparently they put the father's first name before the given name. And the given name was usually a noun or adjective like flower or strong. So really there was no last name. If the father's name was strong warrior, then the daughter's name could be strong flower. And I couldn't even remotely pronounce either of them. So most Mongolians shortened their names for us linguistically challenged tourists.

I rented one of the two available private rooms for $10. The one dorm room slept four and the beds cost $4 each. The place was spotless and had a shared toilet and hot shower. My fellow apartment dwellers were older, quiet and from Finland and Switzerland. I was glad I hadn't chosen my housing from the *Lonely Planet* guidebook, as sometimes their suggestions in my price range could be crowded, dirty, noisy, and with a much younger clientele. Iggy provided a breakfast of sorts every morning consisting of bread, jam, tea and that most horrible of scams big business has run on the world, Nescafé coffee.

Ulaanbaatar is not the main reason to come to Mongolia. It had tall buildings, but not as tall as skyscrapers, and loud crowded streets with cars whose drivers didn't even think about pausing for you as you crossed. The way to stay alive was just to keep walking and trust that they'd miss you. If you hesitated you'd be a goner. While dodging cars I succeeded in getting hopelessly lost, even though I had a map. All the signs were written in Cyrillic and most people didn't speak English so they couldn't help. Luckily it wasn't that big of a city, so eventually I'd end up somewhere I'd recognize. It was worth visiting the museums as well as the large Sukhbaatar square, the big Buddhist temple, and catching one of the cultural shows that included the dance, costumes, and most wonderfully, the Tuvan throat singers. Tuva is a small Republic, a feudal subject of Russia on the Russian-Mongolian border. This form of singing was fascinating in the way a singer could simultaneously produce multiple octaves.

The other must-see was the extensive market. You could buy nearly anything there, but they specialized in selling traditional clothing and tools. You had to make sure to get a receipt for anything that looked old because it could be confiscated at the border when leaving. The Mongolians were trying to protect their cultural heritage by not allowing antiques to be taken out of the country.

It was summer and it was really hot. I noticed that any style of clothing seemed acceptable, at least on the young people, who wore modern styles with skimpy shorts and skirts. But I'd also see older people walking the streets in their traditional long jackets (dels) with sashes, pointy toed embroidered leather boots, and fancy felt hats.

It didn't get dark until around eleven at night, then daylight would quickly follow by five in the morning. So I found myself eating dinner at 10 p.m. There were plenty of bars and discos to keep you entertained until you were ready for dinner or bed. I met a group of young men who invited me to join them at a disco one night. They were from all over the world and a couple of them were working for non-governmental organizations (NGOs) trying to set up a working infrastructure for water and sewage. These altruistic young people gave me hope for our planet's future. I wished local, national or international community service would be required of all young people. And certainly it would be better than any mandatory military service.

The main reason to come to Mongolia lies outside the capital. As we left the city there were few paved roads or phone lines or lights or buildings or cars or airplanes—just vast open quiet space. Mongolians are historically a nomadic people. They move their homes, which they call "gers" (also known as "yurts" in Russian) four times a year to find grasslands for their livestock, which include sheep, goats and yaks. The gers were made from sheep's wool. I saw no agriculture. They lived on meat and anything that could be made out of the milk they got from the yaks. The most common meals centered around mutton, the meat from older sheep. We ate mutton, mutton and more mutton. It reminded me of Bubba and his shrimp in Forest Gump. There was squished mutton, fried mutton, mutton dipped in flour, mutton in a dumpling, mutton with an egg. It was a good thing I liked mutton. You could also find the more durable vegetables like potatoes, cabbage, onions and carrots, which were imported from China.

The only way to get around Mongolia was to rent some sort of vehicle. There was little mass transit and what there was wouldn't take you where you wanted to go anyway. You could organize a trip from your home country, but it would cost you at least double what you'd pay if you organized it locally. I found a little travel agency owned by a Dutch man and a Mongolian woman, Tseren Tours. They said they'd charge forty dollars a day per person if there were three paying people. Their fee included a driver, a translator, food, gas and park entrance fees. The catch was that I had to find the other two participants for the trip. Doing this took me about four days. I went to all the backpacker places putting up notices, checked online, and spoke to almost every foreigner I saw. As inefficient as it seems, it was the way things were done. First I found a young man named Jarne, a social worker from Belgium who'd biked from there to Mongolia in six months. Next I found Claudia, a surgeon from Germany. With three people Tseren Tours would use a Jeep. Any more than that, they'd need to use a van, and that just didn't seem as cool to me. Jarne and I had our own camping gear. Claudia did not but Tseren Tours was able to provide her with what she needed.

Our plan was to travel overland for two weeks, including four days by horse. We were to camp and stay in gers and cover the central part of the country from the Gobi desert up to the mountains, and the itinerary included stops at a couple of volcanic lakes. The plan had a little bit of everything. It was not the most popular route, but then I liked to take the road less traveled.

Claudia, Jarne and I joined our translator, Serge, and our driver, Miga. Serge was twenty years old and acted like the musician Axel Rose, complete with a skull tattoo, long hair, and a bandana, and was constantly listening to loud rock music. We loaded up the Jeep and left Ulaanbaatar. Thank God for Miga, who didn't speak English, but knew the roads and the good spots to see. We headed southwest, stopping at the remains of a beautiful monastery in the mountains. The Stalin regime had killed a staggering number of the monks there.

Our first morning camping brought us rain, a flat tire and a dead Jeep battery. Miga said our bad luck was caused by our taking wood from a sacred local place and burning it, and that we should have brought wood in from outside this area. From then on we tried to be much more careful and respectful. Luckily Miga was a master mechanic because we broke down nearly daily. I didn't want to mention my history of bad car karma to anyone. We stopped at Karakorum, Genghis Khan's original capital city, and it was still being used by Buddhist monks. The monks lived and prayed in the white stucco buildings adorned with hand carved and painted wooden doors and window frames. The grounds were surrounded by 108 white stupas, 108 because it is a sacred number in Buddhism. The stupas are large, round, white stucco monuments that usually contain Buddhist relics. Genghis encouraged Buddhism as the country's religion and there was a peaceful blend of Buddhism and shamanism. Shamanism was an ancient healing art in which the practitioner would connect with the spirit world for wisdom and guidance. Along the way we passed ovoos, mounds of rocks covered with offerings like blue scarves for the sky god as well as bottles, crutches, money, tires, and various other items connected to people's prayers. You were supposed to walk around clockwise three times and pray, but if you were driving by they told us you could honk three times and that would suffice.

We continued south to the Gobi desert and, as expected, it was hot and desolate—mostly rocks, sand, and some tenacious tumbleweed-type plants. Amazingly, out there in the middle of nowhere, we came across a young boy with his herd of camels at a watering hole, and he let us ride them. They were actually quite comfortable to ride and had a nice gait.

We stayed with a family in their ger in a beautiful valley in central

Mongolia while preparing for the horse trip. We were up late at night with the family, as we were quite the novelty. The kids and younger adults stayed awake to sing and take pictures. And they did love to have their pictures taken. They also had amazing voices. There were songs for everything—songs to encourage an animal to feed or have its baby, songs to the sky and the mountains, songs to make it rain, and so on. For such a quiet place, these people sure could make a lot of noise.

One of the most noticeable things was the tremendous amount of excrement—my God, it was everywhere. Most families had three or four gers plus yaks, horses, goats, sheep and a couple of dogs. There were no fences so the animals just wandered around pooping everywhere, and we'd have little choice but to walk, sit, eat, and camp in it. A large portion of Mongolian food was made from yak milk, a bit of a challenge for the lactose intolerant. Milk was used to make a really hard and not so yummy cheese, a runny yogurt pudding, a type of vodka, and the ever present yak milk tea made with a spice which was, as far as I could tell, just salt. They also drank airag, fermented mare's milk. The men would chase the mares and colts on horseback with a lasso, a long pole with a loop at the end like the things dog catchers use. They'd capture the colt, then tie it up. The poor thing would flop around, squealing on the ground, so its mother would stay close by, continuing to lactate, and could then be milked. Mongolians ate all their milk-based concoctions with rock hard bread or biscuits, noodles, and of course, mutton.

After a late night of singing we got up to ride the horses. The Mongolian horse is a small sturdy breed that hadn't really changed since the time of Genghis. There was also a wild horse called the Przewalski, named after the man who reintroduced them to Mongolia and saved them from extinction. Unfortunately we never saw one. The Mongolians used a hard wooden saddle with raised parts in the front and back, but they gave us Russian style saddles that had a bit more padding. We were told to put our gear in our Jeep and that it was going to come with us. We were extremely miffed because we'd expected to carry our gear on pack horses. But later I came to worship that Jeep and view it as an oasis in the desert.

Our weather was totally unpredictable. One minute a hot blasting sun floated in gorgeous blue skies peppered with huge fluffy clouds, then up over the mountain a big dark giant cloud would appear and WHAM, we'd get hail! My God, HAIL! There we were, alone in the valley, because the Jeep would go far up ahead and wait. We were soaked to our bones and freezing. The horses wouldn't even move. They'd just jam up together for warmth with their butts to the wind. Then, ta-da, sun again. It was crazy. The guides wore long wool jackets with brightly colored sashes and tall boots. They didn't seem phased at all by the weather or, for that matter, anything. They just smiled, laughed, and sang.

The scenery made enduring the rain, the cold, the heat, and the physical pain all worth it. I'd never seen the sky so close, the clouds so big, or the grass so green. There seemed to be millions and millions of flowers in purple, blue, pink, yellow, orange, and red, and in every size and shape. The most incredible thing, and the reason I came, was the utter absence of any evidence of people. There were no planes overhead. There were no cars, roads, or signs. There were no houses or fences, and not a power line to be seen. It was profoundly quiet.

Now and then there would be a cluster of gers surrounded by the family's livestock. Or we'd be visited by the occasional horseman who would stop for a smoke, a chat, and a sip of vodka.

The Mongolians were reported to be some of the best horsemen in the world. I couldn't tell. But surely they were some of the toughest people I'd ever met. The horses were really small and quite bouncy. They'd generally trot, the extremely uncomfortable gait between a walk and a gallop that just about knocks your teeth out. I'd been taught to post, which was to sit up in the saddle using your thighs to cushion the bounce like a spring. But I could only do this for so long. Our guides' butts just slapped up and down in the saddle and it didn't seem to bother them one bit. Of the three in our group I was the only experienced rider. Claudia and Jarne had never ridden before, and by the end of each seven hour day we were all walking like Yosemite Sam.

Peeing was the other great challenge for us girls. The inception of penis envy probably resulted from women having to pee in the wild. With open steppes and nary a grass clump to be had, there was little chance of finding an inkling of privacy. In fact it was impossible. I understood then one of the reasons why both the women and men wore long coats in Mongolia. They functioned as a cover while squatting. When you could find a "toilet" by some gers it would be a wooden shack with a hole inside dug into the ground with two pieces of wood placed on either side of the hole to put your feet. I preferred the open air. It smelled better.

By the end of the four days we were sore and stinky so we went to a hot springs that was out in the middle of nowhere. Or should I say we went to pure heaven on earth? This was why I loved to travel—the extremes. Here I was ready to die from pain and exhaustion, and the next moment I was blissfully soaking in a natural outdoor hot spring, had a hot shower, a sit-down toilet, a good meal and a bed.

I couldn't say that our Jeep was much less bouncy than the horse was. There really weren't any roads. There were just dirt tracks zig-zagging around vast open spaces. I had no idea how or if the driver knew where he was going. It seemed he'd just head off in a direction and eventually we'd get somewhere. But the word bouncy just couldn't describe what happened on these "roads." We endured hours of Jeep swallowing pot-holed, rock-strewn, river-rutted, spine-wrenching, teeth-jarring, whiplashing, flip-flopping around the back seat, hang on for your life, backpacks landing on your head, whoop-it-up-you-might-be-dead-any-minute kind of bouncing. Mostly though, it was a lot of fun, and amazingly enough, eventually we got so used to it we could even fall asleep. Now that was pure exhaustion.

Jarne had to head back to Ulaanbaatar to continue with his bicycle tour, so we dropped him off in Tsetserleg while Claudia and I continued on to White Lake with Serge and Miga. It was called that in English. In Mongolian it was called Terkhin Tsagaan Nuur. We stayed two days there, slept in a simple ger (a welcome rest from tent camping) and cooked over a wood stove. We still had no toilet, shower or running water, but hey, it felt like the Hilton.

The gers were amazingly well engineered—portable, warm and quite homey. They were built with a round wooden frame and, depending on the season, layers of felt would be added or removed. They had brightly painted wooden doors and there was usually homemade yak cheese drying on the roof. The roofs seemed to be made of canvas with a hole in the middle for the wood stove (oops, I mean yak poop stove) to let the smoke escape. Small beds, a few brightly painted dressers, a table, two teeny tiny chairs, and lots of photos, including pictures of the Dalai Lama, lined the walls.

There was a set of rules on how to enter the ger and where you were to sit. And, of course, you were supposed to take and try everything that was offered to you. I even tried some snuff, a finely ground tobacco that was inhaled up your nostril. I was told that if we were offered snuff and there wasn't any in the little container, or we really didn't want any, we should just pretend to sniff it to be polite and save face. In some of the gers we visited there was a still to make alcohol out of milk. We were offered that once, first thing in the morning, and it tasted like sake. Personally I liked the fermented mare's milk, airag, because it tasted like yogurt to me.

Somehow on this adventure my stomach survived, I didn't break anything and my old bum just went numb. The last night of the trip we spent camping by another lake, which was actually warm enough for us to teach Serge and Miga how to swim. Everything was perfect until the flies came—swarms of small white silky flies, thousands of them. They were all attempting to land on us to lay their eggs, and after they did, they would die. What a brief annoying life, huh? Really, was it necessary for the biblical Noah to board two of ALL the creatures on his ark? I thought not. We sat on the ground, covered from head to toe with our sarongs, and watched an exceptional sunset. Our lesson was that nothing is ever truly perfect and therein lies the perfection.

It was a bit of a shock getting back to the hustle and bustle of Ulaanbaatar, but it was great to get a hot shower and a pizza with nary a blob of mutton on it. As always it was the extremes—the bittersweet comings and goings, the highs and lows of experiences, that made travel so wondrous. Mongolia was everything I'd hoped it would be and nothing like I'd imagined—just the way I liked it.

China
2005

After seeing Mongolia I figured that while I was in Asia I should poke around China a bit. I had to bribe the train authorities in Ulaanbaatar in order to get a seat on the Trans-Mongolian to Beijing, and somehow I got a super deluxe cabin. There were two bunk beds, a fan and even a hand held shower of sorts attached to the sink faucet. It was quite nice and very different from my usual experience of traveling with an overflow of other people's bags, kids and animals. I shared the train compartment with an interesting middle-aged English woman who worked as a videographer doing individual and family stories by hire. She was on her way to visit her son, who was working and living in China. We spent many hours together both in our train car and in the dining car watching the Gobi desert chug by. The dining car had carved wood details, which made it feel more historic. The food was nothing to write home about, just simple fare of meat and potatoes, and now more Russian in style since the train had come all the way from Moscow. When we crossed the border into China we had to stop to change the wheels of the train since the rail tracks were a different gauge. I heard that Mongolia didn't really want to have the same gauge as the Chinese tracks in order to have one more line of defense against a possible invasion by China. With the crossing to the Chinese side of the border there was a noticeable increase in agriculture and development.

After thirty rather dull hours on the train I finally arrived in Beijing and to the most amazing sea of humanity. Oddly I liked this crazy city. It was pulsing with life and activity, a powerful combination of the ancient and the insanely modern, with things like talking taxis for example. It was loud and hectic, with bikes, cars, buses, trams and rickshaws all zooming about in reasonable order. The people were neither particularly friendly nor rude, but rather had a welcomed indifference to all of us tourists.

I was having a bit of trouble finding any information on how to get around since I was now personally protesting the use of the infamous *Lonely Planet* guidebook. It seemed every tourist had it these days, not just the backpackers, so its readers all ended up in all the same places. Plus my 1999 edition was already six years old, was torn in half and probably more useful as toilet paper. So I was winging it, which wasn't such a good idea considering I could neither read nor speak Mandarin Chinese. It was important to have your destination written down in Chinese characters or you'd be up the creek without a chopstick.

I managed to find a brand new hostel for an exorbitant twenty dollars per night, but it had a hot shower and a TV. The TV however carried only Chinese language stations except for one English speaking business channel. The hostel was really clean and comfy and even had air conditioning, a necessity as it was ridiculously hot in July.

The Forbidden City was a disappointment because it was being renovated, and it was too hot and crowded. But the surrounding buildings were interesting, and you could learn a lot about Chinese history. Even though I couldn't understand what they were saying, I enjoyed tagging along behind the large groups of Chinese tourists with their petite female guides yelling through a megaphone and waving a flag to keep everyone together. Tiananmen square seemed like just a vast cement slab to me, and I certainly had no interest in seeing Mao's body "pickled and preserved" in a crystal box. I could only imagine the 1989 student protests and the indelible picture in my mind of the young man standing in front of a tank. That young man was never seen or heard from again—just one of an incalculable number of Chinese citizens who suffered human rights abuses at the hands of their government. In this regard, China still had a long way to go.

The Great Wall, now that was truly something. I'd signed up for a day tour on the spur of the moment, so I really didn't know what I was getting into. We drove way out of town, and given the size of Beijing, just reaching its edge took two to three hours. Once we got to the wall we were told we'd be hiking on it for six miles, from Jinshanling to Simatai. That was entirely too far to be slogging around in a heat wave, but it did let me appreciate how immense and rather mad an undertaking building the wall really was. Its brick, stone and packed earth foundation followed the curves of the land and some parts were seriously steep. Locals followed the hikers, trying to sell them water, which turned out to be fairly lucrative for them considering the heat and the strain of the hike. At Simatai we geared up in a harness and took a zip line off the mountain's edge and over a river to a boat that took us back to our bus. All in all it had been a grand day, and I was pooped, so I decided to eat dinner at the hostel. Some of the choices were deep fried tongue, goose liver, edible fungus, snakehead eggs (a type of fish) and pig intestine. I opted for dumplings and rice.

As I had limited time I decided to fly south to Guilin rather than take the train. I made it to the Beijing airport quite early in the morning, but it turned out it didn't matter. They changed our gate number about four times and we left late anyway. We foreigners of course hadn't a clue

China | 163

about what was happening, so we just kept following the crowds up the stairs, down the stairs, up the stairs, ad nauseam. I finally did get on the plane and they served us breakfast which included a choice of a Chinese or Western meal. Interestingly enough, the Chinese passengers chose the Western meal and the Westerners chose the Chinese one. So who ended up with the best meal? The Chinese got eggs, sausage, hash browns and fruit, while we, who were trying to immerse ourselves in their culture, got some black runny goo with lima beans.

I arrived in Guilin and began my interrogation of fellow travelers in order to get some clue about what their travel guide said on where to go. I was really regretting not having the *Lonely Planet* guidebook. I couldn't purchase one in China since the government had banned it because of the way the book presented China. The Chinese government didn't want the truth printed. In addition, sometimes the book's information was wrong. In this instance the recommended youth hostel was closed. I ended up settling for a rundown place on the edge of town, then wandered around looking at all the mountains and caves from the outside since the price of admission to visit them seemed too expensive to me.

Then I got lost, which I tended to do, and lo, little Tang saved me. It had been raining and I was in desperate need of a toilet. I must have looked quite pitiful standing in the rain, soaking wet, turning my head from side to side and back to front with a confused uncomprehending frantic gaze. Tang was twenty-seven and a calligraphy teacher who said he lived in a dorm at his school. He took me through the maze of streets and helped me find a decent toilet. I felt indebted to him as I would anyone who could help me find that rare commodity—a good toilet. He also showed me the gallery where he displayed his artwork. I felt I could repay him for his help by purchasing one of his small drawings. Then he took me to an underground mall with a tea shop that was small, dark and smelled exotic. Way in the back of the shop Tang and the shop owner engaged me in the elaborate art of tea making. This consisted of rinsing the tea cup twenty times, pouring here, pouring there, tipping this, slurping that, tap tap tapping on the table, sniffing, nodding, and grunting. I got caught up in all of it, but then had a fleeting thought that maybe this wasn't a good idea. Maybe the tea had been drugged and there I'd be, hidden and alone with two strange men. I'd started to get a cold, my head felt clogged, and I was literally drenched in sweat. I felt dizzy and distracted. And then it happened: I impulsively bought a tiny container of tea for $15, which was a lot of money to me.

I proceeded to take my new found friend out for dinner. At least the restaurant was an experience worth having. Evidently we were in snake season and there were cages of the critters everywhere, not to mention the rest of the menagerie that was available for consumption. Tang walked me home and on the way we had to cross the river and hold our shoes in our hands. People could take a bamboo raft across, but it seemed most chose to wade across. On the other side a man practiced his flute and it was all so lovely. It wasn't until I was lying in bed that night thinking about the day that I realized I'd probably been completely conned by this young man. But then I did get a story as well as a decent toilet.

The next day I checked out of my hotel and took a Li River day cruise, which started in Guilin and ended in Yangshuo. I chose the Chinese tourist boat over the non-Chinese one, not for the more authentic experience as much as for the fact that it was only half the price. I didn't understand a single word of the guide's commentary of course, and the tour guides all talked so loudly! Give a bullhorn to a Chinese woman and watch out— quiet, demure giggling girls become Helgas of Hosseldorf. By the way the predominantly Chinese crowd was responding to the tour guide I could see she was ordering us to board the boat and to sit down. I tried to follow along with the tour brochure as she loudly described what we were seeing and what was pretty and what was not and what each rock was named and so on and so on.

Eventually I just sat outside on the boat deck and was awestruck by some of the most unusual and mystical mountains I'd ever seen. Even the rain added to the experience. I saw water buffalo grazing and swimming, bamboo rafts slamming up against the boat to sell their wares (not that I would have succumbed to purchasing another thing here), delicate ceramic tile roofs, and swaying bamboo trees along the shoreline. It was all truly magical. When the cruise ended, in the market town of Yangshuo, the madness began again with the shouting, crowds and language barrier. But it was the oppressive humid Vietnam-movie type heat that was truly overwhelming and debilitating.

I rode a little tram to my hotel named Happy Hotel, which I lovingly re-named Crappy Hotel. I was with my new best friend Dong Wuk from Korea, who spoke English AND Chinese. We rented bikes and began riding along the famed trails. I felt like I was riding in a postcard—the huge verdant pointy karst limestone mountains, the rice paddies with the workers in triangular reed hats, the women carrying baskets on poles balanced on their shoulders, the water buffalo wallowing in the mud, the thatched roofed houses and the rows of irrigation canals. Then the perfect movie scene screeched to a halt as the hungry cry of capitalism seeped in and the salespeople crowded around us trying to push water, flowers, knickknacks, boat rides and rafting trips.

I stayed on West Street in Yangshuo, where most of the Westerners hung out. So did the gazillions of Chinese tourists. I stayed for three dollars a night in a room situated above one of the many cafés, with hot water and a Western toilet. I was eating my usual gluttonous American breakfast in a street-front café one morning when one of the many tiny ancient faced ladies, slumped over from years working in the rice fields, gave me a near toothless grin and asked for my leftover toast. She hugged me when I gave it to her and then tried to sell me some trinkets from her little basket.

I couldn't imagine what she must have thought of all these strange foreign faces invading her land and her having to learn meaningless words to her like "herro," "tank you," and "you buy?" I wished instead for her to be home with her family, comfortable, safe and happy in these last years of her life. For all I knew she might have been really enjoying herself, but I didn't get that sense. The few Chinese I'd been able to talk to said there wasn't much in the way of social programs for the sick or elderly and that they must rely on their families. I bought everything in her basket.

I realized early on this trip that the world needed to start learning Mandarin Chinese because China would be the country of the future, at least economically. The people were perfecting capitalism, but without a conscience. There didn't appear to be any child labor laws, retirement pensions, concern about the environment, or laws overseeing worker safety or manufacturing standards. The construction seemed to go on 24/7, with the building even going on in shifts throughout the night. The people were obviously hard working and could be so sweet, helpful and easy going. I thought the language sounded pretty and melodic as long as it wasn't coming out of a bullhorn. I butchered the language at every attempt.

Dong had moved on with his travels, but thankfully I met an Australian fellow, Jason, who'd been teaching English there. He not only spoke some Chinese, but he was also an excellent barterer. Jason was able to rent a motorbike, which non-Chinese weren't allowed to do, and we explored the spectacular countryside and villages. On the way back to town the bike stopped working and Jason just shushed someone over and gestured about what had happened. The guy took out a rope and tied our motorbike to his and towed us into town. I thought Jason knew him, but he didn't. This was evidently the normal way things were done: just hiss at someone and they'll come to help. Of course we had to pay our helper a bit, but gee, I couldn't even imagine that happening most places back home.

I think I did all the sightseeing you could do in and around Yangshuo. I explored caves that had mud baths and slides inside, took bamboo rafts down the rivers, biked through traditional villages, and oh yes, saw a very cool sound and light show out on the river. I saw the cheap backpacker version of the show from far away atop the roof of a little boat. The show had hundreds of people performing on the water in dugout canoes and on floating platforms. The costumes were lit up with strands of lights and there were a lot of bursts of fire. There was music, singing, lots of splashing water, and the waving of enormous flags. It looked like it would be quite an extravaganza if you actually had a seat in front of the show to see it in detail.

As a puddle of sweat I left humid Yangshuo and flew west to Kunming. I was supposed to meet the woman with whom I'd shared the train compartment when coming to Beijing from Mongolia. But when I arrived it turned out she was too busy with her family and had to cancel. I was none too happy, as Kunming seemed to be just another huge, sprawling, modern, crowded, loud, neon-lit typical Chinese city. In addition, the hostel I tried to stay in had no private rooms left, and I realized that more and more frequently I was feeling too old, at age forty-four, to sleep in a dorm room with eight other stinky backpackers. Unfortunately though, at the moment, it looked like I didn't have any choice, so I paid for the dorm room.

I immediately booked a flight to Lijiang for the next day and settled down to try to figure out how to spend the evening. As fate would have it I met "Helen," a young Chinese woman studying law in England. She insisted on taking me out to dinner. Granted it was not so expensive, as the typical hot noodle soup only cost about fifty cents. She also took me out for tea and I found out that there really were expensive teas here. It made me rethink my perceived rip off experience in Guilin. It was great finally having a Chinese person to question about politics. She told me Taiwan currently was and would always be part of China and that it should remain so. To her the issue was that two leaders (or parties, the Nationalists in Taiwan and the Communists on the mainland) both wanted to be the boss. As for Tibet, she thought it didn't have the capability of being a sovereign nation and if it weren't ruled by China, it would be ruled by India. She also thought that most Chinese respected the Tibetan people and the differences between the two cultures. The Chinese didn't understand the "religion" in Tibet she said, since most Chinese here were raised under communism so were taught to rely on themselves, without a thought about any "higher power." She felt this was a practical approach and that she herself had done quite well. She also expressed her belief that the land in Tibet would surely be needed to feed the over one billion Chinese people.

Even with the government's current one birth per couple policy, the Chinese population was immense. Every possible spot of land was already cultivated. My new friend ended up inviting me to stay in her nice hotel room, so I didn't have to sleep in the dorm with the smelly backpackers or share one of the horrible bathrooms after all. It was beyond me how the Chinese could tolerate their toilets. They were usually just simple ceramic holes in the ground, or worse, ceramic communal trenches, where you'd scoop up some water to rinse whatever was going down the pike. Rumor had it that many Chinese injured themselves falling off Western toilets while trying to stand on top of the bowl and squat. Indeed, I'd seen shoe marks on the toilet rims more than once.

I flew a quick hour west to Lijiang, which was supposed to be a typical charming old village. It turned out to be more like a Disney World characterization of an old village. It was jam packed with mostly Chinese tourists and every store was a souvenir shop selling jewelry, clothes, leather, wooden products like toy guns, teas, and lots of weird dried stuff I couldn't possibly identify.

I met a Finnish girl named Kaarina and we booked a room together in the youth hostel. At first it appeared quite quaint, but it turned out to be a real dump. Note to self: "Find out exactly when the hot water works when staying in cheap accommodations in China." We then ran around trying to get information on visiting the Tiger Leaping Gorge, which was the thing to do there. We couldn't find anyone who spoke English or maps or any information whatsoever. We ended up catching a bus the following morning to go out there and we just hoped for the best.

It happened to be monsoon season, and it was pouring rain, but we decided to go anyway to try to see even remote shadows of the gorge through the rain. I regretted having given away all my warm clothes and having cut up the remainder to make them cooler when I was evidently in a heat induced delusional state back in Yangshuo. When we approached the gorge we happened upon a café run by a rather odd Australian woman. We warmed up with some terrible coffee and a bowl of noodles, then began the hike to the gorge. The weather had cleared a bit so we were optimistic.

We learned that normally there was an entrance fee and that the hike could take up to two days to complete. Because of the awful weather and recent landslides it had caused, we now found that the park was officially closed. But, lucky for us, that day they were letting people enter at their own risk, and free of charge. So there I was with a twenty year old overly zealous Finnish chick. Neither of us had the proper gear for hiking, as we'd thought we'd be taking a taxi or getting some other transport to see the gorge. Kaarina was wearing one of those see-through plastic raincoats you buy at the dime store and her outfit was replete with a bright green book bag. I looked a little more "together," but that was purely on the outside. I wasn't feeling in shape for this on the inside. Despite all of our challenges though, there was no denying that the gorge was spectacular.

The trail followed the edge of the cliff and would eventually rise to over six thousand feet. As we hiked steadily upward we could see the raging river flowing below us and the huge mountain face towering above. Even with the rain and clouds it was quite impressive. Along the way locals with their donkeys waited for the tourists to just give up and hire their beasts of burden to finish the trail. They all thought I was Kaarina's mother and were saying, "Mama ho?" meaning, "Does your mother want a horse?" I was offered many rides and am proud to say that I never accepted any, probably more to save money than to save my pride.

Along the way we met up with two perfectly outfitted Austrian women and their personal guide. Kaarina and I felt it was prudent to stay close to them, and we all eventually made it to the Halfway House guesthouse, which, as its name suggests, was located midway along the trail. The place was strikingly beautiful, with brand new rooms and balconies overlooking the gorge, semi-hot showers, and yes, the ceramic trench toilet. The lounge had little braziers for the hikers to gather around to warm up and they served really good hot food. The entire thing cost about five bucks each. I was soaked to the gills most of the time while hiking, and what had started as a little cold had turned into something resembling pneumonia.

The next day we kept hiking downhill and made it to the bottom of the gorge. We were going to continue on hiking the trail, but when we heard that the roads out of the park were blocked by landslides, we decided we should focus on getting out of there. There was a small office on the side of the road but they weren't much help to us since we couldn't speak the language. I was beginning to panic, fearing that we would get stranded there, when KABOOM, we heard blasting. They were literally blowing up the boulders which had blocked the roads. Thanks to the Chinese speaking guide the Austrian girls had, we were all able to hire a local man to drive us back to the park entrance. The main road was extremely narrow and had no guard rails. The driver weaved around boulders the size of our Jeep while we stared up at the crumbling cliff face on our right. On our left we overlooked a great abyss to the crashing river at the bottom of the gorge. The drive was terrifying, and was definitely more exciting than the hike had been.

Leaving Lijiang was a bit of a nightmare. I waited for what seemed like forever for a bus to the airport, then waited for a quick flight to

Kunming, where I was supposed to catch a flight to Xian. The airport was crushingly crowded. They announced that our flight would be delayed two hours, which would get me to Xian at about 2 a.m. with no firm hostel reservations and only a pretty sketchy hostel address written in Chinese characters I'd copied from someone else's guidebook. But as had been happening so frequently in China, I got "saved" again.

While standing in the airport in Kunming waiting for my flight to Xian, I was listening to announcements I couldn't understand and looking like a deer in headlights. A young, pretty, well dressed Chinese woman named Lan approached me and asked in perfect English if I needed help. She had been studying law and living in New York City for the past four years trying to "find herself." She was twenty-six and had married an older Chinese man, Fu. Lan's parents worked for the communist Chinese government, which she found rather distressing.

Lan and Fu were also flying to Xian to meet her parents and they invited me to accompany them to their hotel there, where I was able to get a room for three nights. I was so lucky to have met them because the hostel that I'd planned on going to was full and it would have been horrible to contend with that at two in the morning.

In addition, this family invited me to join them every day of their vacation in Xian, and it was a hoot! Lan's father had a local government liaison arrange our transportation with a driver who took us to every possible tourist attraction and to the most amazing restaurants I'd ever been to. Every meal was served in a fancy private room with an enormous round table that had a lazy Susan in the center so the various dishes could circle around for all to try. There were always many people joining us— some family, some co-workers. The many servers brought dish after dish after dish of beautifully presented but unidentifiable food. Eel, fried donkey, and wild mushrooms were pointed out to me. Any offers I made to contribute to the bill were absolutely refused. In fact, I never saw a bill and Lan intimated that the government covered everything for her parents.

These Chinese were some of the most gracious and generous hosts I'd ever encountered. I told them so in one of the many toasts we made over meals. The custom was to stand up, toast your fellows with a tiny shot glass of wine or beer, drink the whole thing in one go, then show everyone the empty glass so they'd have to drink all of theirs and shout, "Gambei!" This was their way of saying "Cheers."

We toured the Terra Cotta Warrior site, which was the burial ground for the first emperor, Qin Shi Huang. Emperor Qin was a very busy man back in the two hundreds BCE. His army conquered all the provinces and unified the writing and the country. In his spare time he built the Great Wall. We also visited the temple that housed Siddhartha's finger bone. Siddhartha later became the Buddha and in many countries temples or shrines were built to house an alleged body part or artifact. What was fascinating was seeing all these supposedly non-religious communists bowing, praying and lighting incense.

I'm not sure if any of them saw the irony in this, considering how they have persecuted the Tibetan Buddhists throughout the years. Were the prayerful just going through the motions and following the group without really questioning what was behind it? This was not a culture that tended to encourage individualism or critical thinking.

We then proceeded to the tomb of China's one and only empress, Wu Zetian. She ruled back in the six hundreds A.D. and managed to stay in power for over fifty years. She helped spread Buddhism throughout China and promote women's rights.

The next stop was at the Yaodong cave dwellings. These had been around for centuries and some were still in use. The caves stayed warm in the winter but cool in the summer. Everything, including the bedroom and kitchen, was inside the cave except for the hole in the ground that was the toilet. This wonderful full day tour ended with a visit to the museum of calligraphy. Huge slabs of stone, with exquisite swirling characters chiseled into them, rose from the floors to the ceilings. Workers on ladders patted the carvings in the stones with ink and then rolled rice paper over them to create beautiful scrolls for sale. Lan tried to translate some of them for me, but sometimes what they said didn't seem as inspiring as just the beauty and creativity of the characters themselves.

While staying with her family, Lan would openly express to me her concerns about her future, her sexuality, her weight, her marriage, her family being so involved with the Communist party, and her desire to study law and return to China to lead a revolution to improve human rights. She continually shocked me with her frank comments. She was especially disgusted with the rampant industrial and population growth in China and with people's lack of concern for the environment, human rights, freedom of expression, and treatment of the poor and mentally ill. And she was most emphatically disgusted with the design of the toilets.

Lan and Fu wanted to go to Pizza Hut to have "tiramisu." They said it was the only "Italian restaurant" around, which made me laugh. It seemed the restaurant staff was a little confused about which country's cuisine they wanted to represent, as the waitresses were dressed in what appeared to be Mexican style garb. They were having a Spanish "special" with sangria and tapas, so I guess they were close, considering Spain had conquered Mexico. Lan and Fu also told me that McDonalds was better in China than in the U.S. I'm not sure that was so hard to accomplish, but the only difference I noticed was that it seemed like there were a thousand people in line in China rather than the usual ten or so at home. The McDonalds employees wore jeans with the iconic golden arches emblazoned on their rear pockets. I have often said how disgusted I feel to see American franchises throughout the world. First of all, they destroy local small businesses, not to mention the negative influence on people's physical health and culture. This holds true for me even within the U.S. It's bad enough destroying the character of our own country's small towns and cities. But it's completely disgraceful to inflict this upon the rest of the world. In general I don't eat at franchise restaurants, not at home, and especially not when I'm traveling abroad. However, Lan and Fu had encouraged me to compare, so one day when I was on my own, I decided to try it. I couldn't find a seat at McDonalds because it was so crowded.

But once again looking lost helped and I was offered a seat by a couple of teenagers who wanted to practice their English. The conversation went something like this: Giggle. Giggle. Pause, "ahhh," pause, "Where are you from?" Pause, more giggling, "ahhh," pause, "What is your name?" Giggle. Giggle. That was usually about it. Sometimes I could even ask them a few questions. If people who approached me didn't speak any English at all, then they just gestured a request to have their photo taken with me. The teenagers I sat with at McDonalds couldn't tell how old I was. They thought I was twenty-eight. I wondered if that phenomenon of thinking, "They all look the same" applied to Westerners too.

I said my good-byes to Lan and Fu and flew back to Beijing. I discovered I was getting pretty savvy about the taxi rip off schemes. The driver tried to overcharge me for the ride from the airport to the hotel, not realizing I'd been there before. First he tried to show me a rate sheet he'd obviously made himself that read "350 yuan," which was $56, to the hotel. I shook my head and responded, "No way." Then he said he'd go by the meter, which after a while I realized was rolling way too fast. So I said it was broken and that I wouldn't pay that either. With gestures I indicated I'd pull the receipt that was printing out of the meter and write down his taxi driver's license number posted on the dashboard and take it to the police so they'd check his meter machine. It was like an old Lassie TV show, where people could infer an amazing amount of information from a few select sounds and movements. He turned off the meter and let me pay what I said I would pay, 120 yuan, which was $20. As a Western tourist I expected to be overcharged, but not almost triple the going rate!

Then when I went to the desk of the hotel in Beijing where I'd stayed before at the start of my trip, the receptionist told me they were full. After I just stood there staring at them, they typed some more into their computer screen, looked at me, and said that there was a room available, but that the price had gone up a hundred yuan, $16. I continued to stare blankly and then said, "Gee," before launching into a calm dissertation reminding them that between my stay with them before and this stay now, I will have stayed a total of seven days, and that I'd used and paid for all their services, including tours and meals, and that I wondered how there could be such a dramatic price increase in a mere week for a loyal customer like myself. I don't know if they understood me or just got tired of me, but I got the same room for the same price I'd paid before. They were evidently not so full after all.

One of my favorite outings in Beijing was to visit the Temple of Heaven. I arrived at about 6:30 a.m. to avoid the tourist onslaught. I didn't care that the temple was being renovated because I hadn't gone there to see the building itself. Instead, I went to see hundreds of local people doing just about everything you could imagine. Every morning groups of people met to do fan dancing, singing, ballroom dancing, hacky-sack, tai-chi with swords, or my particular favorite, walking backwards screaming. I also liked the calligraphy guy. He wrote Chinese characters with water on the cement and so quickly it would evaporate—very Zen. Another great thing to do in Beijing was to go in a rickshaw and visit the hutongs, the old city alleyways. There I felt I was seeing the everyday life of the everyday person, which looked far from easy.

It was encouraging to see the Chinese people out in the open expressing themselves in all these different ways. During Mao's reign in China he started what was known as The Cultural Revolution. This movement was neither cultural nor a revolution. What he wanted was to purge the country of what he considered capitalist or traditional ideology and instead impose his idea of appropriate communist practices. What ensued was a campaign in which millions of people were publicly humiliated, imprisoned, their property seized, and historical relics and sites destroyed or ransacked. It was like a McCarthyism witch hunt on steroids. In addition only certain types of arts—painting, dance, music, for example, were allowed, if they seemed to support Mao's view of communist doctrine. As frustrating as I found this culture at times, I had to remember all that they'd been through. Their bodies and souls had been brutally crushed during Mao's communist dictatorship and people were killed if they attempted to think or act for themselves. Now, with the sudden current onslaught of capitalistic growth and change, the people were having a tough time finding their individuality again. Hopefully, through the resurgence of artistic expression and the advent of an Internet, albeit heavily censored, the people of China could become positive progressive world leaders rather than mindless consumers and destroyers of the earth's resources and minority cultures. We will see which they choose.

On my last day in China I decided to do a meaningless little chore. I liked to do that sometimes, just to see where I might end up. My goal was to find some of those little doughy white buns stuffed with sweet mashed red beans. I'd had them in Japan and loved them and heard that they also ate them in China. So first I tried just looking for them at different bakeries. When that didn't work I tried explaining what I was looking for to various people. But, as you might imagine, gesturing about buns filled with something could be interpreted as a very different thing. Finally I found someone who spoke a bit of English and she wrote out the name for me, "Do sha bao," on a scrap of paper. I proudly returned to all my previous stops and showed them my wee bit of paper so they wouldn't think I was absolutely insane, although now this may have convinced them that I was. I finally found the buns and the lady even warmed one up for me.

While I was gloating yet bemoaning the fact that the bun really wasn't as tasty as it was in my memory, I was approached by yet another young girl wanting to "practice English." I was tired, grumpy and just wanting to be left alone. But somehow she convinced me to come see her school's calligraphy display. I thought it would be obvious by my ripped shorts, dingy stretched out T-shirt, "something the cat coughed up" hair and otherwise total lack of class, that I wouldn't be purchasing any artwork that day. But no, she just didn't get it. I waved good-bye to her and decided to hide out in my room and try to make sense of Chinese TV. I was actually able to follow some of the Chinese soap operas. I didn't even watch soap operas at home, and here I was following them in another language! I took that as a sign that I had clearly been here too long, and it was time to go home.

Costa Rica
2005

My friend Megan had been trying to teach me how to surf in Santa Cruz, and I almost drowned a few times. The water was so cold there I'd have to wear a wetsuit and the big waves and the dark deep water were just plain scary. So I organized a trip to go with Megan to Costa Rica because it was known for having beginner level surfing areas, with small waves and warm water.

We spent one night in the capital, San José, then took a small plane to Tamarindo on the Pacific coast. I was impressed that the airline of a small country like Costa Rica had a female pilot. We stayed right on the beach in a cozy little motel called Villa Amarilla. It was wonderfully convenient to just walk out our door, grab our surfboards and jump in the water.

On one of our breaks from surfing, we went on a day tour of Volcan Rincon de Vieja National Park. We had a full day in the cloud forest, starting with a zip-line which consisted of climbing high up in the trees to a platform, putting on a harness, getting hooked to a line attached above us, then jumping off the platform to zip down the line, ideally with your eyes open, to another platform in another tree. The forests were thick and green, and for us, wet. It would rain off and on while we were there, but because it was so warm, it didn't really bother us. Afterwards we rode horses on the trails below the canopy of trees.

We also went to the Miravalles Volcano, where we could ride a water slide down a hill, visit some beautiful waterfalls, then end the day soaking in silty mud baths. Because we were there off season there weren't many tourists, and though all these activities were the touristy things to do, we had a blast. The government must have realized early on how lucrative it would be to have large unspoiled national parks. Costa Rica's parks provide some of the best ecotourism in the world.

Tourism, however, can be a double-edged sword. We met some locals who told us that they were having trouble finding affordable housing because foreign investors were buying up all the best property.

One night Megan and I went to see leatherback turtles laying eggs in the sand. They lumbered out of the water and up the beach, dug a hole with their hind flippers, then plopped out hundreds of eggs into the hole. We were told that the fertilized eggs were laid on the bottom, and that the mothers were able to create and lay unfertilized eggs on top. They did this so that predators who would dig up the eggs, such as lizards, rodents and birds, would hopefully not reach the fertilized ones. In more recent times the main predators of the eggs were humans who ate them. But with the turtles now near extinction, other humans had become their protectors in areas like the one we were visiting.

Megan could only stay a week, so she went home and I continued traveling by myself. I took a local bus inland to the active volcano, Arenal. There was one fancy and expensive hotel right at its base, but I stayed a few miles away at a smaller, cheaper motel called "El Castillo." My room was clean and had a huge picture window facing the volcano. I'd set my alarm and get up every few hours throughout the night to try to catch a break in the clouds so I could see some flowing lava. At about three in the morning I heard a thump when a bird ran into my window. Apparently someone had gotten my request for a wake-up call. At that moment I was able to see the surreal sight of red glowing magma cascading down from the peak of the volcano. It was a long way off, but still exciting.

Even though I couldn't afford to stay overnight at the Tabacon hot springs resort and spa near Arenal, I could at least spend a day there. The resort had a large swimming pool that was heated by the lava flowing deep underground. There was a bar in the water so you could soak and drink at the same time. The better pools were the natural ones farther back in the park, which you could reach by walking through the jungle and over little arched bridges. The very best hot pools were those near waterfalls, where you could cool down if needed.

After seeing the volcano I headed by bus south toward the Atlantic coast to visit Manuel Antonio National Park. Here the jungle came all the way down to the beach and it was packed with wildlife. I saw and heard howler monkeys that made blood curdling screams. I also saw an armadillo, iguanas, and best of all, a few three-toed sloths. One of them was hanging by its back feet from a branch upside down. It was so big it almost looked like a gorilla. Everywhere there seemed to be white-faced monkeys who'd startle you by leaping onto your backpack looking for food.

When I tried to leave the park I found that the tide had come in and closed off the path, so the few of us who'd stayed late had to hire small boats to get us back to the entrance. I didn't mind at all and was able to find some great food and visit with local street vendors. It was a nice ending to a quick trip, and I felt I'd gotten a good overview of this popular tourist destination. With any luck they'll develop the country slowly, and hopefully continue to protect its natural beauty as well as the local culture.

Morocco
2006

In March 2006 I flew to Mannheim, Germany to meet up with my friend Claudia, whom I'd met in Mongolia. We were headed to Morocco. Before leaving for Morocco we made a quick trip up to Antwerp, Belgium, to celebrate the birthday of Jarne, our fellow tour mate in Mongolia, who was turning twenty-five. The party turned out to be held on the same day as my birthday, but I was turning forty-four. The three of us had a great reunion and we recalled some the incredible adventures we'd had on our overland tour the year before. The Belgians prided themselves on having an extensive variety of beer, each of which was served in its own special glass. Jarne had rented a pavilion for the party and it was wonderful meeting all of his friends. I learned that it was the Belgians who'd invented the "French fry" and they had shops where you could choose from a multitude of dips to lather on the tasty fried potato strips.

Claudia and I then flew on Royal Air Maroc to Casablanca for a layover before continuing on to the city of Fes. During our brief stop in Casablanca we hurriedly took a local train and taxi to see the Hassan II mosque, the largest in the country and the fifth largest in the world.

Arriving late at night in Fes, we were greeted by a driver from our prearranged hotel, the Riad Louna. Unfortunately Claudia's backpack didn't arrive with us. We spent the next three days in Fes exploring the labyrinth of the souk (market) and driving daily to the airport hoping to get her backpack, which they called "le sac." In Morocco they not only spoke Arabic, but most also spoke French, from when it was colonized. Luckily Claudia spoke French, although it seemed we received better attention when I spoke English and threatened to give them a bad review in the *Lonely Planet* guidebook. It turned out that somehow her backpack had gone to the country of Cameroon. Although we spent longer in Fes than we'd anticipated, we didn't waste our time or feel disappointed. Our Riad Louna hotel was in the thick of things right in the souk. We got lost daily wandering the tiny alleyways, admiring the architecture of the madrassas (religious schools), the intricate tile work seen on dozens of fountains, and the myriad stalls selling every imaginable spice, fruit and fowl. One of the fowl was unceremoniously, albeit humanely, dispensed with right before our eyes for a local customer.

One of our favorite stops was an antique shop, where the owner played a lotar, a guitar-like instrument, while we sipped delicious sweet mint tea. Since alcohol was prohibited in Islam, the population made do with drinking this tea and smoking hookahs, the beautiful water pipes with many long tubes for sharing the shisha, flavored tobacco. The highlight of the souk was the tannery, where there were hundreds of clay pits filled with various dyes for coloring leather and wool. Their centuries old technique was used to this day by rugged men with bent backs who stomped the leather with their feet. The leather was then hung out to dry in the sun. Young boys then came with donkeys to load up the dyed leather and rush it through the souk's narrow winding passageways to be delivered to various artisans who'd create a variety of goods, including one of many a woman's addiction, shoes!

The days in Fes flew by waiting for the arrival of Claudia's pack. We were told we'd have to move from our lovely Riad Louna hotel because we'd been there longer than we'd intended and they had previous reservations for our room. The staff was so wonderful that they offered to put us up in a private home for free. Not knowing what to expect, we were just open minded and grateful. But wow, what a gift was bestowed upon us. The home was three stories high, with winding stairways, tucked away rooms and bathrooms, authentic tasteful decor and an incredible view of the city from the terrace. The place even had a kitchen, although we didn't have to cook because the Riad Louna provided our meals. The one drawback was how close we were to a mosque, although it was hard not to be close to one since they were everywhere. In Islam there is a call to prayer five times a day starting before dawn, and with the advent of loudspeakers, the call was deafening. I was awakened abruptly at 4:30 a.m. with what sounded like droning sirens of mantras blaring through our windows. Claudia slept right through all of it.

While we were still waiting for Claudia's luggage we decided to try a hamam, which is also known as a Turkish bath. The hamam consisted of a labyrinth of caverns carved out of stone, with warm water flowing out of pipes in small fountains scattered along the walls. We were the only foreigners so we were certainly the center of attention. We were told to strip down and were then led to the back of the caves. There three women assigned to us gestured for us to lie down on the smooth rock floor on which they proceeded to roughly scrub and bathe us.

Claudia's backpack finally arrived after much yelling and threatening. We overheard the airport staff tell some local women who'd been waiting for months for their belongings that they weren't foreigners so wouldn't be attended to as we'd been. I was disappointed to learn that Royal Air Maroc didn't treat their own people the same or better than they treated visitors, but we were grateful to finally be able to move on.

We caught a local bus south to Timnay to try to hire a guide to tour the Atlas mountains. The bus dropped us off on the side of a road in the desert with nothing else around but a building with no signs. Luckily this building was in fact a place to hire guides, at least one anyway, and that one was Hassan.

Since we hadn't called in advance it took Hassan a while to arrange a driver, but he did finally find one. And, of course, with my car karma, within the first hour our Jeep broke down. Claudia and I found this funny because we'd met in Mongolia and arranged an overland tour that had had more breakdowns than we could count. So with this first one we looked at each other, knowing it wouldn't be the last. The Jeep did break down again, but this time it wasn't on the side of an empty road. It was instead in a small village, where we could wait in a café for Hassan to find another mode of transportation and driver to go with it.

The new driver, Ali, showed up with a dark, rather pimped out Mercedes, replete with velvet covered seats and tinted windows outlined with dangling decorations. Claudia and I were certain that we needed a Jeep because we doubted that a normal passenger car could manage the rough roads of the lower Atlas mountains. But as we really didn't have much choice, we all piled in the car and headed out. At first the roads were reasonable and we stopped at a family farm to eat a late lunch. Hassan had brought the food with us and shared it with the family, who seemed to be struggling financially. The parents and three children all shared a two room house, where they slept and ate on the floor and cooked over an open fire.

It was nearly dusk by the time we set off for the lower Atlas mountains and the sky seemed to darken as the roads worsened. At one point we all had to get out of the car to lighten the load and let the driver try to navigate over a huge dip in the dirt road. In pitch black darkness we continued bumping along, crossing flooded roads, dodging stray animals and wondering if we were lost. We arrived late that night in a tiny mud-walled village, Asaka, where we were to stay the night.

We were now in the Berber part of Morocco. The Berbers are an ancient, traditionally nomadic, non-Arabic people who had now, for the most part, settled down to an agricultural life. As with many "pagan" peoples, when usurped by a more dominant religion, they still practiced their age old rituals, but they did so secretly because their beliefs were frowned upon by the more zealous practitioners of the dominant religion, in this case Islam. You could see the difference between the Berbers and the Arabs right away. The Berbers wore more colorful clothing than the Arabs further north, and the women didn't always cover their heads. Most of the women had permanent markings on their faces, hands and feet, which they believed protected them from the darker forces of life, like bad luck or evil spirits. They seemed more openly expressive to me than the Arab women had. They made good eye contact, smiled more, and seemed more willing to try to communicate with us.

We had a lovely stay with a gracious Berber family, who welcomed us into their two room mud brick home. The parents and their adopted son slept in the kitchen and gave Claudia and me their bedroom. There was no mattress to sleep on, just thin pads placed on the floor. The wife served us the traditional tajine for meals, which they prepared over an open fire pit in the kitchen. Tajine seemed to be served at every meal, every day in Morocco. It was a combination of some form of meat, usually lamb, plus vegetables such as carrots and potatoes, and maybe a fruit such as lemons or prunes. All of this was simmered in a glazed ceramic plate with a pyramid shaped lid and served plain with bread or occasionally on couscous grain. It was always really delicious, but I did get bored eating the same food every day.

We all went on a beautiful hike one day down a dry riverbed before finding a trickle of water running through a gorge with high rock walls. It was an oasis with some trees, shade and a cool breeze.

At night, when I had to get up to use the bathroom, I just went outside in the dark and hoped I didn't step in anything. The family had a rickety old outhouse with a hole in the ground and two wooden planks for your feet. But whenever possible I always chose the open outdoors, as the closed in toilets smelled really awful. After two days we headed back to Timnay, where Claudia and I could catch a bus to continue south to Merzouga.

On the bus we were again looked upon as aliens from another planet. We arrived late at night, which I didn't like but knew that sometimes it couldn't be avoided. On the bus throngs of young men would board at a stop and assail us with "deals." We wanted to have something booked before we arrived because we'd be coming into town late, so we went ahead and chose an auberge (inn). Claudia spoke French so we thought we were communicating fairly well, but we never really knew how much was being lost in translation and whether or not the salesmen were telling the truth. When we arrived late our prearranged ride to the inn wasn't there to meet us. We weren't sure what to do next, so we just waited a while and kept repeating the name of the driver who was supposed to meet us and the name of the auberge where we were supposed to stay to anyone who came up to us. Finally our ride showed up and what a slick character he was, with tight jeans, gold jewelry, thick black hair and a quick smile. Claudia and I climbed into the back of his car while he and his buddy sat in the front and we began to drive and drive and drive out into the desert. Claudia and I clicked into our usual survival mode in which she was quiet and watching for any problems while I disarmed the potential offenders with non-stop chatter and questions.

We arrived at the inn, which sat alone in the desert and we were the only ones staying there. The place was gorgeous and huge, was made of mud, and looked a bit like a fortress. We'd come to Merzouga to explore the desert, which was good because there wasn't anything else to do. We drove all over with our slick host to see fossils, desert flowers and camps of Berbers in dark linen tents. One night we left most of our belongings at the auberge and rented a couple of camels and a guide to go out and camp in the Saharan desert dunes. I found riding camels quite comfortable, and I loved the colors, the shadows, the intricate designs of tiny bug footprints, and the stark open space of the desert. Camping out there was magical, with the stars overhead and the crisp clean air. Our guide cooked our dinner, tajine of course, over an open wood fire.

We could not believe it when after dinner our guide half our age tried to hit on us. We wondered if this were his idea of how we should tip him. We declined the offer of course, and rather than sleep in the tent with him we chose to sleep outside under the immense blanket of stars. The next morning we awoke and ran up to the top of an enormous dune to watch the sunrise. When the sun was on the horizon it was hard to tell the difference between a sunrise and a sunset, and I realized how easy it would be to get lost without any real landmarks. Atop the dune, as far as I could see in every direction, the sky met the earth, bringing home that we are truely mere specks of sand in a vast universe.

When we returned by camel to our auberge we were introduced to the owner's one-way transportation scam. Transportation from Merzouga to the auberge had been included in the price of the hotel stay, but getting back to town was not. Rather than pay for a taxi into town and then catch a bus to our next destination, we arranged to take the taxi all the way to the Todra Gorge, which lay in the middle of the country. We saved a lot of time doing this and it really wasn't that much more expensive. When we arrived to Tinghir, the little town by the gorge, we lucked out again in our search for lodging by just talking to the right person and found a perfect place overlooking a little stream just minutes from the gorge.

We hiked for a day in the gorge and were determined to do it without a guide, which was a mistake since we got lost and it took quite a while to find our way back. But even lost in the mountains, luck was on our side, and we happened upon a tiny encampment with a lovely local woman and her child. She offered us mint tea brewed over a fire, then pointed us in the right direction to find the trail leading back to town.

Back at our hotel we arranged for a driver to take us on a roundabout way to Marrakesh in a beat up Renault car. Often we weren't sure if we'd make it across a washed out road or find our way through the maze of an obscure dilapidated village. The mud buildings blended in with the sand and from a distance it was hard to tell one from the other. We met many wonderful characters along the way. One that stood out was a young man, a deaf mute, with whom we shared our lunch as we all sat quietly under a lone tree on the side of a dirt road cooking kefta, which are lamb meatballs, and tomatoes over a small open wood fire.

We met women with their children working the fields or gathering water from primitive wells with buckets. Their wizened faces shone as bright and varied as the fields of poppies. One woman we gave a ride to handed us a picture of her missing daughter and begged us to notify the authorities, thinking that foreigners might be treated with more deference than peasants like her who toiled on this rugged land. I can say that we tried, but I doubted much came of it.

We made a brief stop at the Cascades de Ouzoud (Olive Waterfalls), which were a welcome cool wet respite from the dust and dirt that had deeply penetrated our pores. The next day we quickly made it to Marrakesh, which felt too busy, too touristy, too loud, and the people too pushy. It was somewhat of a shock to our systems at first after five days out in the countryside, but eventually it grew on us. The giant square, Djemaa El-Fna, was packed with stalls of food, snake charmers, acrobats, musicians, water sellers and every possible local ware you could imagine. So we did what visitors do in Marrakesh—we shopped.

Souvenirs are all too often lugged home on the plane to hang in the closet, sit on the mantle, perch on the wall, or dangle on a wrist, soon to be forgotten in the busy drone of life. But occasionally I do dust off my tajine and attempt to recreate the meal I ate daily while in Morocco. And for an evening I am taken back, as if by magic carpet, to the smells, the tastes, the sounds, and the friendships forged in a beautiful land.

Thailand
2006

In November 2006 I heard from a friend that a good destination for Fall was Thailand. It had nice weather, friendly people, and was a country so familiar with Western tourists that traveling around there was easy. The hardest part was getting there. So after a mind, leg, and butt numbing twenty-hour flight, I finally arrived.

WHY CAN'T SOMEONE DESIGN A COMFORTABLE PLANE? I mean really, couldn't it be like a train with berths, or hammocks? Was it really necessary for the airline to cram us in like that? And what was up with their class system? I say, "out with it," and with the rest of the world's kings, queens and dictators!

I arrived in Bangkok without incident and it turned out to be one of the easiest places I'd ever traveled to. Things went as smoothly as Thai silk. The people were lovely, patient and helpful. Of course, as usual, they started off by asking double the normal price for everything, beginning with the taxis from the airport to the city. In the airport, if you went downstairs you could get metered taxis to town for 300 Baht (about $9) plus tolls, versus the 900 Baht ($28) they tried to get you for upstairs.

My hotel, The Siam 2, was clean and quiet and the pool was refreshing. It was near enough to popular Khao San road, where all the backpackers stayed, but far enough not to be bothered by their noise and crowds. I thought the Thais would speak more English than they did, since they had so many tourists, but I was happy with whatever I could get, because I didn't speak any Thai. I could completely butcher even the simplest of languages, and this one was not simple. It was important to have your destination written on paper in the Thai alphabet, not just in our Roman letters.

I arrived in the afternoon and decided to stay up until nighttime in order to avoid jet lag and switch my body clock. I wandered around Khao San, but this area was a backpacker haven, so I saw more foreigners than locals, which wasn't that interesting. The streets were full of food stalls and clothing, Chinese junk and Thai massage parlors. But everything was pretty clean and peaceful and no one hassled me too much.

After wandering around I was so tired that I figured I'd just sit in my hotel lobby and drink the local beer, Chang. I'd heard this beer had inconsistent quality control so you'd never be sure what percentage of alcohol you'd be getting. As always in these places, you'd meet other travelers. I was fortunate to meet Claire, a feisty young Scottish girl fresh from working in Australia. She was big, buxom and brash. We decided that of all the things to see and do in Bangkok, the vagina shooting ping pong ball Pat Pong nightclub show was the most bizarrely attractive. So we recruited Tom from Italy as our chaperone, since he'd proclaimed himself the Pat Pong ping pong tour guide. Pat Pong was the area of Bangkok famous for the outrageous sex shows. On the way to Pat Pong we stopped by the Saum Lam Night Bazaar, an enormous shopping area touted as the cheapest place in Bangkok, and where the locals shopped. There were indeed mostly locals there and the prices, as with seemingly everything in this city, were ridiculously cheap. Most of the goods in the Night Bazaar were just ordinary things like clothes, shoes and handbags. There weren't many art objects or handcrafts. My companions shopped like mad for all the latest knock off fashions, but I was just looking for a meditation pillow.

We made a quick stop at one of the countless food stalls to eat some reasonably yummy healthy fifty cent noodles, rice and strips of various meats. Then off we went to the ping pong ball show. Pat Pong represented one of the many things I hated about humanity, but I tried to go with an open mind and heart. The narrow streets, in what appeared to be a red-light district, were lined with neon signs, my favorite of which simply read "Super Pussy."

These clubs tried to get you to pay a lot more than the admission fee, so you'd have to stand firm and not allow any extra massages, lap dances, tips, or extra drinks. We got in for a whopping $5, with a drink included. It was dark and smoky inside the club, with black lights so everyone's eyes and teeth glowed eerily. A handful of young girls were on stage and looked to be maybe fifteen years old. They were dressed in skimpy thong underwear, had pasties over their nipples and wore knee-high black leather boots. They wriggled a bit around silver poles and, as far as I could tell, they were completely bored.

They'd visit amongst themselves like teenage girls would do in the hallways of any high school. Then one really skinny girl bent over and stuck a lit cigarette inside her vagina, and she was actually able to "smoke" it! Another girl could pop the top off of a fizzy drink bottle with her vagina, and still another could pull out a never ending glow-in-the-dark tape. There were flying darts shot from the girls' privates that popped blown up condoms held by some of the middle-aged lonely loser men in the audience. My personal favorite trick was the flying banana, replete with a disgusting customer catching it. I noticed the "mamasan" (matron) of this "fine establishment" stayed far away from any projectiles that flew in her direction. The variety of items that could go in and out of these small girls seemed endless, but finally the time arrived for what had drawn us there, the ping pong balls. And oddly, that one was the most boring. A chubby girl would clumsily stick a ball in her and then stand over a glass and plop it rather unceremoniously out and down her legs into the glass. Often she missed, would giggle, pick it up off the filthy floor, and start over. I wanted to laugh, cry and vomit all at the same time.

The most noticeable thing about the whole experience was the audience. There were a few couples who, like us I'm sure, were just morbidly curious. But then there were all the men, even some Thai men. They were all rather homely, balding, with big guts and wedding rings. Some were businessmen and others looked like drunk frat boy types. They were more than willing to have what looked like little girls bounce on their laps. They would gladly hold balloons that looked like penises so the girls could shoot darts at them or catch flying objects with their bare hands or shove bananas up these poor girls' not so private privates. It was all so utterly mesmerizing, and yet, strangely, dull. The girls seemed to be just playing around, giggling, a little sleepy, a little vacant—the way some of us might look at our jobs right after lunch. And that was that. No big deal. And yawning, our little group waved bye-bye to the club, came home and went to bed.

Day two in Bangkok was much more tame—just the ever present wats (temples), which were spectacular with lots of gold, tile, jade, monks and statues of Buddha. It just so happened it was an auspicious, or lucky, day in Thailand that day, so all the monks were out and about doing their prayers and gathering together. Then Claire and I accidentally stumbled upon the long boats (colorful, thin wooden boats with huge long engines) and bargained for a private tour through the labyrinth of canals that wound around the outskirts of the city. We had to pass through locks just like a mini Panama canal passage. The canal ride took us by fantastic little houses and temples and local folks going about their daily lives. It was very pleasant and relaxing. We also went to the obligatory amulet market to pick up miniature Buddha figures, beads and tiny fetish jars with unidentifiable goo and bits in them. I wasn't sure what those weird little bottles were used for but I loved the old lady selling them. A wrinkly monk smoking cigarettes and listening to an iPod was also involved in the sale. I think he didn't want me to get ripped off when I purchased one of the tiny jars for a whopping twenty-five cents.

We then went through the horrendous late afternoon rush hour traffic in a tuk-tuk, a three-wheeled open air taxi—the kind that you often find in the crowded cities of developing countries. We should have taken an air-conditioned metered taxi in order to avoid getting carbon monoxide poisoning, and they were actually cheaper. Tuk-tuks lose their novelty quickly in ninety-degree weather. Our destination was called the MBK shopping country. Yes, that's right, country, and it seemed as big as one. It was overwhelming. But my Scottish companion Claire was a shopping machine and found plenty to purchase. I found some $5 cool cotton fisherman's pants, a must for any hip backpacker. I also learned to be careful trying to catch cabs during rush hour, as they turned off their meters and charged whatever they wanted because of the terrible traffic jams.

Unfortunately I got lazy and didn't take care of business in time regarding the next leg of my journey, so I had to pay a bit more to fly north to Chiang Mai. It was more expensive to fly on weekends and most of the hotels were full because a flower show was in full swing there and would go on for three months. I lucked out though and found a hotel downtown for a reasonable price when I got there. But it would have been cheaper and less nerve-wracking to have booked in advance.

On my last day in Bangkok I decided to try the famous Thai massage rather than go to the river market. The market was supposed to be quite nice but I didn't have time before my flight north. The masseuse said her name was "Ew," at least that's what it sounded like to me. She was just a little wisp of a thing, so who would have thought she could toss me all over the place! She used amazing body mechanics and just pushed, poked and pulled harder if I groaned. After my massage I took a taxi to the airport. The taxis came in a variety of colors—pink, yellow, green and purple—and were quite festive. The Thais drove on the left, which meant I was always getting in on the wrong side.

During my ride I made a few mental notes of things I'd noticed. For example, I never heard any traditional music, only English or Thai pop that blared everywhere. The food, oddly enough, hadn't impressed me. I think that was because I hated cilantro, and there it was in EVERYTHING. And what was up with the 7-11 stores? They were making a killing here, as they seemed to be on every street corner. The cigarette packs had pictures of skulls, black lungs, and rotted teeth. I grimaced as I imagined ads with the young girls from Pat Pong elucidating the effects of vaginal "smoking."

It was a quick flight to Chiang Mai, so my first evening there I toured the Night Bazaar. In fact my hotel was named The Night Bazaar and was right smack in the middle of things. It seemed I was the only *farang*, meaning foreigner, at the hotel. Farang was pronounced as "all wrong," not as "gosh dang." My hotel was nothing special, but it was clean and had air-conditioning. A horrible breakfast was included, with Wonder Bread white toast and Nescafé. The Bazaar was so crowded with mostly Thai tourists there for the flower show that I really couldn't take much of it. Also most the stuff they sold was all the same, row after row. Surely, as a species, we humans will simply end up being buried under all of our crap.

The next day I went to Wat Umong, a jungle temple. I lucked out and met a Thai English teacher who was volunteering with a program that sponsored monks teaching young kids about Buddhism. Everything I loved—spirituality, culture, the outdoors, kids, and education—was all wrapped up right here into one great experience. I got to see a few men get their heads and eyebrows shaved as a requirement to join the monastery. It was a big deal, with all the families there to celebrate. Then I got to hang out with the monks and kids for a while, and all of it with my very own personal translator.

The English teacher dropped me off on the side of the road to catch a *sawngthaew*, which literally means two boards. They were truck taxis with two rows of seats in the back, and as they were shared, they were definitely the cheapest local transport. Tuk-tuks were the most expensive, oddly enough, and in Chiang Mai there were no metered taxis.

So I took a sawngthaew up to Doi Sutep, an amazingly beautiful temple on top of a mountain overlooking Chiang Mai. The temple housed the International Buddhist Center and offered meditation retreats and training in English, which I considered taking. I hated to admit though that the idea of sitting still and quiet for a long period of time scared me. But I was attracted to Buddhism and the calm it seemed to instill in its practitioners. The people in this Buddhist country did seem peaceful, except for their frequent military coups.

As a psychiatric nurse I also noticed that there were no obvious schizophrenics wandering the streets. My English teacher friend assured me that they had them though. She also said there were a lot of hyperactive kids, which I found hard to believe, as the kids I'd seen were all so well behaved.

Boys from Buddhists families trained as monks at some point in their youth. Then they had to decide if they wanted to stay and be a monk permanently, or return to civilian life. Monks couldn't touch women, so the girls in the truck taxi all had to cram in one side so the boy monks could have their space and not touch them by accident. I remembered having accidentally touched my old monk helper in Bangkok, and that must have been why he'd suddenly let out a scream. I'd wondered what had happened, and now he probably had to be reincarnated as a rat or something thanks to me. I finished the day walking down an open market street. I'd had my fill of markets already and was looking forward to volunteering at the Elephant Nature Park.

RUN, DON'T WALK, TO THE ELEPHANT NATURE PARK! Indeed, I felt I could have died right then, a fully contented woman, well, only fully if I knew these amazing creatures would never again be abused, tortured or made to serve Man. The Elephant Nature Park (www. elephantnaturefoundation.org) was situated about twenty-five miles north of Chiang Mai in the middle of a valley with a lush jungle and a river running through it. There were thatched huts for the volunteers to share, with mattresses on the floor and mosquito nets. It was rustic but not really rough. We had electricity, shared toilets and cold running water for showers, which was fine since you didn't really need a hot one. Plus it had the most delicious food I'd eaten yet in Thailand.

There were twenty-eight elephants, forty dogs, probably twenty or so cats, three cows and maybe thirty people including permanent staff.

The elephants had been rescued by an amazing woman, Dr. Sangduen 'Lek' Chailert, the elephant park founder, who'd devoted her life to saving them and trying to change the cruel practice of "taming" them, called the *phajaan*. In the phajaan they take the baby away from its mother and starve and torture it in order to "break" it so it could be trained. Lek discouraged people from riding the elephants because riding actually hurts their backs. She also tried to stop the practice of local people using them to beg on the streets and from being used in circuses where they perform demeaning tricks and are mistreated. There was a long history of terrible cruelty that Lek and the park's staff and volunteers strove to end.

This was one of the greatest experiences of my life. We actually fed and bathed the elephants twice every day. There we were, right in the river with them. I was so blissed out that I was laughing and crying from pure joy. They were all around us in the river, and we were splashing and scrubbing and they just let us. The babies were like any human child, wanting to play and play and not wanting to come out of the water. Each elephant had its own painful story of how it ended up at the park—eyes poked out, foot blown off by a mine, or its mother shot for eating a farmer's crops. And these creatures, who never forgot, had chosen to forgive and let us love them. How lucky could we be?

Volunteers could come for a day or longer. It cost $250 a week to volunteer and that included food and accommodation. I loved this place so much that I decided to stay another week. The volunteers did other work besides washing and feeding the elephants. We helped cook, taught English, helped the veterinarian, and built rafts and fences. One day we planted a field with grass shafts. It was soggy, muddy, scratchy work, but so rewarding since we knew it would become food for the elephants. What Lek really needed was more land, and of course the money to buy it. This was the only place in Thailand designed for this purpose at the time. The hope was that volunteering with elephants could become the new "happening thing" for tourists. It was so much more fulfilling than a ride or a show.

A small group of us went on what the park called the Jumbo Express. This was an overland trip to visit tribes and schools in the northern part of the country to try to teach people to respect and care for elephants. We rode in the back of a truck on bumpy dirt roads, up and down high hills, for at least eight hours. We stopped at a camp where they used the elephants to give rides to tourists in order to check on their condition, which was not good. People should not ride elephants. We then carried on north a few more hours to a Karen village near the border with Burma. The Karen in Thailand were political refugees who'd fled persecution by the Burmese military government. They were also known to be good "mahouts," the trainers and caretakers of trained elephants.

We arrived at their village after dark, but everyone was so welcoming and excited to see us. Lek had come with us and it was a great opportunity to get to know this amazing humble woman. We handed out toys to the kids, helped prepare dinner over the fire and were then invited around to all the homes to meet everyone in the village. We all slept together on the floor of a large barn, where the outhouse had a ceramic hole in it. The weather turned cold at night and I didn't envy the women who got up at five a.m. to beat the rice. They told us they tried to get up before the chickens did so the chickens didn't eat the rice before it was beaten and stored. They used an innovative levered pounding system, then after the rice was pounded, they threw it up in the air so the husks blew away.

After that we went from home to home to treat the cattle and pigs for any injuries and to squirt de-worming medication into their mouths. We lined up the children to de-worm them also. Plus we handed out things like cough medicine, basic hygiene items, clothing and school supplies. All but one of the elephants from this village were out at various camps around Thailand giving rides to tourists. The elephant that wasn't working actually stayed at Lek's park and was called a "leased" elephant, because her park paid for its upkeep. The park did this when an elephant was ill or needed a break from working. Unfortunately one day it would have to be returned to the village. When a village had one of its elephants staying at the park the villagers would send one of their boys to the park with the elephant to act as it's mahout. The hope was that the mahouts would learn kinder healthier ways to manage and train their elephants and would continue those practices when they eventually returned home. In the future Lek planned to send volunteers for home-stays in these villages. There were about forty families in the village we visited and everyone seemed to have a great time.

In addition to the village stay we also zoomed around through the mountains on rough dirt roads in order to stop by schools and distribute clothes and school supplies. The kids would all line up and one by one approach us, put their hands in prayer position, bow and accept their gift. Then as a group they'd sing to us and we'd all take a group photo. Building a bridge between the park and the local people was key to the success of saving the elephants.

As part of the park stay we went for an overnight trip to the mountains to get the elephants accustomed to foraging like they would normally do in the wild. One of the big male elephants ran off and ransacked a village, which we subsequently had to repair. In this area the monks had tied orange scarves around the trees to bless them, as blessed trees weren't supposed to be cut down. It was a clever attempt to save the forest for the elephants. The overnight stay was rustic. We slept outdoors on a wooden platform and cooked over a fire. The mahouts entertained us by playing flutes made out of plastic PVC pipes and together we all sang the children's lullaby we'd been learning, which was of course about elephants.

Back at the park one of the little elephant babies decided a new game was to head butt me, eat the flowers in the garden, then come up on the platform which I'd dashed to for safety. It took three mahouts to get her out. As a result of this new found activity we had to change the fencing structure because the other elephants saw what she did, so now they'd want to try it too. I thought they might be plotting a takeover.

Some of us "old timers" got to change to nicer rooms. However the showers were still freezing cold, we washed our clothes by hand, and the "bamboo bounce" kept you up at night—that was, whenever anyone walked by or turned over in bed, the whole structure swayed.

One of the bull elephants was in musth. That was when they were ready to breed. You could tell because a fluid leaked out of their temples and ran down their cheeks. The males had to be chained during this time because they were so aggressive. The staff brought one of the females over to the male every day and we got to witness "ele-porn." Actually it was really beautiful to watch them nuzzling and caressing each other.

I'd gotten to use my nursing skills a few times when people fell or a mahout cut himself or just plain felt depressed. Most of the mahouts came from neighboring Burma and lived in refugee camps. They didn't speak Thai or English but they had a long history of working with elephants. For the most part they were all sweet and we tried to teach them some English. But there was one mahout who got drunk and cut his elephant with a machete. Needless to say he was let go. We realized it would take a long time to change man's centuries of thinking that these creatures had no feelings. If you could see how the family groups played and protected each other, you'd see how they really seemed so much better than many humans.

The last couple of days at the park were sad because I was preparing to leave. Our little group of volunteers had truly bonded with this place and with each other. I felt completely lost as to what to do next and couldn't stay longer because the next group of volunteers was slated to arrive. I figured I'd take a day or two after leaving to clean up, eat pizza, and ponder my options for where to go. The hill tribe visits to the north sounded like human zoos. Evidently the "long neck" people, a sub-group of the Karen, stopped wearing the gold rings that stretched their necks due to health reasons. But then they realized they could make money from tourists if they continued to wear the rings, so they started it up again. I didn't think I wanted to support that unhealthy practice. At the moment everything I could do in the near future sounded meaningless after what I'd experienced with the elephants.

I then spent an entire day trying to get out of Chiang Mai. The airlines, trains and buses were all booked. Finally I was able to find a third-class ticket on a train going to Lopburi, south toward Bangkok, to see the monkeys. The train left at 6:30 a.m. and was supposed to take twelve hours. It was hotter than blazes, had rock hard seats, was completely packed, and had disgusting holes for toilets. And wouldn't you know it, I had a great time! There were only three farangs—myself, Vern and Hussein. Vern was a big lug from Australia who was having a two day love affair with a cute Thai chick, Nong. Again, Nong was her nickname for foreigners. Hussein was from Yemen and had worked for the Saudis for years as a financial advisor but got fed up with the strictness of Saudi society. The four of us ended up taking over the dining car, where we hung out drinking beer with police, army boys, and the train wait staff and engineers. Who was driving the train then? I didn't want to know.

We finally arrived in Lopburi and, oh my Buddha, what a party was going on there! It was the king's birthday and full moon to boot. A big carnival was in full swing and, wouldn't you know, Nong's mom worked at it. So we stashed our huge packs in a carnie tent and did the scene. We drank weird mini-keg like things of beer and listened to live Thai rock and roll. Finally, a wee bit inebriated, we piled onto the backs of tiny motorcycles with our huge packs crammed between the legs of the drivers, and zoomed off to our hotel. It did amaze me the things I was willing, even thrilled, to do when I wasn't at home.

The following day I went to see the monkeys, my main reason for coming to Lopburi. They had taken over a wat, or stone temple, in the middle of town and they were seriously out of control. One jumped on my back the moment I walked in and I screamed and flailed like a maniac until he jumped off and the park staff gave me a stick to beat the buggers back. It was fantastically funny. There were monkeys everywhere scratching and grooming, tiny babies riding on mothers' backs, monkey fights and plenty of monkeys mating.

I caught a bus to go a couple of hours west of Lopburi to Ayuthaya, the old capital, where ancient wats were scattered throughout the city. Other than having the wats though, it was just another crowded, noisy, dirty city. So before leaving I quickly went to see the famous stone Buddha head at the base of a tree where the wood of the trunk has grown around and nearly enveloped it. Buddha didn't seem to mind though. He looked very peaceful.

Then I was off to Kanchanaburi, which was northwest of Bangkok. The entire day I was the only farang on all the buses. I began to wonder if I were missing important things, or just finding a less beaten path. At the bus station cafeterias, and really almost everywhere I went, no one spoke English. None of the signs or menus were in English or even in our Roman script. So the waiters would just look at me and ask with a smile, "Pad Thai?" This was their staple dish with noodles, chicken and a sauce, and one they assumed I'd know and want.

In Kanchanaburi I decided to splurge and pay $30 a night to stay on Kasem island, smack in the middle of a tributary to the River Kwai. I had to take a boat to get to the island, and it was beautiful.

I had mistakenly been calling the transgender men in Thailand "girlie boys," when they were actually called "ladyboys." It was really an amazing phenomenon in this country. Evidently there was no stigma to this and you could see the transformation of young school boys in uniform growing their hair and nails out and wearing make-up. Some would even decide to take hormones to grow breasts. If they had the money, some day they might choose to have surgery and become a transsexual. They were often quite beautiful and worked jobs in restaurants, travel agencies or boutiques. I had gone to a shop in Bangkok that was having a "Coup

Sale" (yes, capitalism reigned supreme even during the military coups) and had such a good time with the ladyboy salesperson.

In order to get to and from Kasem Island, I had to take water taxis. A very masculine looking woman named "Gow" was my taxi boat driver, and I wondered if there were another term for the girls who wanted to be boys, perhaps "man-girl" or "she-male". Whatever the term, Gow was one of those and she was tough!

Kasem island had little bungalows overlooking the river, a swimming pool, Internet access and soft pop music playing. I believe the words to the tune I was humming along to were "you take my breath ahhwaaay, oooh, oooh, oooh." There were little furry bunnies everywhere and I chuckled to myself that Darwin would be quite confused wondering how they got there. And then there was the most enormous slug or snail on the wall of my personal outdoor toilet. I didn't get close enough to identify it, since I was afraid it might eat me. I decided to name it the "Slugmansnailboy" and hoped it would be satisfied with the offerings I made to the porcelain throne. Don't ask me why they had such beautiful rooms but then put the toilet outside.

I really got off the map when I became obsessed with going to see some bats. I was peacefully lounging on an island in the river in Kanchanaburi and thought I'd go up to Sai Yok Park to see some waterfalls, springs and bat caves. Instead, the *Lonely Planet* guidebook, which I had a love/hate relationship with, printed just enough of the map I needed in order to screw me up. I ended up at Sai Yok Park on the side of the road with my huge backpack about an hour from where I was supposed to be for a hostel and the bat caves. Evidently the bat caves were not at the park.

I went ahead and played in the waterfalls and continued to try to find someone who spoke English or knew anything about the bat caves. I didn't expect everyone in the world to learn English, but it was just such a surprise in Thailand since it was one of the most touristed places in the world. Someone I met thought it might be because Thailand had been lucky and had never been occupied long term by a foreign power. I decided to just keep pantomiming, trying to communicate and be okay with getting lost. I started a "conversation" with the park ranger and he somehow indicated that there was an even better cave in Ratchaburi. This sounded like a good idea to me since I was planning to head south toward the Gulf of Thailand islands anyway. As luck would have it, the city where the better bat caves supposedly were wasn't in the travel guide either.

That was just the sort of challenge I got excited about. The park ranger wrote the name of the place on a tiny piece of paper in the Thai alphabet and I showed it to the bus driver. The bus ride went on for a few hours and then it stopped and the driver took me to another bus, showed the new driver my piece of paper and we took off again. After another hour or so we stopped and the driver said I was in Racthaburi. I couldn't confirm this since I couldn't read any of the signs. I found a little man who drove a sawngthaew, the truck with two rows of seats in the back. I showed him my desired destination and he said or mimed that he'd take me to see the bats for $12. I thought that sounded expensive, but I had absolutely no idea where I was or where I was going, and I'd be the only passenger in the truck, so I agreed. We drove for about an hour and dusk was rapidly approaching, which was when the bats would come out of their caves. I was starting to get a little anxious and was thinking, "Gee, where the hell am I"? But then I figured I'd been thinking that all day.

Finally we got to a temple with huge stone bat sculptures perched on the lampposts lining the driveway. I felt like we had entered Dracula's lair. My driver let me out and wanted to just leave me there all alone, but I said, "No way José, you're coming with me." He looked aghast but followed along and we climbed a hundred stairs, past monkeys and dilapidated Buddha statues, to a huge hole in the ground at the top of the mountain. And then we waited. I climbed down into the hole so I could be right at the edge when the bats came out. My frightened driver crouched up above me under a tree. We were the only ones up there.

We tried to converse, which was a laugh, given the language barrier. His name was "Pinchen" and what a sport he was. At one point he started flailing his arms and screaming and indicated that something had bitten him on the ear. He thought it was a bat, but I was pretty sure it was just a plant thorn or something like that he'd brushed up against. I started getting worried that he might bail on me, but then at precisely six o'clock the bats started to leave their cave. At first there were just a few, but then thousands upon thousands of tiny black fuzzy dots swarmed the sky. They sounded like rain gently falling, mixed with a few of their chirps now and then. The hawks circled around, trying to catch a little winged morsel, but the long winding river of bats just kept flowing out into the twilight. I filmed the bats for a while and then we hiked down the mountain before it got too dark.

I was just beside myself with the thrill of it all, but Pinchen was still freaked out about his ear. I cheered him up by calling him the internationally understood name of "Superhero Batman," and he liked that. He took me to a hotel and I gave him $30 instead of the $12 I owed him. I knew that some people would think doing that was bad because they thought the locals would learn to overcharge tourists. But I felt Pinchen had been a real trooper who'd gone above and beyond the usual tourist request. And it was worth it to see how happy he was when he realized he got to keep all that money.

I spent the night in a pretty nice place, but still no one spoke English. The hotel staff kept trying to get me to go back north to Bangkok to catch transport south, but I insisted that I didn't want to backtrack, that I wanted to continue south from where I was. I was just too stubborn at times for my own good. So instead of going to Bangkok I caught a moped, again with backpack and all, to what was supposed to be the bus station in someplace called Ban Phong. It turned out to be a train station, which was good since I considered trains to be better than buses anyway. There were no tickets left in first class, only in third class—surprise, surprise.

I was on the third class train for eight hours. It was so hot and I was the only farang again. There wasn't even a dining car on this one. It was tolerable because vendors came down the aisles with all sorts of interesting things to eat and drink. They had many clever ways of serving food, such as in banana leaves or in bamboo bowls, and they had drinks in plastic bags with a straw stuck in them. I ate well but was determined I wouldn't use the awful bathroom. The toilets on the train were metal holes in the floor that opened to the tracks below, and with the bouncing and swaying of the train you could imagine what the floors looked like. When I was in these situations I pondered more appropriate styles of clothing for female travelers—for example, pants that could unsnap down the inseam and work like a skirt so they didn't drag on the ground. In the meantime I was perfecting what I called my "camel bladder," with the ability to hold it for an entire day.

Toward the end of the train ride I met a Norwegian man and his Thai wife. They lived in Chumphon, in southern Thailand, and that was where I intended to stay. Chumphon was a junction town from which people could decide to go to the gulf islands or to the Andaman seaside. My new friends recommended that I stay at the Sedu guesthouse, where the manager spoke English well and was able to help me plan the next leg of my journey. I was so exhausted that I realized that staying on one of the gulf islands would be the most relaxing option.

Although the manager at Sedu was a really nice woman who spoke English well, I should not have assumed she knew my tastes in accommodation and activities. She was around my age so I thought she might understand that I wouldn't want to stay in a party town. But it turned out she booked me at Bans diving resort, the biggest on Ko Tao island.

The ferry from Chumphon took about two hours and I met some people who'd been to Ko Tao in the past. I ran into them later on the island and they were horrified by the changes. I got the resort to let me move further away from all their buildings and activities into a little bungalow right on the beach. It sounds great doesn't it? But the truth was that it was small, cramped, hotter than hades and had no mosquito net. During the day there was no end to the sounds of construction, and at night there was no end to the mopeds passing by. I could hear the accents of drunk English boys until 4 a.m., and after that, the packs of dogs howling.

The people who owned the bungalows were really old, and really grumpy. I couldn't blame them. I wished I could talk to them about all the growth and changes they'd seen and lived through on the island with the influx of tourists. I imagined it was depressing for them in a lot of ways. I also spoke with a few business owners and found out that there was no city council, and therefore no rules whatsoever. I didn't get to scuba dive in Ko Tao because there was a terrible storm the day I was scheduled to go. I did end up snorkeling another day though and the fish were beautiful. I was on a tour boat with a few Thai college students and I found it was nice to finally be able to speak in English with some local people.

I took a ferry from Ko Tao and went south to the small island of Ko Phangan. I'd heard it was really crowded too but didn't feel I had many islands to choose from in the short amount of time I had left. Ko Phangan was where they held a full moon party every month during the tourist season, and I was grateful the party was over before I got there. I was thinking how much I missed the elephants.

In Ko Phangan I was picked up at the ferry port by my pre-arranged ride, "Sunny," and when he showed me on a map where we were headed I nearly cried with joy because it looked so remote. On the way to the hotel we stopped and met his family, including his at least one-hundred-year-old granny. We drank fresh coconut milk, then cracked open the coconuts and ate the flesh. His granny showed me how she chewed the betel nut that turned her mouth and the few teeth she had left red. Betel nut has a mild stimulant effect so it was probably keeping granny's heart going. We then stopped in a little fishing village to eat some soup from a stall on the side of the road, and Sunny showed me how to prepare the soup properly with all the available condiments. We finally arrived at Coconut Beach, a laid back rustic little resort at the tippy top of the island, with its own private beach on Hat Khom bay. My room overlooked the water and I had my own private balcony with a hammock. I didn't budge for three days.

The tourists staying there were great and quite a few had been coming to this place for years. A couple of young men from Switzerland had decided they liked it so much that they were going to build their own bungalow up in the hills. And a couple from Australia was staying there with their children for a few weeks. Everyone was so nice and the resort owners were wonderful hosts. There was fabulous snorkeling just a stone's throw away. And almost every day the guests were offered a chance to go on a Piña Colada run in a rickety little blue boat over to a bar on the other side of the bay. We only had electricity from 4 p.m. until midnight, and there was no hot water, but we didn't need it. At last I'd found the one quiet place in the gulf.

Eventually I made it to Ko Samui to attend my prearranged yoga retreat at Yoga Thailand. I arrived on a Friday on the verge of a full system meltdown. My neck was not moving, my tummy was rumbling, I had a heat rash everywhere, and an extremely bad attitude. Much to my dismay the electricity was also out, so there was no fan or hot water. I was a bit peeved after having already pre-paid $50 a day. But eventually the electricity returned, the food was fabulous, and I slept for ten hours.

The next morning we had a restorative yoga class, so I felt a lot better and ready to venture out of the retreat, albeit in a downpour, to explore the nearby town. A German baker, Sonja, saw me waiting for a bus so she picked me up on her moped and we got soaked together on the way to her bakery. Then I came back to the retreat and napped two more hours, went to bed at 9 p.m., and slept another nine hours! Finally, and thank God, the following morning I felt I was almost back to normal, just in time for Mysore yoga. I'd thought it was named after the city in India where this style of yoga originated, but after class I realized that it was really named Mysore because MY just-about-everything was really SORE. The teachers at the retreat were fairly brutal, with their rough hands-on approach camouflaged in spiritual jargon. They wouldn't even let me use the $10 cheat sheet I'd just purchased. Why, you might ask, did they sell it? I was squashed into yoga positions I really didn't think I was capable of getting into. After class the rain let up slightly so I went to see the huge Big Buddha statue. That name summed it up well—it was indeed a big old Buddha.

There were actually a few fairly nice areas on this crowded island, and my little yoga place was quiet and on a private beach. I was feeling pretty rested and healthy. There was no drinking or smoking on the retreat grounds and only vegetarian food was available. But ultimately I felt the facility was a bit too expensive for what I got. Although the Mysore classes in the mornings were kick-butt, there was only the one class offered every day. I'd thought there'd be more classes available. I was, however, grateful for having the time to rest and read, and I believed I'd improved my yoga practice somewhat. At least my sobbing knees, crying ribs and screaming neck certainly thought so.

I met a young woman from Seattle, who was brave enough to rent a moped, the transport of choice in these parts. She was willing to cart me around the island and I think we covered almost all of it. We went to the Namuang waterfall, where I opted to climb to the top. I had acquired a guide of sorts, which turned out to be a blessing since my new friend chose not to go. It had been raining off and on for the past few days so the route was quite slippery, and there were so many alternate routes it was easy to get lost. Along the way there were ropes and rocks to help you crisscross the falls. I was relieved to have my guide "Tom" (Ton, Tun, Tan or however it was pronounced) to help me. At the top there was a pool with a cave under the falls and you could hang on to a rope to guide yourself through the falls and into the cave. It was pretty neat and I was the only one up there beside my faithful guide.

I moved from the yoga place to Buddha Beach, where I rented a bungalow all for myself. I was not up for most of the touristy things to do in Ko Samui, which included elephant trekking (yikes), crocodile and monkey shows (ugh), canopy zip lines (done it), Thai boxing and water buffalo fighting—none of that interested me.

I believed I was now finally ready to return home to my friends, family and even to the rain and my job. The weather in Ko Samui seemed to have been preparing me for home, with stormy skies and big waves. I hadn't minded the rain while on the island, since it made the temperature quite pleasant. I'd even found a more ritzy hotel that agreed to let me use its pool if I just ordered drinks. "Oh, the pressure," I thought. The ocean was too choppy to swim in, and strangely, I'd had enough of life with just sun, salt and sand.

One afternoon I decided to go see a movie and get out of the wind. Rather than renting a moped and drive myself, I chose to pay for a "taxi moped," where the passenger sits on the back and the driver at least knows the roads and traffic. They say more people die in road accidents on Ko Samui than anywhere else in Thailand due to all the tourists who don't know how to ride mopeds, are drunk, or who aren't familiar with driving on the left.

The movie scene was yet another study in Thai culture. You selected your seat at the ticket counter and then waited for an invitation to enter. Like in the U.S. they had twenty minutes of previews. What was different was that a video started which showed the Thai king and all his good works, and the audience was expected to stand and sing the national anthem. They really loved him there.

Every day of the week had a color assigned to it and the Thais believed it brought good luck if you wore the color associated with its day. The Thai king was born on a Monday and his wife was born on a Friday. On Mondays you'd see much of the population wearing yellow shirts, and on Fridays, blue. Many of the yellow shirts had the emblem of the monarchy's flag on them with the words, "Long live the king" in English or Thai, printed underneath.

I'd gone to see some English sci-fi movie about dragons, and it was a nice break. I would have liked to have seen some of the Thai movies that were advertised, like the exploits of two chubby boys off to their stay in a monastery to serve their obligatory time as monks. It looked really cute and would have provided additional insight into this particular Thai tradition.

When I went to the Ko Samui airport to catch my flight back to Bangkok I noticed what a gorgeous airport it was. They even served complimentary snacks in the waiting area and drove passengers to the plane in little trolleys like at Disney World. They served a delicious lunch on board, even though the flight lasted less than an hour. Truly the Thais had the tourist gig down pat. I had to admit that I hadn't been too excited about coming to Thailand, because I generally preferred less touristed places. But really, there were still some very memorable adventures to be had and fantastic people to have them with. Most of all, I learned there was worthwhile volunteer work to be done there by those of us who were blessed with the time, money and desire to do so.

Yemen
2007

When I was in Thailand in 2006 I met a man named Hussein, who was from Yemen. I had only heard a little about Yemen because a friend in the States had always wanted to go and she raved about the architecture there. And it had been in the news with the USS Cole attack. So I didn't know much, but I was intrigued and certainly impressed by how friendly, well educated, and worldly Hussein was. He also loved George W. Bush, and I found that rather odd. But I listened, because when someone from the Middle East liked Bush, you had to wonder why. He felt the U.S. had rid Iraq of Saddam Hussein, a "butcher," and that pleased him. I also learned that Saddam was quite popular in Yemen before the second Iraq war because he helped the country financially and always let the Yemeni people work and study in Iraq.

Upon my return to the U.S. from Thailand I received an e-mail from Claudia, the German surgeon whom I'd met in Mongolia in 2005 and had traveled with to Morocco in March 2006. Claudia said that she wanted us to go to Yemen together in 2007. What a small world it was, and what wonderful "coincidences" happened when you traveled. I immediately agreed of course, and then had the pleasure of telling Hussein that, lo and behold, we'd be meeting again.

After my initial excitement however, I began to worry. The U.S. media and State Department had issued warnings about traveling to Yemen. Not only was the country reported to have had killings of tourists, but it was nearly infamous for kidnappings. There was also ongoing conflict between the many tribes there and the Yemeni government. Yemen had only just recently become a republic in the 1990s after a long and brutal civil war. The various tribes continued to be dissatisfied with the ruling political party and would occasionally kidnap tourists to try to pressure the government to build roads, schools, hospitals, or even to provide free satellite dishes. I'd read that many kidnap victims reported that they had been treated well, including being given gifts. Still, I knew I'd rather not test those rumors.

You couldn't really travel alone in Yemen because of the bad roads, limited mass transit and, of course, the potential danger. So it was best to go on a tour. Claudia and I signed up with a Dutch company called Djoser. There would be fifteen Germans plus me. I checked out another company here in the U.S. but they didn't go to Yemen because of the difficulty Americans had obtaining visas. And I did in fact have trouble getting a visa. I didn't know why, but unlike the Germans, I had to provide a health history, proof of health insurance, and a letter from my doctor saying I was fit for travel. Perhaps the Yemenis had had bad experiences with sick Americans. Or maybe they found out somehow that I'd just gotten out of the hospital where I'd nearly died from dehydration caused by repeated parasite infestations I'd gotten in places like India, the Amazon and Africa.

Not only did I work hard to get a visa, but I also had quite a challenge finding travel guidebooks about the place. I ended up with an outdated *Lonely Planet* guidebook for Yemen from 1996 and one for the Arabian Peninsula from 2004. After overcoming these obstacles I at last arrived in Frankfurt to meet the tour group and leave for Sana'a, Yemen's capital. It turned out to be cheaper to fly from the U.S. to Europe and then to Yemen rather than take a direct flight.

The tour included round-trip airfare from Frankfurt, three weeks accommodation, breakfast, transportation, and all required military escorts. The total cost was about $2000 each, which I thought was quite reasonable under the circumstances, even though it was more than I usually spent to travel for only three weeks. We flew from Frankfurt to Sana'a on Yemenia Airways, and everything went normally except for one interesting detail. The video screens continually showed where Mecca was, with a picture of an airplane, a directional arrow, and the distance. That was so the practitioners of Islam could do their prayers while in flight. Muslims are asked to pray five times each day facing Mecca, which is considered their holiest city because the prophet Muhammad was born there.

We arrived in Sana'a, went to our hotel and went to bed and at 5:00 a.m. I heard, "ALLAHhhhhhhhh!" The call to prayer blared all over the city from a multitude of mosque public address systems. The sun wasn't even up yet. I rolled over and grabbed my earplugs. I considered myself lucky because my hotel room had a fan running to help drown out not just the mosque but also the start of a city waking up with the sounds of cars honking and buses revving their engines.

Every room had a symbol on the wall showing the direction of Mecca so Muslims could face it to pray. I prayed for a little peace and quiet. I also pondered this custom, which was not a requirement by law, but was certainly a cultural expectation in Islamic countries. Could you imagine church bells ringing loudly five times a day and everyone stopping what they were doing to pray? In some ways it might be nice for us to pause, relax and give thanks for our blessings. But everyone should be allowed to do it in their own way, and hopefully, with an appreciation for nature and the planet, and not just for a particular ideology that does not always result in peaceful tolerance and coexistence.

The tour schedule required that I get out of bed sometime between 6 and 8 a.m., depending on the program for the day. A few times on the tour we had quite nice rooms, but more often the beds and pillows were hard, and everything was dilapidated, dusty and just plain worn out. The showers usually had their own heaters and sometimes they worked. They tended to only provide a weak drip of water that alternated between hot and cold, but they were at least wet and somewhat refreshing. After my "shower" I'd brush my teeth with bottled water, put on one of the two changes of clothes I'd brought, and hoped I didn't smell too bad. It probably didn't matter too much anyway, since all of us were in the same situation.

Breakfast for tourists was always the same—old white roll-like bread, a hard-boiled egg, a triangle of processed cheese, strawberry jam, Nescafé, and orange juice from concentrate. The Yemeni breakfast was a great dish called "fool", which consisted of spicy beans and flat bread. Although it tasted better than what we were served, it probably would have been a bit of a shock to the Western stomach first thing in the morning. Yemenis ate with their hands, while tourists got spoons. They sat on the floor and we sat in chairs. We got Kleenex as napkins and the locals used a sink with laundry detergent powder to use as soap. The toilets were "Turkish" style—a ceramic hole in the ground, with no toilet paper, just a spigot for water with which you rinse yourself and the ceramic hole in the floor. Voilà, a tree is saved.

"Yala yala!" meant a lot of things like "okay!" or "let's go!" and it was always yelled, not spoken softly. Claudia said "these people yellow a lot." I never corrected her because I thought it was a cute mistake, and I knew exactly what she meant. Those people did yell a lot. They sounded like they were angry, even when they weren't, like when they'd yell, "Yala-yala!" and the sixteen of us would load into four Land Rovers with our drivers, Achmed, Muhammad, Walid and Sale. I was lucky to be in the lead vehicle with the tour guide, Arif, so I had the opportunity to ask a lot of questions. Claudia had to translate everything of course since Arif didn't speak English and I didn't speak German or Arabic. He was funny, sweet, knowledgeable and he enthusiastically shared the love he felt for his country.

Even early in the morning in Sana'a it was so packed and so noisy, mostly from the hundreds of honking cars, that you could barely hear yourself speak. There would also be donkeys or camels pulling carts about, weaving in and out of traffic. The streets were lined with shops selling everything from personal items like food, perfume, and clothes to household goods like cookware, tools, and hookahs. The women were covered from head to toe, including their faces and eyes, in a black garment called a burka. The young schoolgirls wore green abaya uniforms that went from neck to foot, with their hair covered by scarves. They weren't old enough yet to have to hide their faces. The little boys wore whatever they wanted and played foosball or soccer in the streets after school. Fridays were like our Sundays, so the kids were out of school and every Internet café was full of boys playing video games.

It was an ongoing argument among some Muslims whether or not the Quran said women must cover their faces. The south of Yemen, which had been run by the Turks, the British, and the Soviets at different times, was less strict than the north. The north was more tribal, and had less outside influence. The western part of the country had more African influence, so the women there wore head scarves but had their faces uncovered and wore more colorful clothing. I had the opportunity to speak with some women while there, and they said they preferred being covered, that they felt more comfortable because they could be more anonymous and could look out and not be seen. As such, they'd get less harassment.

Yemen is mostly known for its amazing architecture, which changes from place to place. Sana'a was the most famous because of its "Old City," a UNESCO World Heritage Site. The city was packed inside a protective wall with the occasional arched gated entrance. The buildings were all a red color painted with intricate white stucco designs. The windows, called takhrim, were made from alabaster and stained glass. And every door seemed different, either wooden and carved, or metal with bright colors and artistic overlays.

Most older cities in Yemen had souks, or markets. The souks had tiny shops just crammed into an even smaller space than those on the main streets, and had narrow pathways made of either dirt or cobblestones. To the southwest of Sana'a, along the coast, lay the granddaddy of all souks, Bayt al Faqih. Yes, you are probably pronouncing it properly. "Faqih, Faqih." I thought our guide Arif was teasing me when I first heard him pronounce it, and I couldn't stop laughing. This was one of the oldest souks in Yemen and was open every Friday, as it had been for hundreds of years.

There were thousands of stalls and so many people were packed in there that you could barely walk or breathe. Each section had its own personality and specialized in a different type of product. The multicolored grains and spices displayed in enormous woven baskets were weighed out using centuries old methods and tools. The food section had huge fryers filled with splattering oil and batter covered meats and vegetables. There were textiles, tools, kitchen wares, plastic shoes, music and hookah pipes. The pipes were much bigger than those I'd seen in Morocco, with much thicker and longer inhalation tubes. There were also healers treating bare chested men by putting suction cups on their skin, or by making small incisions on their foreheads, in order to remove "bad blood". They would also wrap prayers from the Quran around their arms to ward off "evil" or illness.

But the gat section was always the busiest. As alcohol and drugs were not allowed to be ingested by Muslims what they did instead was chew gat (pronounced "got"). This was the main social activity for the men in Yemen. Evidently this was also true in Ethiopia and Kenya. Gat was grown almost everywhere, was sold almost everywhere, and was chewed daily. They said it has only a mild stimulating effect, but everyone looked totally stoned on it. They'd buy bags of this stuff starting at around two in the afternoon and then sit around and chew until one of their cheeks was packed with it. It was a status symbol to have the biggest cheek, as it indicated affluence and stamina. This was a real problem for the economy, as the men spent up to half of their meager income on it, not to mention how little work got done while sitting around chewing. In addition most of the available water went to grow the gat trees in this desert country, creating a dangerous water shortage.

After perusing the gat section we came upon the most difficult part of the souk to see, the meat section. Here partially skinned carcasses dangled from chains. There was a calf's head hanging with its eyes still open, and down below on the ground was its body. Then we saw the thighs of a camel, which they ate in Yemen, and chickens squawking, tied together and watching their brothers be stripped and quartered. On the ground all around the entrails were being devoured by scrawny, filthy, ravenous dogs and cats, growling and hissing with their eyes flitting about. I really didn't mind this open slaughtering, because I figured that if I were going to eat these animals I should know and appreciate where my meal came from and give thanks to that animal for giving its life.

Soon after the butcher section we got to see the live animal section—mostly cows, goats, chickens, some donkeys and camels. The camels were often attached to a mill of sorts, where it walked around and around to extricate cooking oil from olives. Sadly we also saw many disabled children being rolled around in wheelbarrows to beg for money. The wheelbarrow was the main form of transport in the souk. Faqih, Faqih was a thought provoking place.

In Sana'a we also got to try our first traditional Yemeni meal, the salta. It was like a stew cooked in a wrought iron pot over an incredibly high hot flame. Restaurants were usually open to the street and packed with men. Those that served families had private curtained rooms for them so that the women could uncover their faces in order to eat. Other common meal choices besides the salta were roasted chicken, lamb, camel, lentils, beans, rice, and even pasta served with a small blob of tomato paste. There was also a dish that was a thin layer of eggs on the bottom of the pan. And there was always bread. They had many kinds of bread in Yemen, but the most common was a large flat one that was easily folded to enable you to scoop up the rest of the meal with your hands. In countries where the food was eaten with your hands you usually ate with your right hand only. My understanding of the reason for this was that, because there usually wasn't any toilet paper in these countries, the left hand was used with water for cleaning yourself after using the toilet.

Meal times were never peaceful. The places were packed, with everyone yelling and running around, with the waiter (if you could call him that) flinging pans of food onto the tables, usually with a cigarette hanging out of his mouth. My favorite time was when Claudia ordered fish and it was slammed down on the table in front of her on a sheet of newspaper, with the head, tail, eyes and all. Bottled water was available everywhere, as was mint tea.

Unfortunately plastic had not served this country well, and really, maybe not even the world. The city streets and even the countryside were littered with everything made from plastic, especially the bottles and bags. In the countryside it looked like there were plastic bag bushes and a plastic bottled layer of earth.

Of course you could always order Coke. I even found Mountain Dew. They also had alcohol-free beer, but why bother? And after every meal they served a black tea with milk. The tea was good but it was disappointing that a country that was famous for its coffee (Mocha came from there) now only served Nescafé. I'd witnessed this, sadly, all over the world. Delicious high quality beans were grown, then the Nestlé corporation ruined them and sold this crap back to a poor country at a profit. Yemen was also famous for its honey. The bees fed primarily on acacia trees and I was told that some honey could sell for $135 a pound. The one time we were served honey it was on a delicious dessert that was sweet bread drenched in it.

Our first night in Sana'a Claudia and I were wandering the Old City with my friend Hussein when we stumbled upon a large colorful tent. The men sitting outside it told us they were having a bachelor party and invited us to join them. To invite us the men would put their hands on their heads, which meant, "We so welcome you, we would stand on our heads." Here weddings, like just about everything, the men and women did separately. In fact it was difficult for local Yemenis to meet someone to marry and the mothers usually did the matchmaking while they were bathing together in the hamams. The men in Yemen would greet each other with multiple kisses, first kissing one cheek, then the other, and repeating this several times. And men frequently held hands when walking down the street. Occasionally we saw what was obviously a married couple holding hands, but in general men and women wouldn't touch each other in public.

There were at least a hundred men in the party tent and Claudia and I were the only women. Because we were foreigners and not Muslim we weren't held to the same standards and rules that the Yemeni women were held to. The groom sat in the back of the tent on an elaborately decorated throne. The rest of the men were seated around the interior of the tent on pillows and all of them had large wads of gat in their cheeks. Musicians played music on the traditional ud, which was like a big round guitar, and they danced. The most popular dance was done with the jambiya, a curved knife worn daily by most men in Yemen on the front of the body and held in by a colorful woven belt. The knife covers used to be made from rhinoceros horn until it almost caused their extinction, so now the covers were made from lime green or brown chiseled leather. The men wore long white shirts which hung down to their ankles and a Western style coat jacket that was a carry-over from British influence. They also wore a traditional scarf tied in a variety of ways on their heads or around their shoulders. We were told that at weddings the women wore long, bright beaded gowns, gold jewelry and lots of make-up, all covered up by the black burka if there were any men around. The women held their own separate parties but we never saw any of those going on.

I went to a hamam (bathhouse) once in Sana'a. I was the only foreigner, so I was, of course, the center of attention. The hamam was a labyrinth of caverns carved out of stone similar to the one Claudia and I had gone to in Morocco. The women were not as friendly as those in Morocco though, and I had to bathe myself because I wasn't assigned to someone to bathe me. It seemed that wasn't the custom in Yemen. No one spoke English, so it was difficult to communicate, but I felt my gesture to connect by being willing to be naked with the Yemeni women was appreciated. It was a nice, albeit unusual, way to finally meet some women there.

After Sana'a we headed north. Our scheduled visit to the city of Sada was cancelled due to tribal conflicts, so we were now only going as far as Shahara. On the way we stopped at a few villages. You could immediately see the difference in the architecture. Now we saw much simpler mud buildings, but they were still many stories high in order to house extended families. The first floor was the kitchen, the second floor was the women's quarters, the third was the extended family area, and finally, at the very top, was the gat chewing room. Somewhere in the mix were the bedrooms. People slept on pads on the floor and a man could have up to five wives. I imagined sleeping arrangements could get a little confusing in these homes.

This leg of the journey required military escorts provided by the government. Our escorts ranged in age from fourteen to eighteen. They barely had facial hair and were carrying Kalashnikovs and chewing gat. "Guns and Gat" became the mantra of this trip. At the base of Shahara we had to switch vehicles and use the local tribe's own Toyota trucks. We did this not only to support the tribe financially, but also because only these Toyotas could make it up the road! I'd been over some rough terrain in my time, but I'd never been on roads like these—narrow, treacherous, steep, and littered with boulders and rocks. Terrifying! We were told that Toyota designed these trucks specifically for this road and then made commercials about them. As we bounced around in the back of the trucks the butts of the guns belonging to our stoned military escort boys would poke us in our sides. We'd catch glimpses of the cliff's sheer drop off, then Claudia and I would look at each other and smile, knowing that the terror was worth it.

We finished the harrowing journey in the dark and were immediately settled into our accommodation when we arrived. We stayed overnight in a *funduq*, which is a home turned into a hotel. The men and women of our tour group had to sleep separately, even if they were a couple. We slept on pads on the floor, with all the women in one room and all the men in another.

In the morning we awoke to a breathtaking view. Shahara was a village located nearly 9500 feet up a mountain. It was common for villages to be situated on the top of mountains because they were easier to protect.

This also freed up the mountainsides and valleys for planting in extensive, amazingly constructed terraces. Through the years Shahara's location had helped it hold out against many invaders. Until the advent of the airplane that was, because during the 1960s civil war the town got bombed into semi-submission. The main attraction was the bottom tier of what used to be a three tiered stone bridge connecting the villages on the two mountains. It reminded me of an Indiana Jones movie and put "Vertigo" to shame! It was truly an engineering miracle, built by the architect Salah al-Yamani in the seventeenth century.

At the top of the mountain, as in every village, there were cisterns that collected rainwater. The women, in their black burkas, came daily to collect water, which they filtered with old T-shirts, then returned home over steep mountain paths, with the full brightly colored plastic water buckets balanced on their heads.

In all the villages we visited we were met by throngs of children yelling "kalem, kalem!" (pen, pen) or "sura, sura!" (photo, photo). Of all the places I'd traveled I'd never encountered a people so eager to have their pictures taken. Everyone wanted theirs taken except for the older women. All the people we photographed really wanted was to see the photos. Unfortunately though, some were beginning to figure out that they could ask for money.

In one village, at the tippy top of a mountain, a woman dressed in black and surrounded by children waved Claudia and me over to her. We were shocked to have been approached by a woman. Through gestures and my little Instant Arabic book we had a wonderful conversation about religion, our countries, our families and traditions. She was so comfortable with us that she uncovered her face and even showed us scars on her belly. She then showed me how to properly wrap my head scarf so it would completely cover my face. When her son-in-law showed up, she quickly covered up and it was noticeable how she withdrew.

We had had many conversations with men about the covering of women. One group of college boys told us that they felt women being covered helped men "control themselves." During this conversation they also said that Muslims are adamantly against violence and they did not agree with religious extremists. They accepted all religious books and prophets, which were said to have come from God. But they believed, of course, that the Quran and Muhammad were the final, definitive ones. When talking about politics they were able to separate a people from its government, and that was why it was okay with them for me to be from the U.S. They didn't really like their own president, Saleh, as they believed he wasn't taking the country forward. Their president had a difficult time finding harmony among all the tribes. And, as was so often the case, they said he stole or wasted a lot of money. For example, he built a forty million dollar mosque rather than spending the money on schools or hospitals.

After Shahara we headed east to Marib. We again needed a military escort due to conflicts between the tribes and the government. The conflicts could be over a tribe wanting more legislative representation, or simply wanting a school, hospital, or paved road to be built. We passed so many military checkpoints that I lost count. The soldiers loved to hand us their guns and take pictures with us. It looked really strange to see them all wearing their traditional clothing and carrying old-fashioned weapons, but then having cell phones attached to their belts, out in the middle of nowhere.

The larger cities were given codes by the government. Green meant okay to visit, yellow meant be careful and stay near the hotel, and red meant too dangerous to leave the hotel. Marib was a red city, but they let us tour it with a police escort. Marib had ancient temples, which were over two thousand years old. Some believed the Queen of Sheba came from there. The temples were also known as the Sun and Moon temples and were covered with Sabaean text. There was also an old dam which had a lock system like the Panama canal. A new dam had been built nearby, but reportedly hadn't been used because of political conflict. It was such a waste to have the water evaporate rather than being used.

The old city of Marib sat on the outskirts of the modern town and had been abandoned. The mud houses were decaying, eerie and mystical in the setting sun, with the muted sound of the day's fourth call to prayer in the distance. We stayed at a hotel called the Land of Two Paradises, and I asked, if you needed two paradises what was up with the first one? The hotel was filthy, buggy, hot and miserable. It was as far as you could get from even one paradise. I considered it a blessing to get up at 4 a.m. to check out and cross the Ramlat as-Sab'atayn desert, this time with a non-military Bedouin escort.

We were told we needed the escort because there were still land mines remaining from the civil war between the Royalists and the Republicans in the 1960s, and the Bedouins knew where they were. I'm not sure if that was true because we didn't seem to drive along any particular path. We just drove east, really fast, through the middle of the desert. We stopped and ate with a Bedouin family in their tent and hung out with the camels for a bit. The women's head coverings were different here, made from a thin black piece of material with shiny black beads which dangled around their faces. After our lunch stop we took one of the Land Rovers for an insane ride up and down a particularly large dune. I was the only woman brave or stupid enough to do it and only my constant screaming kept my lunch down. The long journey in the desert was trance-inducing and so disorienting, with only sand, the occasional mirage, dots of camels on the horizon and the dust stirred up by the vehicles.

After the desert we ended up in Wadi Hadramawt. Wadi meant riverbed and normally had a river running through it, although most we saw had no water. There was a brief rainy season in the summer, which made the valley greener, with palm and acacia trees, and agriculture. A common sight was young women covered in black and wearing the local style straw hat in the shape of a witch's hat. They were either working in the fields or leading a herd of goats around.

This area was one of the more affluent governorates, an administrative division, due to its fertility. Even the people were heavier. The men wore sarongs because of the historical connection of trading goods and workers with Indonesia. You could also see the Indonesian influence in the bright colorful flowers painted around the windows of the buildings.

The most noticeable place in the area was the village of Shibam, also known as the "Manhattan of the Desert." It was called that because shooting up out of the flat landscape were a patch of tall, thin, tightly packed mud "skyscrapers." Although multistoried buildings were common in Yemen, for some reason here they were even taller. The inhabitants often didn't even go down to the street to get around, but instead, crossed over the roofs.

At times you'd see blue eyes beaming out amongst the Arab faces. They'd lock with ours and the person would smile at our apparent genetic connection. Because of all the trade there, Yemen had been exposed to many cultures throughout its history. The Sunni and Shia Muslims seemed to be living together in peace. We were told that there were even a few Jewish communities left, although most had gone to Israel in 1949 with Operation Magic Carpet, when Israel paid for Jewish people to relocate there. We saw some doors with the Star of David carved into them. We were also told that Jewish architects were responsible for the design of the houses and windows you'd see in places like the Old City of Sana'a. Occasionally we saw remnants of Soviet style block houses, and we even saw a Christian church standing empty.

Saying farewell to Wadi Hadramawt, we headed south toward the port of Mukalla on the Indian Ocean, which was just another crowded, noisy and dirty place. We were supposed to head from there back west along the coast to a fairly good sized city named Ataq. It had become a red coded city however, so the visit there was cancelled. This turned out to be a good thing, since we went to Bir Ali instead. We stayed in three-sided mud huts that were open in front facing the pristine turquoise water and white sandy beach. It was a much needed pause in this fast-paced tour. There were no locals swimming because, in an Islamic country, wearing a bathing suit was considered almost being naked, which I guess it was when you think about it. The Yemeni people evidently fished but rarely swam and, needless to say, if the women wanted to swim they'd have to do so in a private pool.

The next city, Aden, was once an important world shipping port and had become Yemen's winter capital. It was a big fairly modern bustling city. We even went to a mall where I had to have a slice of pizza at Pizza Hut. Pizza Hut and Kentucky Fried Chicken were the only fast food franchises I saw in Yemen. I didn't like the fact that these franchises had not only taken over our country, but they were now attempting to spread throughout the rest of the world. What a shame it would be if the entire planet looked like an Anywhere, USA strip mall. I had to admit though that the pizza slice I had there was much more familiar to me than the Yemeni pizza I'd tried, which didn't have tomato sauce and had some weird sweet sauce instead.

It was here in Aden that I again noticed a cemetery with no grave markers. I came to find out that in the Muslim religion a person is to be buried, but the grave not marked, so that all are remembered equally and humbly in death.

After Aden we headed north toward Sana'a and stopped in Taiz, a big old loud dirty city sitting in the middle of a valley surrounded by mountains. We stayed three nights, using it as a hub to visit nearby villages. I must say, it grew on me. It was here that I finally decided to try the gat. I figured it was the most pervasive cultural experience in Yemen, and I thought I should know why. I bought a small $10 bag of pre-picked leaves. Taiz was known for having the best gat in the country. But $10? That was a lot of money, as the average income was only about $350 a year. You could find cheaper gat, especially if it came with the leaves still on the branches.

We ended up at a gat chewing parlor. It was decorated with plush couches and pillows, furry rugs up on the walls, multi-colored fabrics, and lots of hookahs (water pipes for smoking) were scattered about. Our guide Arif showed me what I was supposed to do. Basically you stuck the leaves in one of your cheeks and chewed. It tasted AWFUL! It was bitter and nasty, but I kept chewing, determined to see what was up with this stuff. Arif suggested I drink a Coke with it to help it go down. You didn't swallow the bulk of it, just the juices, and that was why the bulk built up as a big wad in your cheek. Then I tried to smoke shisha (tobacco) in a hookah to help with the horrible taste. I kept chewing and chewing and chewing the gat, but nothing ever happened. Arif told me it could take up to three hours to feel the effect, which was described as a "push." They said it was a bit of a stimulant, but I never felt anything. And when I looked around the room I mostly saw people sitting and looking zoned out, certainly not acting as if they were stimulated. I chewed it for about an hour and a half, but there was no effect for me whatsoever. Then I just couldn't take it anymore. It was too boring just sitting there. I could see why it was destroying the economy. What a complete waste of time and money.

During our stay in Taiz we visited quite a few villages. One was on top of Jebal Saber, the local mountain. Here the women wore bright wraps, often had their faces uncovered, and put henna decorations on the hands and feet of the tourists. We were told that the women ran quite a few of the businesses because they could sell more goods to the soldiers stationed at the bottom of the mountain than their own men could.

Staying in one place for a few days meant that we had the opportunity to wander the city on our own. Claudia and I found a restaurant that served particularly tasty fool, the typical Yemeni meat and bean casserole. The owner would put newspaper down to serve as a tablecloth, and he paid close attention to our needs. We tried to communicate with him using my dictionary, and as a reward for my efforts, he gave me his prayer beads, called *tasbih*. They had thirty-three beads and were used like a rosary to keep count of the prayers being said.

We also went to Gibla, where there was a beautiful old mosque, elaborately painted inside, which had been built by a queen who'd ruled there until she was ninety-two. Another village, near the Red Sea, was called Khokah. Its beach was disgusting, with thousands of dead crabs, a dead dog and a dead flamingo on it. Rather creepy, but in keeping with the "Wild West" feel of the place, we stumbled upon what looked like a Harley Davidson motorcycle convention. The bikes were all Hondas though, and decorated with sheepskins, rugs, bells, feathers, lights and beads. Then just when we thought we'd seen it all, we found what was called a "national park," with Yosemite-like cliffs, forests, and, amazingly, baboons!

Our three week trip was coming to an end. I was feeling a little overwhelmed by this whirlwind tour. It seemed like we'd seen every single village in the entire country, but there were even more surprises awaiting me. Our final village before returning to Sana'a was Manakah. We stayed again in a funduq (house turned into a hotel) nearly at the peak of a sheer mountainside.

What was special about this place was the family that ran it. A father and his sons did everything. We never saw the women. We were told that the men did the cooking and they certainly did all the serving of the delicious meals. But it was the dancing and music that were so impressive. They played the ud and drums, but what was most astonishing was how loud they could clap and how well they could whistle! Then they'd get up and dance. They did the jambiya knife dance, a dance with rifles, and one in which they twirled gracefully, using the long sleeves of their white tunics. They reminded me of Sufi dancers in the way they just kept twirling faster and faster and would stare off into space as if in a trance. We all got to join in and it made me again wonder what the women did. Did they get to dance and play music? I hoped so. And I loved this family. They were so sweet and friendly and always laughing. One of the young sons asked me if America was in Asia, Africa or Europe. It was so refreshing to meet someone with no preconceived ideas about us.

I met so many wonderful people on this trip, and not just from Yemen. One couple on the tour was a German man and his Iranian wife. He had converted to Islam in order to marry her. They said they went to Iran every year to see her family. And I met a man from Jordan who said that Jordan was so progressive that I could just fly in, rent a car and drive wherever I wanted to. I spent a couple of wonderful afternoons with my friend Hussein's family. We ate lunch on a cloth, sitting on the floor, then moved to the couches in the living room to have tea and talk.

Hussein's nephew had autism and Hussein volunteered at the one and only autism clinic in the country. It was started by a woman whose daughter had autism, and the mother realized she was never going to get help in Yemen if she didn't organize a framework in which to do it herself. All the staff were other mothers who'd trained themselves to care for their autistic children. I got to visit the clinic and meet all the staff and kids. They were doing wonderful work with the kids despite the scarcity of resources.

Since I was a psychiatric nurse Hussein arranged a visit for me to a mental hospital. It was fascinating, and I was allowed to meet the patients and the nursing staff. The nurses all wore full burkas that covered their faces. They also wore gloves to cover their hands. But this didn't stop them from openly sharing with me the challenges of treating mental illness in this country. The main problem here, as it was anywhere, was the stigma, and the resultant difficulty of getting people to seek treatment. I met one patient who had deep scars on his wrists from ropes used by his family to tie him up.

The hospital patients all seemed well treated and would gather around me out of curiosity. The men, but not the women, asked me for cigarettes. I was given a private tour by the medical director, who even allowed me to take video of and interview the patients and staff. The patients presented with the same major mental illnesses Americans had like schizophrenia and bipolar disorder. What was different was the content of the delusions, as the subject matter reflected the culture. For example, some thought they were an Islamic prophet instead of Jesus. The staff also said that gat use could trigger a psychotic episode. Mostly men used gat, but increasingly women were starting to use it too. The treatment at the hospital was similar to Western standards. They used the same medications plus therapy groups, crafts and recreation. The hospital was a bit run down though, and all the men were crammed into one room with mismatched linens. But it was clean and they had plenty of outdoor space in which to roam.

During my time in Yemen I'd been enthusiastically welcomed everywhere, and often showered with gifts. I thought back about my initial reservations about visiting this country, sighed, and felt grateful that I didn't succumb to the negative propaganda we'd been fed in the U.S. about the Middle East. I'll continue to explore this part of the world, so rich in history and passion. And I'll try to bridge the great gap that governments and politicians create between people, when in truth, as travel always proves, we are all so much alike.

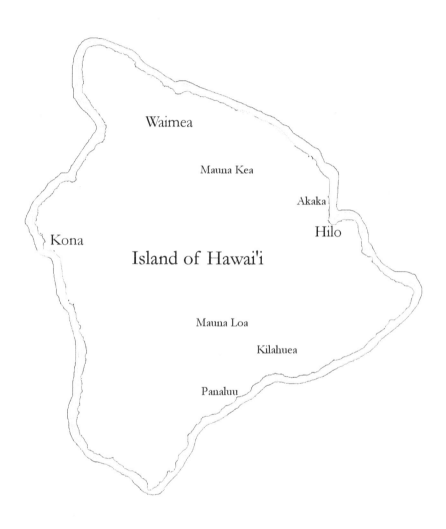

Waimea

Mauna Kea

Akaka

Kona

Hilo

Island of Hawai'i

Mauna Loa

Kilahuea

Panaluu

Hawaii
2008

In 2007, before I went to Yemen, I'd been hospitalized for five days due to severe dehydration. Three times during my travels I'd gotten giardia, an intestinal parasite. Although I say it was giardia, only once were the doctors able to confirm it. The other two times they couldn't verify what I had, but it was treated with strong antibiotics. When I first moved to California in 2004 I immediately started having symptoms of an intestinal parasite, including severe diarrhea and abdominal cramping. I knew where every bathroom was in my city of Santa Cruz. Over the next three years I went to five different doctors, including a naturopath. No one could figure out what I had, and one doctor told me it was irritable bowel syndrome. I lost twenty pounds and had intestinal bleeding. But I continued to travel, and would just always have plenty of Imodium on hand.

For many people intestinal problems could be a very real part of travel. And I came to learn that the medical community even in the U.S. could frequently misdiagnose or miss altogether what was really happening with a patient. Luckily I was nurse, did a lot of my own research on the Internet, and talked to everyone I met about the issue, just in case they'd experienced or knew someone who'd had the same symptoms and had found a treatment. It was as a result of this research, that my life was saved. Through this process I knew exactly which medications I needed to be on. The next challenge was getting a doctor to prescribe them.

I really thought I was going to die before any doctor would listen to me. I'd never been hospitalized before, and was reluctant to go until I realized that if I didn't, I'd surely end up in that "great toilet in the sky." So I went to the emergency room and begged them to admit me. They drew my blood and discovered that I was so dehydrated that I was at risk for a heart attack. They immediately started potassium IVs and heart monitors and I was there for five days. During this time they finally started me on the exact medications I'd been asking for.

I improved immediately, but the doctor told me, "You can never travel again." I stared incredulously at him and explained that telling me this was like telling a concert pianist you were going to amputate his hands. Instead of following his instructions I went to Yemen. That trip was arduous yet wonderful, but when I returned I realized that I needed to give my body a good long break, so I decided to take the year 2008 "off" and only travel within the U.S.

This, luckily, included Hawaii, so Carson and I decided to celebrate Valentine's Day on the romantic island of Hawaii, also known as The Big Island. We found a reasonable deal for a two night stay in Kona at the King Kamehameha hotel, and we rented a Jeep so we could drive around the perimeter of the island and stop and stay whenever we felt like it. As Kona was the main tourist destination on the Big Island, it seemed like it was just one big traffic jam at all times of the day. It was nice to have our own vehicle so we could escape the congestion and explore the island on our own.

Before leaving Kona we went for a scuba dive, where the highlight was being able to hear the humpback whales sing under water. If you didn't want to dive, it was easy to snorkel right off the beaches, and there were many places where the green sea turtles would swim right around you. My hope was that the tourists wouldn't harass them.

Our main goal was to see lava on the active Kilauea volcano. We were all geared up with appropriate hiking shoes, binoculars, water bottles, bandanas, sunscreen, hats and cameras. The road that led to Kilauea came to an abrupt end, where the lava flowed over it years ago, then hardened. When we arrived and checked in at the guard post however, we found out that a few months earlier the lava flow had shifted direction. For many years the flow had gone down to the water and, upon reaching it, it would produce a huge spout of steam. But not now. We were terribly disappointed but decided to hike up the volcano anyway, and were able to detect a tiny glowing spot off in the distance as evening came upon us.

As we continued driving around the island we found interesting places to stop, and things to do such as a beach swim, where the ocean had pockets of hot springs, or a quick dip in the Akaka waterfall. We stopped for lunch on the opposite side of the island from Kona, in the more mellow town of Hilo. This place felt less touristy, a little more run down, and there wasn't really that much to do. So we continued on to Waimea.

Waimea was located on the northern part of the island and seemed different from the rest of the island because of its green rolling hills. We spent the night there so we could join a tour up the Mauna Kea volcano. The group tour van took us up the inactive volcano, over thirteen thousand feet, to watch a panoramic view of the sunset before starting our stargazing from the observatory. Visitors could view the famous constellation of the Southern Hemisphere, the Southern Cross. Even though Hawaii was in the Northern Hemisphere, this constellation could be seen at certain times of the year.

It was funny being in a tropical paradise like Hawaii, watching young people all bundled up and driving their cars to the top of a volcano with their snowboards attached to the roofs. The snowy slopes had sharp crystalline ice formations jutting up that were caused by the volcanic terrain. I had to go searching for Carson at one point, as he'd wandered off when he became disoriented because of the altitude. When I found him he explained that he wasn't used to being so far away from sea level.

As we drove down the volcano, preparing to return home to California, we shed our Arctic parkas and marveled at the diversity of the ecosystems that existed on this tiny Big Island.

Ushuaia

Argentina

Drake Passage

Deception
Astrolobe
Brabant
Anvers
Lemire Channel

Paulet
James Ross

Snow Hill

Antarctica

Antarctica
2009

By 2009 I felt healthy enough to resume my international travels. Since it was January in the Northern Hemisphere heading south seemed like a good idea, so I flew to Rio de Janeiro in Brazil to visit my cousin. I had purchased a round-trip ticket to Rio since I intended to fly home from there after Carnival. Before Carnival I planned to fly to Argentina to try my luck at finding a boat to Antarctica.

Most people organize their Antarctica tours from their home countries, and they do so well in advance. I knew that buying a ticket locally, for almost anything, could be cheaper than buying it from the U.S. This approach however requires that you are not on a tight schedule. It also helps if you are alone because it's just plain easier to find space for one than for two.

Ships to Antarctica left from Ushuaia, the southernmost city in Argentina. After arriving there from Rio I immediately started talking to various tour companies in search of a berth that might be open due to a cancellation. I left my name and the phone number of the hostel where I was staying at a few of the tour offices, and they said they would call me if anything opened up. I had chosen the Freestyle hostel from the *Lonely Planet* guidebook because it was centrally located and cheap. The hostel was also quite understanding about my inability to predict how long I would be staying, since at any moment I might get the call that a berth had opened up.

While waiting for a cancellation I had time to sightsee in Ushuaia, which had a fascinating history. Ten thousand years ago a couple of native tribes actually lived there, the Y'amana and the Ono. By the 1800s Argentinian and British explorers were establishing themselves in the area and brought with them diseases that nearly decimated the indigenous population. They also brought crime, so they built a penal colony. The jailhouse still stood and visitors were allowed in to view this dark, dank and cramped facility. Downtown Ushuaia was a quaint but bustling town packed with tourist shops and restaurants catering to all those awaiting departure to Antarctica. One night I joined a group of young backpackers I'd met at the hostel to listen to some music in a local pub. It was fun to hear the Argentinian band play old Beatles tunes. All of this activity happened during their summer, which was our winter in the Northern Hemisphere. During their winter this place was a ghost town.

I participated in a few other activities with the backpackers I'd met at the Freestyle hostel. We took a Jeep ride in the surrounding mountains to visit a dogsledding kennel, but there wasn't enough snow this time of year to actually go dogsledding. They did let us meet the animals however, and learn about the process of training and caring for the dogs. Our little group also took a lovely hike through Tierra del Fuego park which was situated at the very tip of the Argentinian land mass. The motto of Ushuaia was "End of the World, Beginning of Everything." They even had a map that adjusted the countries so that Ushuaia and Antarctica were at the center of things. It was really just a matter of perspective, wasn't it?

After three days, I finally got a call telling me there'd been a cancellation, and it just so happened it was on the ship I'd wanted most of all, the Alexsey Maryshev. This ship had been a Russian research vessel and carried only fifty passengers and twenty crew. It was one of the smallest ships available, and I knew that with fewer passengers, I'd have less time to wait in line to get on land in Antarctica. We left the port of Ushuaia, Argentina, late in the evening on the nineteenth of January 2009.

I was one of the youngest passengers, as these trips were normally pricey so they didn't cater to the usual budget backpacker. The average age was mid-sixties and one man was eighty-nine years old! There was a large group from western Switzerland, so all the information had to be said twice by the tour leaders—in English and in French. Passengers were from the U.S., Canada, England, Belgium, France, Switzerland, Holland, Germany, and Ireland, and there was even one woman from Russia. This was a well-traveled group, with yet another dream destination now being crossed off their lists.

The Drake Passage between Argentina and Antarctica was so rough it took over two days to reach the closest point, a tiny strip of land called the Antarctic Peninsula. This area was surrounded by islands, and was teeming with wildlife and astounding ice formations.

The ship, food and sleeping berths were quite luxurious. There were even hot showers. There was an "open bridge" policy, so we got to hang out with the staff as we watched the beauty float by. We lived on the ship for the eleven days of the tour, but every day we made two three-hour zodiac trips. The zodiacs were rubber inflatable rafts that held about ten to twelve people, and had outboard motors. The staff would take these off the ship and put them in the water with enormous cranes. The passengers would then walk down metal gangways to board the boats, and we'd then motor close to shore, step out of the boats into the water, and wade onto the rocky beaches.

All of this maneuvering was awkward, since we were all dressed in multiple layers of bright red survival gear, which made us look and walk like oversized replicas of the penguins we'd come to see. It really wasn't that cold, fluctuating between forty and sixty degrees Fahrenheit. But it was reassuring to have on the gear in case you fell in the water, or God forbid, got left behind on shore!

The crew was attentive to our safety, and at the start of the trip we were required to run through a drill that reviewed how to board the lifeboats. The lifeboats were large, orange, completely closed-in floating containers. They could hold nearly twenty people if they were crammed in like sardines. The diesel smell from the life raft's engine was nauseating. The tour ships had been known to break down while visiting Antarctica, and you could imagine how complicated a rescue would be. As claustrophobic as I was, I couldn't see myself surviving in one of those rafts, and I just hoped I'd never have to try.

We managed to get a couple of sunny days, but mostly it was windy and stormy, which made the zodiac rides quite exciting. Once we landed we'd immediately be surrounded by noisy honking penguins. Depending on the location of the landing, we'd see a different species of penguin each time including the Adele, Gentoo or Chinstrap. There'd be thousands of them waddling about or sitting on their nests or feeding their chicks. We were allowed to sit quietly among them and they were not afraid. They'd saunter right up to us, as curious about us as we were about them.

Antarctica, a big cap of ice surrounded by ocean, sat at the bottom of the planet. It had whales, seals, penguins and, of course, birds. The most aggressive of all the animals was the leopard seal, and we were lucky, although shocked, to see one grab a penguin and smack it repeatedly on the surface of the water to strip it of its skin so it could eat it. A few times we were able to see humpback whales off the bow of the ship, waving and breaching and showing off their flukes. And each day we caught glimpses of the albatross, with wingspans of up to eight feet. It was hard to gauge their size, as they were dwarfed not just by the immense ocean, but by the most impressive sight of all, the icebergs.

An entire art gallery could be filled with nothing but pictures of the massive ice "sculptures." The variety of shapes and sizes and colors was mind boggling and the ephemeral blue glow was simply breathtaking. As our zodiacs floated by these beauties, we'd all get quiet and try to absorb the magic of this place. I felt overwhelmed knowing just how small we humans were, but how big the damage we could do to nature when you put all of us together. It would be unconscionable if we lost all of this because of our shortsighted greed and waste.

Some of the research areas and old depressing whaling stations we visited clearly illustrated the difference between man's creations and those of nature. There was no question as to which was more spectacular. Luckily, no one country owned Antarctica. A treaty signed in 1959, and ratified by forty-seven nations, prohibited new territorial claims and banned military activity, weapons and nuclear testing. What the treaty did allow was scientific research. Any nation could come to do research, as long as it shared it with the rest of the world.

The ship offered daily lectures by on-board scientists covering a wealth of information about the history and wildlife of Antarctica. Every day felt like you were seated in a swivel chair spinning and viewing a three-hundred-sixty degree IMAX movie filled with activity, color and drama. Except here you also got to experience the smell. Whewie, pwewie. The stench of penguin poo hung heavy in the air and had saturated our clothes. But even that just contributed to, and completed the sensory overload of this amazing adventure.

Before we left Antarctica for our journey back to Ushuaia the staff put on a barbecue, and it was fun to see the juxtaposition of such a suburban custom taking place in these spectacular surroundings. Unfortunately I got food poisoning and spent the night in the bathroom. Everyone, including me, wore a scopolamine patch behind their ear to avoid potential sea sickness over the Drake Passage. The patch made people really tired, so luckily I slept through most of it. When I'd get up to try to eat something I couldn't help but laugh, watching all of us struggling to walk down the corridors or up and down stairs as we sailed across the rough seas. All we needed was some slapstick three stooges music to be played to complete the picture.

As we passed through the Drake Passage we crossed what was called the Circumpolar Current, where the ocean flowed eastward, around and around, in a clockwise direction relative to the ship. This was also where the Antarctic Convergence happened, where the cold Antarctic waters met the warmer sub-Antarctic ones. I loved to imagine being at the bottom of a spinning planet, a tiny speck in the midst of all that movement.

If there were just one word to describe this voyage, it would be "wow." That word passed my lips too many times to count. As we pulled into Ushuaia the sun was trying to set, but that far south at that time of year it didn't stay gone for very long. Still, it was a warm welcome and I was happy to be on land again, even with my wobbly sea legs.

So my shaky legs and I flew from Ushuaia up to Buenos Aires to take some tango classes. Buenos Aires was a beautiful city and it was easy to find tango dancing, as it seemed to be on nearly every street corner. A couple, usually young, fit and dressed to the nines, would just start dancing. A crowd would gather, and when the couple finished, they'd pass a hat to collect tips. I decided to try my hand, or should I say my foot, at this complicated dance style, and went to one of the many tango dance halls scattered throughout the city. There older local people were dancing. Everyone sat at tables surrounding the dance floor, and if you were a lucky lady, a gentleman would ask you to dance. I didn't know the fancy footwork of the tango, but my dance partners were quite patient and accommodating.

After a couple of sightseeing days and dancing nights in Buenos Aires, I moved on up the coast by taking a ferry to Montevideo, Uruguay.

Uruguay | Brazil
2009

The ferry I was on from Buenos Aires crossed the Rio de la Plata inlet and arrived in Montevideo, Uruguay, just in time for the Iemanja celebration. This celebration came from the African Umbanda religion and was to honor Iemanja, the goddess of procreation. Hundreds of devotees gathered on the beach and launched boats with images of the goddess in them out to sea. There was plenty of music, dancing, eating and drinking going on. People would gather around a woman or man dressed all in white and who appeared to be in some sort of trance. This special person seemed to be channeling spiritual energy by dancing around the image of the goddess, saying prayers and smoking a cigarette, since smoke was supposed to enhance the connection with the spirit world.

I continued traveling by bus up the coast of Uruguay, and happened upon paradise in Barra de Valizas. This tiny village with sandy streets was home to youthful hippie artist types. Fresh off the bus I met Jimena and Juan in a café and they invited me to stay at the hostel they owned, Satori. Satori was a Japanese word for awakening or epiphany, and the name suited this very Zen-like accommodation. Satori was situated right on the beach, with a view of both the ocean and sand dunes. There was no electricity or running water. The four or five guests the cottage could house all slept in a dorm room and we all ate communally, donating what we could to the meals.

One of my favorite things about staying there was the shower—a bucket with holes in the bottom that we filled with water that had been heated on the wood stove. Frequently I'd be joined in the shower by rather large toads. I couldn't seem to drag myself away from this place and spent days wandering the beach and dunes, happening upon whimsical artwork in the sand or other equally mesmerized travelers.

One afternoon Juan, Jimena and I went for a horseback ride inland, following tree-lined trails to a hidden lake. We all jumped in and swam while the horses rested. In the evenings I'd meander down the sandy trails to find something to eat at one of the candlelit porches of some beach shack. Slowly, as the sun went down, the hippies would gather to display their hand made jewelry, clothing or artwork for sale on a blanket set out on the sand. No one really bought much, and it was mostly just an excuse to gather, play drums, dance and socialize.

Finally I tore myself away and boarded a bus to continue north up the coast. We stopped for many hours at Chui, Uruguay's bizarre border town with Brazil. On one side of the street you were in Brazil, the other, Uruguay. There was some confusion at immigration. In fact the bus had driven right by it. I talked to some other travelers and found out it was my responsibility to obtain an exit stamp in my passport from Uruguay before crossing into Brazil, which I hadn't done. I had to pay for a taxi to go back to the Uruguayan immigration office, pay for my exit stamp, then pay for another taxi back to Chui. Then I had to wait until the bus office opened to buy a ticket to Brazil. Luckily I was able to get one because I'd met quite a few people who'd had to stay a few nights in Chui trying to figure out all this border crossing confusion.

Once all of that was sorted out, I headed to Florinopolis and the island of Santa Catarina. There I began to feel a little lost. The place was lovely, but I wasn't really connecting with any locals, and I certainly didn't connect with the other tourists. Most of the travelers at the hostel were much younger than I was and they all seemed obsessed with their computers. I looked wistfully back on the days when travel meant a total disconnect with home so you threw yourself intimately into the present. Also, most of the other tourists were on their way to Carnival in Rio, so they were probably deeply involved in planning the logistics of that. I was headed to Rio too. The difference was that I had family there and I was going primarily to see them.

My cousin-once-removed, David, had married a vivacious Brazilian woman named Helena and they were filmmakers. My favorite movie they made was called *Bananas is my Business*, which was the story of Carmen Miranda. They'd filmed many documentaries about various aspects of Brazilian culture, like the samba dancing schools and the way the music and written word were intertwined. I'd tried repeatedly to get them to let me work on films with them, but they always said, "You don't speak Portuguese." Brazil had been a Portuguese colony since the 1500s and declared its independence in 1822. So before embarking on this trip I actually took a Portuguese language class. Unfortunately I found it difficult to overcome my habit of slipping into Spanish. The languages were similar, but not the same, and although the locals seemed to be able to understand my Spanish, I could never seem to understand their Portuguese.

David and Helena lived in a beautiful home perched below the massive Christ the Redeemer statue, Cristo. It overlooked the lagoon and Copacabana beach. Rio is a spectacular city situated on the Atlantic ocean, with bays and inlets punctuated by conical shaped mountains scattered throughout. After arriving I soon realized how incredibly exhausted I was, and I spent days just sleeping in my air-conditioned room.

Now and then I'd venture out into the oppressive heat to explore Rio. Over the course of a few days I managed to climb up to the Cristo statue, take the cable car to Sugarloaf mountain, pay my respects at the grave of Carmen Miranda, and ride on the back of a motorcycle to the Rocinha favela.

The favelas were enormous "slums" that covered Rio's surrounding mountainsides. It was interesting to note that in Western countries the wealthy built houses on hills for the views, but in Rio it was the poor who had the prime real estate. The social structure of the favelas was fascinating. The inhabitants had come up with their own ways of surviving, replete with punishment for those who broke the rules. For example "microwaving" was putting a body, dead or alive, in a stack of tires, then burning it.

The company I went to the favelas with organized these motorcycle and walking tours and donated part of the proceeds to establish local day care facilities for the favela residents. Our group of five, led by a beautiful tough tattooed young woman, walked safely through the labyrinth of the favela. Everywhere you looked there were tangled masses of wires transmitting stolen electricity. The shack-like houses were built from cement, pieces of scrap wood and metal, and were stacked one on top of the other. They all had blue plastic tanks precariously balanced on rickety roofs to collect water. Through the maze of narrow paths and alleys we met shop owners, graffiti artists, samba dancers, and the young students who benefited from the money that these tours provided.

One day I took a local bus to Sugarloaf, the thirteen hundred foot high granite mountain shaped like a conical mound of sugar, thus its name. On the buses there were always a driver, and a helper who collected the fares and assisted the passengers getting on and off. I was one of three women on the bus. When it was stuck in traffic, suddenly one of the thousands of young boys who begged on Rio's streets tried to break into the back of the bus by crawling through the window. The bus driver's assistant rushed to the rescue, punching the kid and dislodging him from the bus. It was a frightening and sad experience to so closely witness the desperation of the poor in this country.

But through all their struggles it was evident that Brazilians sure knew how to party. Carnival or Carne Vale means, "Farewell to the Flesh." Carnival was the way to have one last fling before lent. In Rio the streets were packed day after day, night after night, with neighborhood parties, food, dancing, music, floats and people in costumes. The costumes were very skimpy! I didn't make it to the arena where the float competition was televised around the world, and I was actually fine with that, as being in the streets with the locals seemed more authentic to me. In fact, after a few nights of it, my family did what most locals did—they left town. We went up the coast to Buzios and stayed with friends in their lovely villa on the beach.

I'd gone from seeing the cold isolated majestic icebergs of Antarctica to the hot steamy samba chaos of Carnival and finally to this peaceful refuge on the beach with family, friends, good food and a soft bed. What a perfect note to end on.

Tibet
2009

When I was in Yemen in 2007 I'd had the opportunity to record some video in a mental hospital. Using that footage I'd put together a short film called *Mental Illness Around the World.* My hope was to create a series that looked at how culture and religion affected mental illness and its treatment. The film was well received at the Santa Cruz film festival, so I felt encouraged to continue with the project. I spoke with Lan, my friend who'd I'd met in China in 2005, and whose parents worked for the Chinese government. She thought her father could get me an interview in a mental hospital in China. So we arranged to meet in Beijing in September of 2009. I also had plans to travel to Tibet after visiting China.

The only obstacle I faced on my flight from the U.S. to China was being seated next to a guy who stunk of garlic. You know that smell, right? We had a lot of it in Santa Cruz, that pungent hippie odor. It was overwhelming, and I felt nauseated. It took me a couple of hours to figure out what it was and where it was coming from. I tried giving the guy some gum, but that didn't help. The smell was oozing out of his body. Nearly in tears, I talked to the flight attendant, and she knew I was telling the truth because she could smell it too. She compassionately moved me to a wonderful aisle exit row seat, and I'll have to remember this technique in the future when I want a better seat! Unfortunately I had to move away from an interesting American couple who'd been seated behind me and smelled just fine. They'd traveled all over the world and were fascinating. I spent many hours standing in the aisle visiting with them, which helped make the time "fly by."

I landed in Beijing and was again faced with the challenge of my taxi driver not being able to read letters from the Latin alphabet and my not knowing Chinese characters. We did eventually make it to the home of the English couple I'd met in Malawi years before. We had stayed in touch and they'd been living and working in China for two years after moving there from India. As I've said many times, the English are the greatest of travellers.

We went out for dinner one night, but not for Chinese food. Instead, we went out for Ethiopian. My friends said it was the only restaurant of its kind in Beijing. I loved Ethiopian food and this food was good, but really it was the restaurant itself which was so beautiful, and the dancing which was so interesting. I thought I'd seen most styles of African dance, but no, this was weird stuff, with the dancers popping and snapping their shoulders and necks like chickens on meth or something.

I spent a couple of nights at my friends' house, then moved to a hotel in Beijing to meet up with Lan. She had now divorced her husband and was preparing to marry a Russian fellow she'd met while studying law in the U.S. They were in China to meet her parents and to start preparing for an elaborate Chinese wedding. We all went out for the usual totally bizarre Chinese foods, like sea cucumber, goose intestines and chicken feet.

It was so nice being in China with Lan. She spoke both English and Mandarin Chinese, and she was such a joy to be with because of her struggles, questions, curiosity and humor. She had a unique perspective on cultural issues between the U.S. and China, the similarities and differences, the good and the bad. I was feeling healthy, with minimal jet lag, and my body, mind and spirit were on an even keel. The weather in Beijing however was atrocious. The thick overcast sky coupled with occasional rain added to the thick smog. It was gross, heavy and depressing. It burned your eyes and you could taste it in the back of your throat. I hoped it would be better when we got to Lan's "small" home town. I wondered what small could mean in this vast overpopulated country.

The next day we caught an ex-military plane to Guangzhou in the south. Lan's parents, who both still worked for the government, picked us up in a huge black SUV with our very own mafia looking driver. A three hour drive north brought us to their home town, Chenzhou, which Lan described as a "tiny village" of seven million, or something crazy like that. It was a verdant, humid, hazy, rather hilly place. We were taken immediately to a fancy private party room in an enormous multi-storied restaurant where we met all Lan's family, ate gobs of food, and drank and toasted dozens of times. The custom was to say nice things about someone sitting at the table, then yell *gambei* (cheers) and chug the wine or beer. Yes, they chugged wine.

I was then dropped off at a luxurious hotel where nobody spoke English. It seemed everything was paid for by the government since Lan's father worked for them. I had no idea what Lan's parents did for the government. Lan described her father as a mayor of sorts. It did feel strange to be totally spoiled by the Communist regime, since I could only imagine what her parents might had done to people during Mao's dictatorship. Even if I had spoken Mandarin, I doubt they would have told me. The communists presented themselves as being a government of equality for all people. But in its practice, it was anything but fair.

In the morning, I had my breakfast, which was a porridge of rice soup, dumplings, and noodles. A hard-boiled egg was also offered, I imagined because I was American. They also brought me a glass of milk. There was no point trying to explain that I was lactose intolerant, as they reportedly are. It is interesting that the only mammal to drink milk in adulthood is the human, and we don't even drink the milk of our own species. In my room I'd watch the one and only English speaking television station, which seemed to be a Chinese government propaganda channel. The shows they presented were about tea, Chinese history, and Chinese arts and science. One story was about the "angry youth," who were conservative nationalistic young folks who said they were sick of hearing all the criticism about China.

The hotel staff gave up their office just to let me use their computer. Being a guest of a government official had its perks. On the other hand, I later realized that my password for signing into my email account didn't automatically go away after I quit using the computer, which meant that anyone had access to my account. While in China I was always careful about what I wrote in my e-mails, just in case I was being monitored.

My first application to request entry to the mental hospital near Lan's home town had not been successful. We re-filed and, while we were waiting for the latest response, Lan and I went to get a massage. The massage chairs were lined up in such a way that the customers could visit with each other while being worked on. First your feet were soaked in warm water with herbs, and while you soaked, they massaged and pushed on pressure points on your head. The masseurs were two cute young boys. The massage was done fully clothed and they used a cloth to rub you with instead of oil. After they massaged your body, they'd return to work on the pressure points on your feet. Next they put heated glass jars on your skin, which they said were to suck out all the toxins. After the massage we went to replenish our toxins with beer and pizza and to practice English with Lan's niece. Lan's uncle ran a teahouse, where we got to participate in a simple ceremony. It was pretty down to earth, pleasant and not complicated like Japanese tea ceremonies were.

The next day brought the news I'd been waiting for. Our application to visit the mental hospital had been accepted! At the hospital they took down all my information, while the head of propaganda photographed me and scrutinized my nursing license. The entire time I had an entourage following me around. But I got two interviews, one with the head of finance, discussing the nuts and bolts of the hospital, and another with the lead psychiatrist of the women's unit. Lan did a great job translating and interfacing between me and the staff. They wouldn't allow me to see the patients or their rooms, or even the activity rooms or the pharmacy, which was unfortunate. But hey, I was amazed we got as far as we did.

We got a call after we left, and they told Lan they regretted permitting the interview because they thought the hospital looked shabby. I tried to pass on how impressed and grateful I was to all of them. During the interviews I'd pointed out that I hadn't seen any mentally ill people wandering the streets like we had in the U.S. I was told that the police drove around, and if they noticed someone acting strangely, they picked that person up for evaluation. I didn't mention during the interview that I'd heard that political dissidents had been placed in mental institutions indefinitely in order to keep them quiet or to discredit them in the public eye. I spent the rest of my time in China worrying that my hotel door would be broken down by police wanting my video footage back.

After the hospital interview we went to meet yet more wealthy friends of Lan's family. We searched and searched for the place where we were to meet them before finally ending up at a modern style building, still under construction, but open to the public, with dust flying about and reeking of glue. And even with all this work going on, they were blaring techno disco. The place was appropriately called "Boom Boom." We went inside with Lan's cute little mom. The lights were flashing, the music was pounding, the smoke machines were billowing, and there were young boys and girls dancing on the bar counters to some strange music which told a story in English that was about aliens. Lan's mom was trying to dance along.

As always, there was food. We ate non-stop all day long, and I couldn't understand how the people stayed so small. I was excited about the lobster Lan wanted to get us, and I thought, "Yay, something I'll really like." But no, after we saw the poor fellow alive, he was chopped up raw and served sashimi style. We were also served soup with turtle and scorpion. And, oh yes, the full body of the black creepy bug floated on top of the soup.

While in Lan's hometown of Chenzhou, we tried to find some nature. We went on a day trip to a nearby cave with her uncle and his friend, a car salesman. The cave was huge, beautiful and had a river running through it. But unfortunately the experience was marred by a large Chinese tour group in front of us with a bullhorn, which shattered the silence and peace, and by the men in the group who ignored the "No Smoking" signs.

Lan and I got into an argument about saving nature versus succeeding in business. It was abundantly clear that in China the rapid industrial growth had caused terrible environmental damage. Lan had changed since I'd first met her in 2005. She used to want to help the world. Now she openly admitted that she just wanted to be what she called "a parasite," and make money doing whatever she had to, no matter what the consequences were.

On the drive home there was a sobriety checkpoint. Our driver asked the police officer, "Are you crazy, do you know who this car belongs to?", and we were promptly waved on. I now had such mixed feelings about Lan and her family. On the one hand I didn't agree with the special treatment government officials received, but on the other hand I couldn't thank Lan's family enough for their hospitality. They completely financially supported my stay. They welcomed me into their humble home, which was surprisingly small, but clean and cozy. Lan's mom let me help her cook. They adored their daughter, who had struggled with depression and mood swings, impulsive marriages, and divorce. These people, who obviously had some clout, seemed to live simply and bent over backwards to please Lan and to do everything possible for me.

On my last night in Chenzhou we all went out to a mall to eat dinner, and to celebrate our success at the hospital, and to say our goodbyes. Lan's father drank a bit too much and sent our driver to go find him a traditional flute. He sat there in a booth, with his rosy cheeks and his eyes squinted nearly shut by his big grin, playing the flute for us, while we all cheered him on. Lan's family wrote a letter for me to carry in case the authorities became suspicious of my large video camera. I invited Lan to come with me to Tibet, but she'd succumbed to her government's propaganda and believed the Tibetans would try to kill her.

I left Lan and her family and flew west to Chengdu to try to get the required government permit to go to Tibet. My first four days in Chengdu were spent filling out paperwork and making phone calls to try to get the permit. It seemed like a full-time job. If I hadn't had gifts to deliver to people in Tibet I'd probably have skipped it and just gone to areas nearby in western China that were reportedly more Tibetan anyway, and involved much less hassle.

When I was back home in Santa Cruz, just before this trip, a Tibetan co-worker and many of her friends had given me small presents and photos to deliver to their families in Tibet. They were no longer allowed to return since they'd left illegally. Many Tibetans risked their lives hiking over the Himalayas to escape and get to India, especially Dharamsala, where the Dalai Lama had also escaped to and where he was still living. The Chinese had for years persecuted the Tibetans living in and around Tibet's capital, Lhasa. But many of the areas in western China, near Tibet's borders, had been left relatively untouched by the Chinese and were therefore places where the Tibetans were more easily able to maintain their traditional culture.

The issue with my permit was that, with the upcoming Chinese holiday celebrating sixty years of Communist rule, everything had become even stricter because of the risk of protests by the Tibetans. I was finally able to fax off my request to the Chinese government with the details of the personal tour I'd signed up for in Tibet. Every traveler had to have a government approved guide with them every day, nearly every waking moment, that they were in Tibet. This made things quite expensive and complicated. It also meant that approval was slow, to say the least. There was also confusion because the staff at my hostel who were helping me arrange everything thought I wanted to trek the entire time and hire a "yak and yak man." I certainly did not want to do that because I was way too out of shape to trek at all. I wanted the "drive-by" tour, thank you very much.

The time I'd allotted for seeing Tibet was diminishing, since I'd wanted to leave China before the anniversary celebrations started. So I was left with only half the time I'd wanted to spend there. If all were approved, and that was a big "IF," I'd be in Lhasa for four days, then go north to see a lake, mountains, monasteries, nunneries, hot springs, and caves for three days. I had to eliminate the option of taking the famous train to Lhasa, since this would have added even more time to the trip. I decided I'd fly and I hoped I wouldn't get altitude sickness since I would suddenly fly into a city at an altitude of nearly 12,000 feet. I also decided to travel alone, because it would be too much trouble to try to find travel companions that late in the game. I'd also requested that my guide and accommodation be Tibetan, and wondered if that too had slowed down the process.

While waiting in Chengdu I saw the pandas, the Wu Hou shrine, and visited the "Tibetan" street, where I ate yak stew. The frustration with sitting and waiting for the permit was that I didn't feel comfortable leaving

Chengdu to go somewhere else in China in case there was some problem that needed to be dealt with right away. So there I sat. It rained and rained and rained. I hadn't seen the sun in two weeks and I couldn't remember what a shadow looked like. I heard the Chinese government had seeded the clouds so it would rain, which would alleviate the smog, so the air would more likely be clear for the anniversary celebrations. I felt that messing with Mother Nature would surely backfire someday.

One day, while I was waiting, I decided to go for a massage. It took me a while to find the address I was looking for, and when I did, it was a tiny little hole-in-the-wall with about eight tables all lined up in a row with people being massaged. The clients were all fully clothed. I stood at the entrance and finally a man waved me in. I was wondering why he was looking above my head, but didn't think much of it. Then I briefly wondered why another man had sunglasses on indoors. When I got called over to my table, my masseuse had her eyes shut tight, and that was when it dawned on me that they were all blind. It was not such a great massage, but my little lady masseuse was so sweet. She worked on a lot of pressure points and overall I felt better.

Afterwards I went to see a Sichuan opera at a huge "tea house," which was really fascinating. They had music, dancing, and singing, which were okay, but it was the hand shadow dancing that I really liked. This was where, behind backlit screens, the performers made all sorts of images with their hands that told a story. I also liked the "face changing," where, like magic, they shifted the colors of their masks. The puppetry was also good, and they even put on a skit, which was still funny even though I couldn't understand what they were saying.

All in all, it was a good day. But I still waited for my Tibetan travel permit. I didn't want to leave town until I knew I'd been approved to go to Tibet and could then purchase my plane tickets. Every day I asked myself, "What can I do today?" My days were running into each other. I'd shuffle downstairs in the mornings, still in my pajamas, and wait in line to get some coffee. Then I'd sit in the garden staring at the plants and listen to the fountain mix with the rain. Then I'd mess around on the Internet in an increasingly paranoid state, not wanting to write too much in my emails, just in case some government official was watching. Fortunately Sim's Cozy Garden Hostel was a nice place, relaxing, and with a wonderfully helpful staff. The owner, Sim, was a Chinese version of a hippie and operated under a tremendous amount of stress at he tried to keep both his customers and the Chinese government happy.

On Thursday the seventeenth of September in the year of our Lord 2009 I'd been at Sim's for seven days, and hoped seven was a lucky number. The previous day I'd ventured out with Kevin, a young German traveler staying at the hostel. We went to Peng Le, an old town built alongside a river—a polluted stinky river. We saw a bunch of shop stalls, traditional architecture, and farmland. Yawn. But at least it was a day out. Back at the hostel I'd thought I'd do my laundry and watch movies on my room's DVD player, but of course it was broken. As I was waiting for it to be fixed, I was staring out at the depressing haze and pondering an alternative plan to visiting Tibet. I was ready to give up and get the hell out of there.

Suddenly there was a knock on my door, and BAM, I had my permit! My mind started racing about what to do next, and flights seemed to be top priority. I tried to book them on the Internet, but the airline would only accept cash for tickets to Lhasa. So then I hoped I'd be able to pull out enough cash from the bank to be able to pay for the plane tickets and the tour all at once. I rushed to the bank, but its ATM would only let me get the set amount my bank back home would allow per day. I was so frantic I had to chuckle through tears of irony and frustration and impatiently wait to see what tomorrow would bring. Hopefully the ATM would then let me pull out enough cash. Hopefully Carson, my boyfriend back home, could contact my bank in the U.S. to okay it. Hopefully it would all unfold as it needed to. Before I fell into a fitful sleep I prayed, "Dear Universe, let me let it happen as it is supposed to."

In the middle of this mess I'd communicate via e-mail with Carson, and my friends and family in the U.S. I'd tell them to be grateful for the bureaucracies at home, because they were so much more efficient than those I was dealing with in China. I couldn't say everything I wanted to say on the Internet because I was certain I was being monitored. I'd met a young man from Switzerland who'd been taking pictures of some of the minority tribes in western China. He said he'd seen tribes people being beaten and even shot by the Chinese military. We'd meet and whisper our shared insights and suspicions. I saw Communism for what it was—a nice philosophy, but nothing more, as I'd never known of a country able to put it into practice fairly, or for that matter, even humanely.

To hell with the Big Dipper roller coaster on the Santa Cruz, California, boardwalk! Oh how I'd screamed when I rode that. But my roller-coaster day at Sim's Cozy Garden Hostel beat that hands down. The morning started with my pot of French-press coffee to get my blood moving and my brain firing. Next I took a shower and wandered down to the hostel's reception and travel desk, which was always packed. I walked to the Bank of China, but, "No," they couldn't change travelers' checks or U.S. dollars, nor would they allow a cash withdrawal on my credit card. My debit card had already been maxed out for the day's withdrawal of $300. I started to panic, but was then able to catch a ride with a man on the back of his moped to a bigger branch of the same bank downtown. He took me on all the back roads to avoid the police, because he said it was illegal to have both of us on his moped. In broken English he continued to say that if the police stopped us, I was to get off, walk away, and pretend not to know him.

We made it to the bank and the sweet moped man said he'd wait for me while I went in. Here they at least changed my travelers' checks and cash, the wee bit that I had left, into Yuan, the Chinese currency. I still didn't have enough though, because I'd been told that all my travel arrangements for Tibet had to be paid for in cash.

During all of this, my longtime boyfriend Carson, the amazingly supportive love of my life and man of my dreams, kept trying to contact my bank in the U.S. to see if they would increase my withdrawal limit. He put up with my tears and hysteria on the phone in stellar form, and somehow found a PIN number for my other credit card, which I'd never had to use before. Then I waited some more because the hostel office said the travel agent getting my plane tickets would come by and let me use a credit card to buy them. That would leave me just barely enough cash to pay for the rest of the tour. I waited and waited and waited for the travel agent, who came over an hour late. When he got to the hostel he realized that he couldn't run a U.S. credit card. I just sat there and cried.

Through all of this the hostel had assigned me a "helper" to assist with arranging my travel plans. All the backpackers had a helper, which was why the travel desk was always so chaotic. My helper's name was "Jodie," which was the English name she had given herself. She felt so sorry for me that she decided to walk with me to a nearby bank and see if she could help me get a cash withdrawal on my credit card even though I'd been denied before. With her good energy and the new PIN number Carson had obtained for me, the cash just kept coming out of the ATM like a jackpot at a casino. I was so excited to be able to get money out that I ended up with a good three inch pile of 100 Yuan notes! I was at long last able to pay for my flights and my tour in Lhasa, all for about 10,000 Yuan ($1500).

The stress never seemed to end. I'd paid extra for rush delivery of my

Tibet Travel Permit, but the night before I was going to fly to Lhasa it still hadn't arrived. It finally showed up late at night, leaving just enough time for me to try to catch a few hours' sleep before an early morning departure to the airport. The police had stopped by the hostel twice already to check if Sim were running his hostel and travel agency properly. I suspected that my fear of being hassled by the Chinese government was going to be an ongoing issue, probably even more so in Tibet than in China. I asked myself if the trip would be worth it all.

In the morning, after a long wait on the runway in the incessant rain and smog, we finally took off and broke through that dismal layer of pollution, and I could at last see the sun high above the clouds. When we landed in Tibet I was greeted by two adorable Tibetans, my driver and my guide, who were waiting for me with a scarf, water, and smiles. It was so wonderful that I burst into tears. The warm sun twinkled as it reflected off a green river winding through the snowcapped mountains, their peaks just below the fluffy white clouds. The air was crisp and clean, in sharp contrast to the unbreathable smog of China. Buddha statues and prayer flags dotted the landscape, and the peace and quiet lifted a week's worth of stress from my shoulders in mere moments. I had to pinch myself to make sure it weren't all a dream, and that I had indeed finally made it to Tibet.

As we neared Lhasa we could immediately see the Chinese influence, with all the construction going on, the garish signage and row after row of stalls selling cheap Chinese made trinkets and clothes. The Chinese had taken over, except for a small section of old Lhasa, where the Tibetans were allowed to have shops and restaurants, and to keep their monasteries. The Chinese government had sent so many Han Chinese to occupy Tibet, in order to now make the Tibetans be a minority in their own country. The Chinese takeover of Tibet was all about controlling the water that the mountains in Tibet provided China and its burgeoning population. My hostel was located smack in the middle of the tiny Tibetan haven in the old part of Lhasa. It was a beautiful, brand new, Tibetan style place with incense and decor right up my alley. From the hostel's rooftop I could see the mountains all around me, and it felt like I was so close to the sky that I could touch the clouds. And just over in the distance was proof that I was actually in Tibet, the iconic Potala Palace.

I was handling the high altitude, over 11,000 feet, but I was a little giddy. My guide, Tselhamo, had given me a Chinese herb to help stave off altitude sickness, but the belches it caused were horrendous. Surprisingly, beer helped. Tselhamo said we should have no problem meeting with and distributing the gifts I'd brought to the families of my U.S. based Tibetan friends.

I had not gotten to Tibet gracefully, but there I was, puffy-eyed from crying, and grateful. And man oh man, oh man, Lhasa was incredible, mystical and magical. It was also swarming with Chinese military, decked out in riot gear, carrying guns with bayonets. They were marching around everywhere, even in the koras (pilgrim paths) around monasteries, and it was a bizarre juxtaposition with the little old Tibetan ladies twirling their prayer wheels. The fact that the Chinese were celebrating the 60th anniversary of the Communist takeover of China this week didn't help matters. It only increased the police presence.

And then, out of nowhere, as I was walking around the main square, I suddenly heard my name being called out. The couple I'd met on the plane coming from the U.S. to China had ended up in Tibet at the same time I was there! We spent the better part of our remaining days in Lhasa together, and I knew then that we'd become fast friends.

I saw so many monasteries, but every one of them was different and fantastic—dark, old, and covered with ancient peeling paintings and statues of Buddha and Buddhist teachers. The people would gather around the monasteries, and do repetitive prostrations and prayers. And the smoke laced with the smell of yak butter candles and incense burning was thick in the air.

I was pleased that my lovely hostel was located smack in the center of the old Tibetan part of town, so I could walk everywhere and still come back for a decent toilet break. I visited the Potala Palace of course, and yes, the painful history of the place was palpable. The Dalai Lama had lived there, had trusted the Chinese to abide by a peace treaty, but had instead been violently betrayed by them. The Dalai Lama is to Tibetans what Jesus is to Christians, the holiest of holies, but the Chinese government wouldn't allow Tibetans to have a picture of him anywhere.

The Chinese government's oppressiveness was why I'd been so worried about delivering the small gifts I'd been entrusted with by my friends in the U.S. to give to their family members still living in Lhasa. Tselhamo helped me find all of the addresses and families I was looking for. It was so moving to see the joyous, tearful and grateful reactions of the recipients to the photos and small tokens, like necklaces or bracelets with pictures of Buddhist saints, that had been sent by loved ones they'd probably never see in person again. They were allowed to speak on the phone, but knew they could be monitored, so they never really got to speak about what was actually happening in Tibet.

These families all lived in housing that had been built by the Chinese and the houses were large and clean. The Chinese had also built roads, schools, and hospitals and were working on an infrastructure to better manage utilities and waste. The improvement of the Tibetan standard of living brought about by the Chinese would have all been well and good if there hadn't been such flagrant religious persecution and seemingly intentional obliteration of the traditional Tibetan culture and way of life. The Chinese required the Tibetans to study Mandarin Chinese, and I reluctantly came to understand that, for practical purposes, it was probably a good idea to know the language of those who had taken over your country and continued to occupy it.

The families who'd received the gifts were all so grateful that they all wanted to feed me. I'd eaten so many yak *momos*, that I was about to explode. These were little dumplings filled with yak meat, and then steamed or fried. One family took me to see a traditional Tibetan dance and music show. It seemed I'd finally reached the age though where some singing I heard sounded more like screaming, and I had to put toilet paper in my ears to deafen it. There was a lot less dancing than I'd hoped for.

There was a large dark dance hall with a stage, surrounded by seating for the audience in the form of restaurant booths, where food and drink could be served while watching the show. I was the only foreigner. During the singing some members of the audience, usually drunk men, would climb up on stage and put a white scarf around the performer's neck. They'd have their picture taken with the performer, who was all the while screaming, or singing. Your interpretation depended on how old you were and if you spoke the language.

One day my guide Tselhamo took me to a monastery in Lhasa to see a big group of monks arguing about the Buddhist scriptures. This was a popular tourist stop. What was interesting was to see the wide age range of the monks, from a seven year old boy to a toothless old man. The monks would get in each other's faces and yell, then slap their hands as if to say, "So there!" after having made their point. I like the tenet in Buddhism that asks the practitioner to always question the teachings. When we finished viewing the monks we caught a local bus to return to the hotel. The bus was stopped and boarded by the Chinese police, who walked up and down the bus aisle looking for anyone suspicious. It was creepy and demeaning.

While in Lhasa I'd hoped I might be able to film different aspects of how Tibetan culture approached and treated mental illness. I was able to go into a Tibetan hospital, which was separate from the Chinese hospital, and talk to the pharmacist about herbal treatments. Unfortunately the pharmacist was Chinese. Tselhamo told me that she had rarely seen or heard about mental illness among the Tibetan people. She guessed that some people in the countryside might attribute mental illness to "bad spirits." But in general the Tibetans would seek out a shaman of sorts to analyze their urine, phlegm, and pulse strength. They'd discuss how they had been sleeping and eating, and if any other stressors were occurring in their lives. For the treatment of any minor physical or mental disturbance they'd use herbal medicines, prayer and meditation. There was a medical hospital for any major trauma, where doctors used a combination of Western and Eastern medicine.

I liked to try pizza wherever I went, just out of curiosity, so I had a "Hawaiian" pizza while in Lhasa. Instead of ham they used yak meat, and it was not so tasty. It was fatty, greasy and rather gamey. I also tried their barley beer, which was a bit tart and really good.

I've noticed during my years of traveling that I'd start to reach a saturation point when I stayed somewhere too long. And that was now happening here. I'd start to get annoyed at petty things, like the fact that the toilet paper rolls didn't have enough paper on them, or the toilet didn't flush well, or that the bed was actually really hard. And hadn't the hostel served the same food for breakfast yesterday that they did the day before, and the day before that? And weren't the people a bit overly ingratiating? I'd really enjoyed my stay in Lhasa, but it was clearly time to move out of the city and see some of the countryside.

Nam Tso lake was about a four hour drive north of Lhasa. On the way, Tselhamo, my two drivers and I stopped at Yambaje, a huge hot spring. You could see the billows of steam from far away. Its natural course had been changed into about five huge hot water pools. In general I prefer hot springs in their natural state, but in this instance, I could say it was fabulous. You could move from tub to tub, each with different herbs or plants added to them, like rose petals or lavender. There were only a couple of Chinese men there, and one of them wanted to race me in an underwater swim. I opted out and just applauded his amazing skill. They also served hard boiled eggs cooked over the steam.

We continued to drive to the lake, which was purportedly the largest high altitude salt water lake in the world. The turquoise blue water surrounded by snowcapped mountains reminded me of Lake Tahoe on the California-Nevada border. But Nam Tso was not as built up. Instead, there were Quonset hut type buildings lined up in a row and you could sleep and eat in them. There were about eight different huts in one area by the lake. Some were for sleeping, some were stores of sorts that sold basic items, and one had signs that read "oxygen restaurant yogurt" and "film oxygen battery." The oxygen was available to purchase in case of altitude sickness, but my private tour carried its own. There were generators at night, which provided electricity until 10 p.m. There was no running water, and the one and only group toilet was, yes, you guessed it, a hole in the ground.

The food was cooked over an open fire in the hut of the family that ran the place where we stayed. The food of course was yak meat, which we'd bought off the back of a truck. The yak carcass was still there, and the seller would cut off a piece of meat from it and weigh it in front of you. The meat sellers were described to me as being from the Kham tribe. The men had red scarves woven through their hair and beautiful carved bone jewelry. Historically they'd been known as the "warrior tribe," but with time they had been absorbed into Tibet and Buddhism.

The family who ran the place we were staying had a new baby. She was so cute and quiet and wore pajamas that had an opening in the back for her little butt to hang out. I figured that it at least cut down on the garbage of diapers. The family joined Tselhamo, our two drivers and me for dinner.

The lake was spectacular, and my guide, drivers and I walked around Tashi Do, the peninsula jutting into it. There was a monastery on the peninsula with thousands of bright prayer flags flapping in the wind off every peak, rock and tree. The flags came in blue, white, red, green and yellow, with each color representing an element. Blue was space, white, air, red, fire, green, water, and yellow, earth. Prayers were printed on each flag with the idea that the wind carried them out in order to effect positive change in the world. We met one monk who'd been living in a cave by the lake for fifteen years. He let us come inside his cave, which was covered with images of Buddha and various saints. He also had candles, incense and his sleeping pad. It didn't look very comfortable, but he had a cleverly designed solar cooker outside that could heat water and food.

On the path leading up to the peninsula there were many large prayer wheels that you could walk by and spin saying, "Om mani padme hum" over and over. There was no standard translation for this prayer, but some said that "mani" and "padme" spoke of the "jewel of the lotus flower," which was sacred in Buddhism. The prayer was also said to invoke blessings from Chenrezig, the embodiment of compassion. Throughout my trip we saw many pilgrims walking with their hand-held prayer wheels or beads. Honestly, there was so much praying going on that I could see how the Tibetan culture had seemingly gotten little else done. On the other hand, if you were so busy praying, you'd have little time for bombing, conquering, robbing and raping the land.

I didn't sleep well and didn't know if this were due to the incessant barking of dogs, the roar of the generators, the high altitude, the freezing cold, the itching from the bed bugs, or the bad gas the dinner had given me. But morning finally came and we left to drive to another monastery, Reting, that I'd read about in the *Lonely Planet* guidebook. We made it, albeit over incredibly bad roads—all rocks and gravel and potholes. It wasn't the worst I'd been on, but pretty bad. This monastery was famous because three of the fourteen successive Dalai Lamas had been chosen from this area and because the complex had been nearly destroyed during Mao's Cultural Revolution. Sadly, the place was disgusting, dirty, worn down, and didn't seem to be treated as the holy ground it was touted to be.

When I just HAD to go to the toilet I was shown an outdoor area that was just a shoulder high wooden fence around an open hole in the ground.

While I squatted over the hole, three of the thousands of wild dogs that infested this country jumped down in the hole to eat my fresh deposit. I thought I was going to puke. There were only male monks staying there, and I had to ask myself, "Be it a frat house, a locker room or a group of monks, do all men live like pigs?" The upside of the monastery visit was seeing the restoration being done to the artwork on the inside walls. The paintings were quite beautiful, colorful and intricate, and were being touched up by the monks.

Taking time to visit that horrible place caused us to add five more hours of nearly impassable roads in order to get to the next stop on the itinerary, the Tildrum nunnery. I'd originally planned the itinerary with ideas and recommendations from the *Lonely Planet* guidebook. The draw of the nunnery was that it had hot springs. We drove on and on over bumpy, slippery, curvy, potholed dirt paths that were too narrow to even be called roads. There was lovely scenery though, with mountains and the river and the yaks, goats, sheep, horses, old stone houses with bright doors, stupas with fluttering prayer flags and scarves, and nomadic brown tents, which were much simpler than yurts. And still we kept driving. I had to ask myself, "How is it I always seem to end up on these routes with no other travelers?"

We were out in the middle of frigging nowhere. And as we were trying to drive across yet another rocky river, where the "road" had washed away, we got stuck. "Yes," I thought, "this also seems to happen to me a lot." And of course it chose to not just rain, but to hail instead, right at that moment.

Now, not only did I have my little twenty year old translator-guide Tselhamo, but I also had two drivers, so they could take turns. I hadn't asked to hire that many people, but that was what I got. Both of the drivers got out of the truck, and without their shoes on, were trying to dig us out by hand. Then they attached a prayer scarf and tied it to another truck to try to pull us out. A prayer scarf, for God or Buddha's sake? I suggested to Tselhamo that this would never work, and that we'd need to find a real rope or chain. So off we went searching while the "boys" messed around with scarves. We found a rope, which worked, and we got out. Brains over brawn (or limp scarves) wins out any day. I suggested to my entourage that they all make a "note to self," namely, never go on a road trip without a rope, jumper cables, a spare tire, water and a flashlight. My list went on and they all smiled and nodded although the drivers didn't even speak English. I also had to make a note to myself that these people were always smiling, and perhaps I could learn from that. And even though we didn't need it, they had at least remembered to bring the oxygen.

Finally we got to Tildrum, exhausted. This nunnery was nestled between two mountains, and like the monasteries, it was covered with flags and scarves. The four of us grabbed all our belongings and started hiking up and down the stairs to get to the nunnery, which had sleeping rooms available for tourists and locals on pilgrimage. As we neared the nunnery I became more and more disgusted with the mounds of garbage and feces everywhere. I was shown the room where I was supposed to stay the night, and it was filthy and smelled horrible. From the room I could see that the hot springs were full of plastic bottles, bags, empty cans, old clothing, shoes and much more unidentifiable garbage. Nevertheless, a few brave local people were actually bathing in them.

I was ready to cry and scream at the same time, but as calmly as I could, I said, "No way" and explained how I'd had life threatening intestinal problems due to parasites, and that staying there or getting in that water could be deadly.

I'd seen a lot of poverty and stayed in some very basic places all over the world, but nothing anywhere had been like this. I wanted to try to understand how this happened. I thought it might be the increased use of plastics, especially given the tremendous influx of the Chinese to the area, which happened so rapidly that a basic infrastructure for handling waste had not yet been developed.

We left and drove back to Lhasa. Even the drive was pushing my buttons, with the winding roads at night, the drivers smoking non-stop, then being stopped at police checkpoints every few miles for no reason. The police would say we'd have to be at the next checkpoint at such and such a time, and if you arrived early you'd be ticketed for speeding. So everybody speeded, then stopped on the side of the road to smoke and pee and wait to arrive at the next checkpoint at exactly the right time. It was an interesting idea to try to control speeding, but it obviously didn't work. If there were ways to get around a rule, human beings would find it.

Then it hailed again. And with the lightning and traffic the nightmare seemed to go on and on, testing the minute amount of patience and tolerance I thought I had left. Perhaps I just didn't have any more at all. Perhaps I was done with this sort of rough independent travel. Perhaps it was time for me to just give it all up and go on cruises and organized tours. So be it. And then I sighed, nodded to myself, and with a smile of resignation, knew that that would never happen.

Most people didn't take the route I did. Instead, they went to the Mount Everest base camp, then headed back to Lhasa or went on to Kathmandu. I'd heard the road to Mount Everest was good, but that it took three days from Lhasa and was always jam packed with tourists. I didn't have time to take that route and I usually liked to avoid tourists. Well I sure did avoid them. I thought the off-the-beaten-path route would be okay, since the *Lonely Planet* guidebook said it would be. Unfortunately, a lot of it wasn't that great. What I can say is that, as always, there was a story to tell from the challenges and hardships. I survived. And in retrospect, some of it was quite funny and certainly educational. I met beautiful people who struggled terribly with the oppression and downright abuse by the Chinese government. And ultimately, I could ask myself how dull and dissatisfying would it have been to say that I'd driven in a nice car, on a perfect road, stayed in luxurious clean hotels and took photos of a lovely mountain surrounded by folks in Gore-Tex?

Baja Mexico
2010

There were few experiences in my short life that could rejuvenate my soul like being covered in whale snot. It was like being blessed with nature's holy water. And to think I hadn't known about this special experience, or how close by and easy it was to have it at the gray whale breeding lagoons in Baja California, Mexico. In the U.S. there were laws keeping people at a certain distance from these magical creatures, but in Mexico they found a way to let you pet and snuggle and learn and love these majestic animals without hurting them.

There were three lagoons on the Pacific Ocean side of the Baja peninsula—Guerrero Negro, San Ignacio, and Magdalena. Whales came to breed and give birth in the lagoons every year between December and April. As the gestation period was about twelve months, a female could be pregnant during her migration north, then return to give birth the following year.

There were a few ways to get to the lagoons. Most people rented a car on either the U.S. or the Mexican side of the border near San Diego, California, and then they drove south. Or they flew to Cabo San Lucas on the Baja peninsula, rented a car, and then drove north. Carson and I took the road less traveled. We flew from San José, California, to San Diego, then caught the Flyer bus right outside the airport terminal. The bus dropped us off at the trolley stop on "C" street, where we caught the blue line trolley to San Ysidro, on the U.S. side of the border with Mexico. It was an interesting ride, which gave us an overview of some of San Diego's finest cultural elements, like a mural proclaiming "All American Pride and Glory," which stood right next to a Bail Bonds sign. At the end of the line we just got off and walked across a bridge to Tijuana, Mexico. There were no Mexican or American guards or customs officials. I'd never left the U.S. or entered another country so easily!

After a short block and a half walk, we arrived at the ABC (Autotransportes de Baja California) bus terminal. For about $10, paid in either dollars or in Mexican pesos, the bus would take you to Ensenada. The buses were comfortable, clean, except for the bathroom, and they played dubbed American movies that I really wouldn't have wanted to see in any language. But it was a quick hour-and-a-half trip, and voilà, we were in Ensenada.

There were many hotels, but we chose the Hotel Ritz, which sat on the corner of 4th and Ruiz, an easy walk to the waterfront. Our room cost about $35 and had a lovely balcony overlooking the city. It was a huge balcony really, but the funny thing was that it had no chairs. We wondered if those cost extra. The staff spoke English and were wonderfully helpful. We walked around the harbor, then ate fish tacos at Lupitas right on the waterfront, where we watched the fishermen bring in the day's catch.

We'd come to Ensenada to spend the night in order to catch a small plane down to Guerrero Negro the following day. The small plane company, Aero Servicio Guerrero, only flew on Mondays, Wednesdays and Fridays, and charged about $240 round trip. We took a taxi to the military airport early Friday morning and thoroughly enjoyed our four hour flight delay by watching the daily life at a military transport facility.

While I was still in the U.S. I'd been in phone contact with Aero Servicio Guerrero to arrange our flights, and felt like "family" with the airport managing staff Carmen and Ruben. They were used to dealing only with local people and were wonderfully trusting that we would show up to pay, since they didn't have an international billing system in place. They checked and weighed every passenger's luggage, which seemed like an incredibly large amount to squeeze onto such a small plane. We watched them load not only suitcases but also boxes of medicine and food, and even a satellite dish. There were thirteen passengers, which made my superstitious mind a bit nervous until I realized the pilot would make fourteen people.

The plane landed briefly at Isla Cedros before making its final approach to Guerrero Negro. The entire flight took about an hour and a half and was an adventure in and of itself. The take-offs and landings were exhilarating, as the plane was so small you could really feel it tilt with the pilot's steering or bump with every gust of wind. Not to mention that the runways tended to end at a sharp drop off into the ocean. We were seated right behind the pilot, who, once we were in the air, spent most of his time chatting on his cell phone. As we headed south the mountains were on our left, the wide open Pacific Ocean was on our right, and the scenes below were extraordinary, with the crashing of the waves on the shoreline. As we neared Guerrero Negro we flew over miles of rippled sand dunes on either side of the winding inlet to the Scammons Lagoon. The Mexican name for the lagoon was Ojo de Liebre, Eye of the Jackrabbit.

After landing at the military airport in Guerrero Negro, we easily caught the one and only taxi waiting there, which took us into town. They must have known we were coming because all the other passengers were locals, who wouldn't need a taxi. Most of the passengers had been firemen and were huge, which caused me to again wonder how strict they were with the plane's weight limits.

We'd made reservations with Mallarimo, a Mexican owned facility that had a motel and restaurant and offered whale tours, which was everything we needed all in one place. Guerrero Negro had only one road and no stop lights. There were a few shops, one bank, taco stands, and of course whale tour sales shops, because that was the biggest attraction here. We saw a salt mining company and heard that it supplied at least twenty-five percent of the world's salt. There were beautiful sand dunes and migratory birds. But it was the whales that drew the crowds.

Our motel was lovely, quaint and comfortable. I'd packed summer clothing with bathing suits and sarongs, only to realize that there it was usually cool and windy. So we ended up wearing our jeans and fleece the entire weekend. On Saturday we left early for our pre-booked tour to see the whales. Arturo, our guide, was well versed in history and science and covered it all on the drive to the bay. We boarded our *panga*, a small motor boat, and headed out into the lagoon to find some whales, or to let them find us.

The Mexican government realized long ago that by protecting this lagoon and the whales it could bring in a fair amount of money from the annual visits by tourists. We met people who came every year to engage in this rare experience of touching whales. Almost everyone we met was Mexican, including the tourists, business owners and all their employees. This led me to believe that the local people and not foreign investors were benefitting from the tourism. My hope was that the area could stay small and continue providing personal intimate experiences for the type of tourist who seemed able to appreciate how special this place was.

The boat ride out to the lagoon took about twenty minutes and passed lovely white undulating dunes, tugboats pulling barges piled high with salt, migratory birds and sea lions. The boat drivers were on their radios with the three other tour boats in order to keep them all notified about whale sightings. We saw lots of whale blows and plenty of whales up close, usually mothers with their babies. The whales bred here earlier in the season, so by now, March, most of the males had already headed back to Alaska. We also saw a lot of dolphins. And toward the end of the afternoon we were gifted with seeing a breaching whale. It was right off the bow of our tiny boat and it leaped out of the water thirteen times in a row! It was spectacular. But no whale came close enough to touch. I was of course disappointed about that.

So when we got back to the dock I simply boarded another tour boat and thank goodness I did. We ended up in a rather shallow part of the lagoon. The whales, two mothers with their babies, started to play with us. Evidently they liked the sound of the motor and they wanted to scratch the top of their heads and backs on the bottom of the hull. Amazingly, the mothers encouraged their young to come up close and let us touch them. The mothers seemed to want us to use our hands to scratch the barnacles that were stuck to their heads. For nearly an hour we were surrounded by whales nudging our boat, snorting on us with their blowholes and splashing us with their tail flukes. I was crying and laughing with pure joy.

We spent the next day taking two more tours to see the whales. Both trips were equally gratifying. I came away from this experience even more dedicated to the preservation of this planet's beautiful diverse wildlife. I wished the human species would realize how lucky we were to share this tiny speck of the universe with such gentle amazing creatures. I wished we'd figure out a way to live harmoniously with the rest of nature and speak out against the senseless slaughter and unnecessary captivity of wild animals. I wished we'd control our population and stop the reckless use of our resources. I imagined living on a planet where all I saw were cement parking lots, strip malls, SUVs, trash and smog. And that made me really sad.

Carson and I then headed home on an even smaller plane to Ensenada, then took the bus to Tijuana. There was a huge line waiting to get up to the customs office on the Mexican side, so we hired a van that could get us to the front of the line, then would take us to the airport on the U.S. side. While passing through customs I was amazed that they didn't even question the bags of salt we'd brought back, because to me they'd looked a bit suspicious.

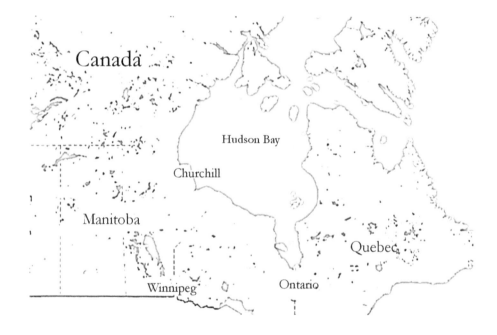

Canada
2010

In August 2010 Carson and I left our home in Santa Cruz, California, for a short trip north to Churchill, Canada. Although it was such a small place, Churchill was teeming with wildlife, and with different ways to see it. Our main objective was to swim with the migrating beluga whales, but we also hoped we could catch sight of a polar bear or two. Our flight stopped in Winnipeg, Manitoba. From there we had the choice of taking a train or flying in a small plane up to the tiny town of Churchill on the shores of Hudson Bay. We chose to fly because it was faster and we only had a week to see everything.

It was possible to find our own hotel and book tours in Churchill once we arrived, but we had limited time, so we had pre-arranged a stay at the Lazy Bear Lodge, which also had a tour office on site. This wonderful homey inn was clean, comfortable, efficient and authentic. The owner had built it in the form of an old log cabin. The few staff were friendly and each performed multiple duties. There were only a few companies in Churchill that organized and operated the sightseeing activities, and Lazy Bear was one of them. We signed up for everything they offered.

We started by taking a bus tour to see the historic sites, including the Polar Bear Jail, where bears were kept if they consistently got too close to town. Churchill had a bear patrol, which drove around shooting off noise makers to scare the polar bears away. Because of the roaming bears, it was recommended that visitors not walk alone or after dark. There were many signs posted along the coast of the bay warning people not to venture too far, since a polar bear was hard to spot amid the white rocks and it might find you before you saw it.

Hudson Bay was huge. We joined a tour that would boat up the coast to look for bears. We all had to dress in bright red bulky water survival suits in case we fell overboard or the boat sank. We did see a bear in the distance standing on its hind legs, as if posing for us. But it was the boat ride itself and the sheer immensity of this bay that were so impressive. And having to pee in a bucket on the boat, behind a tarp being held up by the captain, with the other passengers just on the other side of it, was a funny experience for someone like me obsessed with this necessary human function.

We went to Churchill first and foremost to see the beluga whales and we did, in every manner possible. First, via boat, we were surrounded by the snow white mothers and their gray babies. Our guide put a microphone in the water so we could hear why they were called the canaries of the sea. Next we kayaked alongside the whales, which would come right up to the boat out of curiosity. Finally we donned dry suits, which meant that, unlike wetsuits, no water could get in, and we jumped in the water with them. There'd been a big storm a few days before we arrived in Churchill, so the water had been stirred up and was cloudy. We could only see blurry white shapes darting by, but still, it was incredible being in the water with them at eye level and hearing them sing with our own ears.

Although we'd seen a few bears along the shores during boat trips to see the whales, we opted to take a tundra buggy to try to see more of them. The buggy was a vehicle shaped like a bus, but with big tall wheels, so it could not only travel through the snow, but more importantly, the polar bears couldn't reach the windows and nab us tasty tourists. We were told that only pregnant females would create dens. The other polar bears entered a physiological state called walking hibernation, where they remained awake and active. We were incredibly lucky to see a mother with her two cubs. We also saw two adult males eating what appeared to be a beluga whale carcass. It might have been remnants left by the Inuit, the natives in this area, who were still allowed to hunt the whales. Scattered around Churchill you could still see stone structures called *inukchuks*, which were large thirty foot tall sculptures made from flat stone slabs and piled up in the shape of a person. They were used as directional landmarks by the native people, but we never saw or met any native Inuits.

Although the Inuits were allowed to hunt the whales I loved so much, it didn't bother me as much as what was really affecting the whale population, and for that matter the polar bear population too—the effects of global warming. I get weary from repeating myself about the need for the human species to pay attention to what we're doing to the planet, and to make the necessary changes now.

In the evenings we'd dine at different local restaurants, our favorite being the Tundra Inn's Pub Grub Lounge. There we got to meet locals, who, although they weren't Inuit, had spent years in the area and had great stories to share. Everyone was so friendly, and the man who owned the one and only grocery store in town even gave us some free dried arctic char to eat, which is a fish in the same family as salmon. At our lodge we were told that because a solar flare had occurred, we should be able to see the northern lights, even though it wasn't the season for them. I'd set our alarm clock for 2 a.m., get up and look out our window to the north, searching for the lights. It wasn't until the last evening that we realized the lights were behind the lodge to the south, and because we were already IN the north, we didn't need to look that way. It was a spectacular show of green lights, which we learned was the most common color. They'd start in one part of the sky, then ripple, grow, and spread to take over the entire night sky, with the lights quivering like a surreal backdrop to an alien invasion.

On our last day we decided to take a helicopter ride so we could get an overview of all we'd seen and experienced. We could see the three street town of Churchill, nestled between Goose Creek and the expansive Hudson Bay. In the creek were thousands of white and gray specks of beluga whales, and over the land we then discovered where large numbers of polar bears had been hiding. There were at least forty in one area, all sunning themselves with their legs spread out behind them like old dogs. We also flew over a herd of caribou and the huge Fort Prince of Wales. The fort was built in the seventeen hundreds and was used to protect the comings and goings of fur traders. I was happy that those days had passed, and that now these animals were protected—at least the polar bears were. The other animals such as beaver, fox, and caribou could still be hunted at certain times of the year.

We hadn't come to Churchill so much for the history, although there was plenty of it. We'd come to see the whales and bears. My hope is that these magnificent animals will still be around in plentiful numbers and in their natural settings so they will inspire awe in future generations.

Papua New Guinea

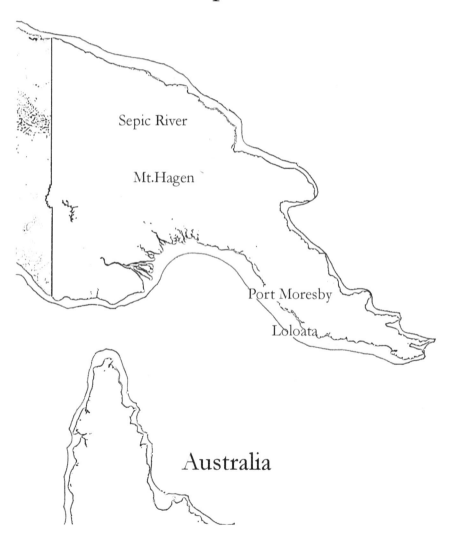

Sepic River

Mt.Hagen

Port Moresby

Loloata

Australia

Papua New Guinea
2011

When I was twenty-seven and traveling in Australia I'd met a couple of young men who'd offered to let me sail with them to Papua New Guinea, with the warning that there might be pirates along the way who would kidnap me in order to sell me as some sort of mistress on the black market. That was, of course, if we weren't all just robbed and killed. I decided not to join them. And then the years passed and many other travel adventures were undertaken and I didn't think much more about Papua New Guinea. That was until I saw a small advertisement in a travel magazine called *International Travel News* that intrigued me.

I began researching travel to Papua New Guinea and discovered that it was a very expensive destination and that it was best to join an established company since getting around could be difficult and dangerous. There were few roads and no mass transit, so the only way to get around the country was by small planes. There were also few lodging choices, and the ones that did exist were quite fancy because they catered to businessmen and well-off tourists. One of the companies I researched was French, and they said they took tourists hiking and camping in the forests in search of having a first encounter with tribes who may never have seen a white face before. I forwarded this website to Carson as a joke, inviting him to join me. It was a joke because I knew I couldn't travel rough like that anymore, given my age and history of intestinal issues. I also didn't believe in that sort of travel because I wanted to minimize the negative effects tourism could have on indigenous people. Carson didn't take it as a joke though and made it perfectly clear that he would never travel to Papua New Guinea.

After extensive research I decided to go and ended up signing on with the company New Guinea Travel, whose ad I had first seen in the *International Travel News* magazine. It was run by a wonderful man named Greg, who had been leading tours to Papua New Guinea, and nowhere else, for thirty years. He was passionate about that country and sent me every book, article and DVD he had about the place. Carson's curiosity was piqued, and eventually I was able to convince him that our tour, arranged by Greg, would provide clean safe hotels, and that we probably wouldn't be stumbling upon any active head hunters or cannibals. So he finally decided to join me.

To get to Papua New Guinea you have to stop in Sydney, Australia, and, as always, I had complaints about air travel. This time Carson and I had paid $300 extra for Economy Plus seating on United Airlines. Well, don't bother. We literally got a mere two inches more space, and as much as I liked the bulkhead, the first row of seats in each section, the downside was that the seat dividers didn't lift. I tried sitting in every possible position, but I couldn't get comfortable. The flight attendant felt sorry for us however, and plied us with mimosas and fluffy blankets to try to make up for it. Fourteen hours did fly by (pun intended), with the meals, movies, TV, books, magazines, and the usual indecipherable announcements.

We had planned our flights so that we could spend two days in Sydney before heading on to Papua New Guinea. Sydney was a beautiful clean city with so much to do. Our hotel, the Hyde Park Inn, was really nice and had a balcony that overlooked Hyde Park, where we could see some cathedrals and the ocean in the distance. Our room even had a kitchen. I was starting to feel spoiled traveling with Carson, since he liked, and could afford, to stay in better places than I was used to. To minimize jet lag we tried to stay awake during the day in order to switch over to the local time. So, since we'd arrived at 6 a.m. we had the whole day to walk around and sightsee.

Everything we were interested in seeing was within walking distance. First we went to the top of the Sydney Sky Tower to get an overview of the place. There we started a conversation with another couple, Leo and Huia Koziol, who turned out to be the founders of the New Zealand

Maori Film Festival. They'd actually lived in Santa Cruz, California, where we were from. What a small world it was after all! They were in Sydney to see the Australian Aboriginal Film Festival, being held at the Sydney Opera House. We decided to go to the festival not only as a way to see the Opera House, but also because we were so involved with the Santa Cruz Film Festival back home.

We took a short walk down to Darling Harbor to see Wildlife World and the Aquarium. Since we wouldn't have time to explore Australia's Outback we decided that, although we didn't like zoos or seeing caged animals, we should go to these places in order to see the typical Australian animals—kangaroos, koalas, cassowaries, the duck-billed platypus, dugongs, sharks, poisonous spiders and snakes, and Rex, an enormous crocodile. This country had such cute little furry creatures, but they also had some of the most venomous icky buggers in the world.

The next day we went to the film festival at the Opera House called The Message Sticks Indigenous Film Festival. They screened films about indigenous people from around the world. We saw Shifting Shelter 4, an anthropological study of four Aboriginals over the course of twenty years. The four were revisited every five years, beginning in their teens. The director explored their life plans, beginning in their youth, to see what obstacles they faced in realizing their dreams. The most common obstacle seemed to have been pregnancy and relationship issues, compounded by drug and alcohol abuse. One of the subjects, Ben, was there after the film to answer questions and play songs on his guitar with audience participation. The audience asked him many questions and one was whether the school system encouraged kids to reconnect with their heritage or taught family planning. He was none too keen to talk about family planning, and his answer about heritage was, "I'm around bush tucker all the time!" Bush tucker was food from the wild.

After the festival we took a ferry from the Opera House to Darling Harbor, where we got amazing views of the city and the Harbor Bridge all lit up. There were also fireworks, which I loved. I enjoyed seeing things up in the sky that weren't usually there, like fireworks, hot air balloons, and once, what I'm pretty sure was a flying saucer.

After a quick two days in Sydney we headed to the airport to catch our flight to Papua New Guinea. We'd arranged to arrive a couple of days before the tour started so we could go scuba diving on our own before meeting our group. It was a short flight to Port Moresby, Papua New Guinea's capital. Our prearranged ride wasn't there to meet us at the airport, so we waited outside. It was entertaining to watch the families who came to meet the young adults who'd been competing in various sports in Australia, and had returned home on the same flight as ours.

Our van finally showed up and the hour-long trip from the airport to the island of Loloata was intriguing. We passed men in local dress of leaved skirts and body paint, preparing for some special event. Then we caught a boat to the island. The weather was a bit windy and the seas were rough, but it didn't detract from the island's beauty. The staff at the island's scuba diving resort were welcoming and friendly, especially Rebecca, a young native woman who told us all about her difficult childhood and a lot about the culture of this unique country.

Our rooms were simple but clean and air-conditioned, and the food was delicious. Even with the rough water, we tried to scuba dive the next day. We managed one dive, but the visibility was poor and Carson got stung by jellyfish larvae, so we gave up. Our dive master was a local who'd grown his hair into dreadlocks and taken on a Rastafarian character. He and the boat ride turned out to be much more interesting than the dive itself. As was so often the case, the intended goal wasn't always the best part of an adventure.

On the paths to and from our room we'd see many wallabies grazing and groups of huge blue crested "pigeons" that looked more like peacocks.

And twice we nearly stepped on some highly venomous striped sea krait snakes!

We went on a wonderfully unusual "city tour" of Port Moresby with a couple we met at the hotel who were from Colorado and were in search of a soccer jersey for their grandson. They and our driver were willing to take a detour in order to go visit the local mental hospital. Because of my profession as a psychiatric nurse, the administrator gave me a tour of the grounds. The patients were allowed to do the gardening and the grounds were clean and well-manicured, with plenty of trees and flowers. I was allowed to film and interview the staff and meet the patients, but not film them. The patients' common room was a large empty round cement structure with bars that the patients stood behind and stared out at a TV hung on the wall. We could only smile and stare at each other, since I couldn't understand their language. There were over eight hundred different tribes and languages on this mere half of an island. In addition to their own tribal languages, most also spoke Pidgin English that was so distorted I couldn't make out the words.

The other half of the island belonged to Indonesia and was referred to as West Papua. We were told that the Indonesian government mistreated the tribal people there. I felt it was sad and unfortunate that governments thought they could arbitrarily draw a national boundary line on this island, and countless other places on the planet, and separate the original inhabitants who'd been living there for millennia.

The hospital only housed male patients and many had committed serious crimes. They'd come from far and wide, since this was one of the few facilities available in the entire country. The staff reported that increased marijuana use had become a contributing factor to an increase in psychotic breaks leading to hospitalization. The staff also explained that the locals made their own alcohol called Jungle Juice. It was so strong that it could lead to behavioral changes and violence. The hospital treated schizophrenia and bipolar disorder, but more commonly the staff saw depression, usually caused by relationship issues. I was told about suicides, where people overdosed or set themselves on fire. The people in Papua New Guinea were torn between the foreign Western religious influences of Catholics, Lutherans, and Seventh Day Adventists, and their own traditional beliefs of a powerful spiritual world in which sorcery was the cause of death or illness. Both the medical and mental hospitals struggled with insufficient funding and were understaffed. I thought it odd that we faced the same issues back home in one of the wealthiest countries in the world.

During the tour of Port Moresby we were told about the bad reputation it had for the *raskols*, who'd rob you at knife or gunpoint. This was why tourists tended to have guides and drivers with them everywhere they went. We never saw any violence though and felt reasonably safe. We were told that most of the crime in Port Moresby happened on Friday nights, after workers had been paid and had money to spend on drugs and alcohol.

We left Loloata island and joined our tour group at the fanciest place in Port Moresby, the Airways Hotel, which was near the airport and was over-the-top luxurious. I was deeply disturbed by the contrast between the extreme poverty and so much seemingly unnecessary opulence. The hotel had a happy hour with free martinis and a pool on the roof overlooking the mountain range. I realized these businesses provided jobs for local people, but I could only hope that some of the money we spent actually ended up back in the local economy in order to improve the standard of living for the people who lived there.

Our tour group consisted of three Australian couples, one couple from San Diego, Carson and me, and our guide, Mary Jane. She was a Canadian currently living in Reno, Nevada, and she occasionally helped Greg with his company's tours. She'd lived and worked in Papua New Guinea, so she really knew the intricacies of getting around this complicated country. She would be our tour leader for the entire trip, but we'd also be joined by local guides at each stop. Not only did Mary Jane know this country intimately, but she was also an experienced guide down to the smallest detail. She'd constantly amaze us by pulling out hand sanitizer wipes, drops of deodorizer for the trench toilets, granola bars from Trader Joe's, bubble wrap to pack souvenirs in, and even breath mints, joking that those would have to suffice as our in-flight beverage service on the small planes we took.

The following day we flew from Port Moresby to Mount Hagen and toured around a bit in our van, with our own driver and a local guide. We went shopping at "Best Buy," a store totally unrelated to the electronics chain stores in the U.S. Thankfully we'd seen no chain stores whatsoever. We also went to an outdoor market, which had beautiful fruits, vegetables, handcrafts and tables full of live chickens. We were told the produce was all organic. The people were amazing gardeners and had been for hundreds of years. I hoped that the Monsanto corporation, a seed and pesticide giant, wouldn't get a foothold there and cause the country's farmers to lose the right to use their own seeds and methods of farming. I'd heard that Monsanto had a nasty habit of pressuring farmers around the world to stop using the seeds they had been saving and using for generations, and instead use Monsanto's seeds that were developed to be used with the company's pesticides, such as Round Up.

The locals all wanted their pictures taken, and with the colors of the market, and peoples' sincere curiosity and smiles, everywhere you turned was a photographer's dream. People would come up to shake our hands, and with a big grin say, "Appy noon" ("good afternoon" in Pidgin). We ended the day by checking in at Magic Mountain, a rustic lodge built by our local guide and his family. It had just opened so few tourists were staying there. There were large black tanks filled with water that was heated by the sun, so we could have hot showers in the evening. Unfortunately Carson and I didn't figure out the hot and cold taps had been reversed until the last day.

Our separate cottage was surrounded by a noisy jungle with near deafening sounds of bugs and bird calls. A mystical fog blanketed the valley below, with mountain peaks jutting out, looking like surreal floating islands. The family running Magic Mountain treated us to a small show called "Turnim Head," a courting dance for the men and women, where they bump and roll their foreheads together like certain birds of paradise do. Pim, the lodge owner, also organized the Tumbuna sing-sing, the highlight of any trip to Papua New Guinea.

This event took place on a clearing at the top of a nearby mountain. Clans, or tribes, from the surrounding areas competed here annually and were judged on who had the best costumes, body paint and dance style. Sing-sings had always taken place as a way for a tribe to celebrate any number of events such as weddings or the birth of a child. But things changed when Christian missionaries began arriving in Papua New Guinea in the early nineteen hundreds. In order to decrease the warfare the various tribes engaged in, which started with disputes over land, women or pigs, the Christians began to organize these competitive but peaceful gatherings. Every year three sing-sings were held which tourists could attend. The Tumbuna was the smallest, with perhaps a hundred tourists total, and was reportedly the most intimate of the three.

We got to wander around the grounds and view the sing-sing preparations, including face painting and applying leaves and head gear. Most of the headdresses were made from a variety of bird of paradise feathers, were highly valued, and had been passed down for generations.

The dancers decorated themselves with mud, paint, feathers, beads or shells, and the designs varied depending on the tribe and their particular customs. As they passed by the spectators, the dancers stomped their feet, jumped up and down, or made menacing gestures with their spears. The Mud Men tribe wore large gray clay masks with grotesque expressions and attached long sharp bamboo fingernails to their hands. The Huli Wig Men donned colorful tall headdresses made out of their own hair. One group was painted like skeletons, and the women's group was, well, let's just say they were very bouncy.

In the middle of the show it rained! We were told that it hadn't rained there for the sing-sing ever. They also said they'd been noticing changes in the climate and weather patterns, but I wondered if most people there were even aware of the concept of global warming. The rain didn't dampen the spirits though, of the tourists or the Papuans, who gathered in a circle and jumped and sang and laughed while we cheered them on, waiting for the rain to stop, which it did. The Papuans also performed mock warfare and mock wedding ceremonies. The weddings involved the groom's family giving pigs and kina (seashell) necklaces to the parents of the bride. This culture had a quite complicated bartering and compensation system in place, and the people had become relatively advanced in their math and oratory skills. The sing-sing ended with a pig and yam roast, and it appeared that everyone won the competition.

One of the trip highlights was a surprise event scheduled to honor the opening of the Mount Hagen Tourism Bureau, and our small group of ten were evidently the honorary tourists. We were lead through a gauntlet of dancers, drummers and hundreds of locals waving and smiling at us as if we were royalty, even though we were dressed in our jungle pants, boots and floppy hats.

Every day we were taken to local villages to be shown how the villagers lived, and were given a glimpse into their world. Because the people who inhabited this half of the island spoke over eight hundred different languages and had so many different cultures, there was just too much to learn, understand, experience and absorb in the short amount of time we had.

While visiting the different tribes we witnessed *mokas* (complex loan systems), spirit dances that prepared villages for war, and various rituals that crossed the young over to adulthood. One afternoon we had lunch in an orchid garden, where there were over thirty-thousand varieties, and we were always searching for birds of paradise. Around every corner was a surprise!

Along the roadside there were mounds of produce for sale, like betel nuts, which people chewed with lime and pepper. This mild stimulant turned the chewers' mouths red and could cause them to lose their teeth. We'd also see people gathering to gamble with card games or with games of darts. There were some paved roads, but mostly they were just bumpy dirt. Carson was smart to have brought army jungle boots, and the rest of us envied him while we ineptly negotiated muddy trails and slippery bamboo bridges in ridiculously inappropriate tennis shoes. The Papuans, of course, went everywhere barefooted.

Because there were so few roads we had to fly in small six-seater planes. This meant that everywhere we went the pilot would have to make two trips to get all ten of us to our destination. Trans Niugini Tours was the main travel company in Papua New Guinea. It owned the few lodges available as well as most of the vans, drivers, guides, and even the planes and runways. So any travel agent arranging either private or group tours, including ours, would have to go through them. Still, there were very few tourists and the ten of us were often the only foreigners at any given place. We were a novelty to the local people and were regularly waved to, especially by kids who wanted to "high five" us as we drove by.

When meeting tribes, there was a standard ritual Mary Jane, our tour guide, had taught us to do each and every time. First we'd have to shake everyone's hand. Then one of our group would say a formal, "Thank you" for having us. At the end of the visit we'd again shake everyone's hand and thank them for a wonderful time. They'd then thank us and request that we please send our friends and family to their village.

One of our hotels in the highlands was called Rondon Ridge, and our local guide there was named Raymond. The locals had their tribal names given at birth, but were then given Christian names when they were baptized. Over ninety-six percent of Papuans describe themselves as Christian. Raymond didn't want to tell us his tribal name, saying it was sacred. I didn't know if this meant only he could know his tribal name, or if only the people from his tribe could know it, or if he were just making it all up. Raymond was wonderfully amenable otherwise and answered nearly all our questions. He did shy away from the topic of homosexuality however, saying that subject was taboo.

The position of women in society was way down the totem pole in Papua New Guinea. In fact boys were separated from their mothers at a young age and raised by the men. At the mental hospital I visited I was told stories about women who would drown themselves with their male child to avoid giving him up. The men and women slept separately, the men in their own huts, and the women in huts with the pigs.

All tenets of Christianity hadn't been absorbed by everyone, so polygamy was still widely practiced, and even a self-proclaimed Christian man could have as many wives as he could afford. A bride price was paid to the bride's family and could be somewhere around thirty pigs and ten thousand kina (about $5,000). If a woman later wanted a divorce she had to pay the bride price back. We met a woman who did this, and it was no easy task. Physical abuse was common. There was great respect for ancestors though, and after someone died, their bones were well treated and placed in miniature decorated mausoleums. They were also spoken of with reverence and even exaggeration. Raymond, for example, described his ancestors as being nine feet tall.

Boys all went through some sort of initiation before they were considered to be men. What this entailed varied, depending on the tribe. For example, the Huli Wig Men grew the hair on their heads without a haircut for eighteen months so they could then shave it off and create a wig, which they then decorated with pig fat, clay, flowers and feathers. They even incorporated Western items like buttons or logos they'd cut out of a piece of cardboard or metal.

Girls were considered to be women when they started menstruating. They would then stay in a separate area of the tribal compound for up to six months, and would be taught by the older women what would be expected of them. A woman's menstrual blood was believed to weaken the men if they came into contact with it. Men would defecate in secret places because they believed women might gather the feces and use them to create spells against them. Because brides could come from different tribes than those of their husbands, the men were concerned that the wives might turn against them. In the past, during some of the wars between tribes, women and children would be taken captive and the men would be eaten by the winning tribe. With the spread of Christianity, this practice was mostly eliminated.

In the villages there was no electricity, no hot water, and only rain water for drinking. The toilets, which were perhaps constructed just for us, consisted of a hole dug in the ground which was surrounded by a wooden platform for your feet while you squatted. Usually there was a thatched fence around it for a little privacy. In the tourist lodges, on the other hand, the toilets were Western style and functioned well. We also had electricity and usually hot water. The water was channeled through UV filters and then boiled for drinking.

From Mount Hagen we took a small eight-seater plane to another area in the highlands to stay at the Ambua Lodge. Ambua was a Huli word meaning yellow, a popular color for them. Planes were the main form of transport in Papua New Guinea, and landing on the tiny dirt or grass airstrips was always exhilarating. Ambua Lodge was perched on a hillside, and each of its rooms was an individual thatched hut overlooking the Tari valley below. Sounds of raging waterfalls, cicadas, frogs, birds and the occasional human calling out emanated from the thick forest behind the lodge. Due to the advent of cell phones, we were told that communicating with a loud whooping call had become less and less frequent. In the jungle behind the lodge we crossed swaying bamboo bridges spanning rough and tumbling rivers, in search of wildlife. There were never many mammals on this half of the island, and those that had been here had mostly been eaten. Throughout the trip the animals we saw were primarily in captivity—the famous tree kangaroo in a cage, a pet cuscus possum, and baby crocodiles being raised for their meat and valuable skin. In the wild we did see enormous fruit bats, and, amazingly, a Ribbon Tail bird of paradise.

The local people were beginning to realize that they must save the birds, at least for the tourists to see live and not just for their feathers in the headdresses. Ironically tourism could be what might end up saving this island's connection to its culture as it is catapulted into the modern world. We witnessed bizarre juxtapositions of barefoot grass-clad tribal men with cell phones handing out business cards. These tribespeople respected the environment and their traditions, especially when they could make a living sharing them with the outside world. Even so, there was a problem with modern trash. Traditionally everything they made or used was biodegradable, but now we saw plastic trash in most places as a result of Western influences.

Around Ambua we visited a local school, where we saw students ranging in age from twelve to twenty-five, and being taught together in one class. This was because keeping teachers in these remote areas was difficult. As a result students went to school when they could and started up where they'd left off. The students expressed an interest in being nurses, teachers, engineers, and, of course, pilots. When we arrived we sang their national anthem with them, resulting in a lot of stares and giggles. The anthem went:

> O arise all you sons of this land
> Let us sing of our joy to be free
> Praising God and rejoicing to be
> Papua New Guinea!
> Shout our name from the mountains to seas
> Papua New Guinea!
> Let us raise our voices and proclaim
> Papua New Guinea!
> Now give thanks to the good Lord above
> for His kindness, His wisdom and love
> For this land of our fathers so free
> Papua New Guinea!
> Shout again for the whole world to hear
> Papua New Guinea!
> We are independent and we are free
> Papua New Guinea!

Papua New Guinea gained its independence from Australia without a fight in 1975. We heard repeatedly from Papuans that they were not ready for it, and that they struggled to maintain a decaying infrastructure. They continued to strive for the development of a functional government that could pull together the disparate tribes while honoring their cultures and protecting the environment they so directly depended upon. They hoped to achieve this without greed or corruption on the part of the officials.

And that was a tall order.

We also visited a shaman who used bones and stones to do his magic. The stones were five to eight inches around, were smooth and black, and appeared to be old cannon balls left from foreign wars fought there long ago. We heard stories about the Papuans being used by both Allied and Japanese forces during World War II, and saw remnants of the destruction from a war these people could not have fully understood and were powerless to avoid. While here the shaman created what I would come to think of as a Harry Potter style horcrux, where he did a ritual to put a part of my soul into a small round stone sequestered in a gourd as a sort of protective talisman. All for a very reasonable fee.

The Highlands remained comfortably cool, with a predictable afternoon rain, but we were ready to set off on a Sepik River boat trip. There we came to know true heat, humidity, and *nat-nats*. Nat-nat was the Pidgin word for mosquito. With the humidity came swarms of nat-nats and grasshoppers, like a biblical plague. We flew on a small plane from Ambua to Timbunke (easily confused with Timbuktu, but only similar in that both were in the middle of nowhere), and landed this time on an even shorter grass runway.

We were met with cheers and handshakes by all the students at the local school. This was where we began our voyage on the MV Sepik Spirit, a boat that looked somewhat like an old Mississippi River paddleboat, but without the paddle. Not only was this form of travel unique, but it was luxurious. Inside the boat were many examples of the wood carvings the Sepik area was famous for, but best of all, our rooms were air-conditioned. Trans Niugini Tours organized the groups so that each had the boat to themselves. There were only the ten of us, our guide Mary Jane, and a handful of crew. The boat had three decks. The common area, kitchen and dining room were on the first floor, the state rooms, all with a view, were on the second, and the staff and captain's quarters were on the top deck.

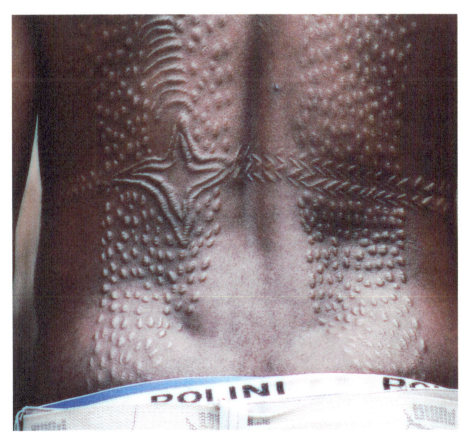

We left our floating hotel every day and boarded a smaller jet boat to visit villages along the way. The river changed levels frequently because of the changes in weather, and at times, if their stilt houses flooded, the people had to actually live on their dugout canoes. The women fished from tiny unstable boats made from hollowed out trees and they caught mostly catfish. These tribes would also garden when possible. Mostly they lived off fish and sago palm, whose insides were made into a starchy mush, then baked into a flat bread. And that biblical plague of grasshoppers? The staff collected them from all the decks, and even gathered some from inside our rooms. The bugs were then salted and baked into a nice crunchy snack that Carson was brave enough to try. "Tastes kind of like shrimp," he said.

The tribes in this area prided themselves on having been head hunters and not cannibals. They felt that eating a person was far worse than just killing him and shrinking his head. They also venerated the crocodile, so much so that a boy's initiation into manhood involved a month long scarification process that left the skin on his back and chest looking like crocodile hide. The Sepik Spirit's manager, a white Canadian named John, had been living in this area for many years and was invited by a local tribe to actually have this painful initiation process done to him. He explained how they cut the skin with sharp bamboo knives, which they believed released what they considered to be the tainted birth blood of the mother. The wounds were then filled with mud, ash and oil so that they'd welt up and thicken. The patterns created were truly beautiful.

We then visited one of the largest spirit houses in the area in the village of Palembie. The house's thatched roof was curved, and on the front was a sculpted form of a woman with her legs spread apart as if giving birth. The tribal belief was that a woman could give birth to a baby, but it was the men of the village who turned the boy into a man. And that was what happened in these spirit houses.

Women were not normally allowed to enter, but we were told that foreign women could, because the spirits couldn't see us. The structure was an eerie place, with many carved masks, flutes and the huge *garamut* drum. The drum was made from a carved out tree trunk, sat on the ground, was about eight feet long and stood waist high. Two men would pound it with clubs, in quick alternating strokes. The sound was used to communicate with the spirits and all the villagers. There was also an orator's podium, which resembled an intricately carved stool, and we weren't supposed to touch it. In these spirit houses the men, one by one, would slap a handful of leaves on the podium while making their opinions known in what was a sort of democratic senate.

The people of the next village, Yentchen, performed a crocodile sing-sing for us that included all the children. Some of the little boys wore tiny penis gourds. Penis gourds were sometimes the only thing a male had on. Not only could they serve as protection, but they were also considered a decorative enhancement. Kanganaman village was especially friendly, with the kids laughing and all of us chasing each other. The dancers wore masks made from reeds that covered their entire bodies. One of the tribal women ran around laughing and teasing the dancers, so we joined in by forming a conga line, which brought roars of laughter from the villagers. In Kaminimbit we witnessed the ethereal flute dance done only by men pacing and swaying gently in a circle. At Mindimbit we watched men in the process of carving the masks and sculptures we'd been seeing, and we were astonished to see what could emerge from a rough tree trunk hewn with stone age tools. The women were busy cooking sago over open fires, drying fish, and weaving twine for the edges of the penis gourds, that, as the country progressed, would one day only be sold as souvenirs.

To get to these villages we boated down narrow estuaries and swatted at hundreds of nasty malaria ridden blood sucking mosquitos. The Australians in our group, being used to particularly intrusive flies, were smart enough to wear hats with nets that covered their faces. At one village we pulled up to a man who actually swam out to greet us, and all I could think of was what could be in that water!

After each full magical day we re-boarded the Sepik Spirit and were grateful for its cold air, hot showers and delicious buffet meals. All in all we traveled over a hundred miles of rivers, from the Sepik to the Crossmeri (meaning angry woman), and up the Karawari, ending at the Karawari Lodge, another of the beautiful Trans Niugini Tour accommodations. The Lodge was built many years ago, just after World War II, and it was filled with huge, intricate carvings including the Kamanggabe, or spirit sticks, that were used by Papuans to detect where to find the enemy in times of war.

The evening's entertainment was a surprise performance by The Karawari Bamboo Band. There were at least ten performers, all dressed in *bilas* (traditional finery) and playing guitars, including an electric one, a keyboard, and, in the center of it all, what looked like a bamboo pipe organ. The pipe organ had three tiers of huge bamboo pipes roped together, like a marimba on its side. A very athletic man leapt about, slapping the ends with flip flop sandals, which made a wonderful percussive sound. Many of the locals had shown up and we all shared the universal language of dance. What a perfect ending to our tour of contrasts.

There was no air conditioning at this lodge and the electricity stopped at 11 p.m., which meant that there was no working fan at night to move the hot muggy air around. The mosquito nets over the beds seemed a bit holy, and not in the spiritual sense. It was a rough night.

The morning brought a beautiful view of the surrounding lush green valley, the river passing by and the myriad butterflies in all shapes and colors. We boated to the shortest grassy airport runway yet, with a thatched roof "terminal" shack and naked children serving as "ground crew." We watched a dilapidated old tractor help unload a large freezer that looked like it should never have been able to fit onto our tiny plane. But of course it did, in this special place, where the unbelievable happened every moment of every day. Where else could you have just left your beautiful hotel, be in the only car on the road, and see a group of men with machetes carrying a pig hanging from sticks on their shoulders, its gut cut open, its entrails dangling, but still breathing. And all the men smiling and laughing, wanting their pictures taken and inviting you to come to the "Mumu" where they roast the pig underground with hot rocks and Taro root. Where else but in Papua New Guinea?

We flew breathlessly close to the mountains and clouds and watched the patchwork of gardens below grow smaller and smaller. All too quickly we changed planes in Mount Hagen, then arrived in Port Moresby, where we were again stunned by the opulence of the Airways Hotel. This reputedly "nicest" hotel was our least favorite. It just didn't seem to belong there. There were armed guards at the gates, and that didn't make us feel welcome like we had felt everywhere else we'd been throughout the country. Some dignitaries or business tycoons might come to Papua New Guinea and only see this hotel. I hoped not, for the beautiful and timeless soul of the country lay just outside those fancy gates.

Bhutan
2011

My friend Claudia, who I'd met in Mongolia and traveled with to Morocco and Yemen, was going to meet me in Paro, Bhutan. She was flying from Germany, where she lived and worked as a surgeon. I was flying from the U.S. There was only one airline that flew to Bhutan, Druk Air, and it could only be accessed from Bangkok or Kathmandu. I had to stay overnight in Bangkok before catching my flight to Paro. My hotel in Bangkok, The Great Residence, was wonderful, and a bargain at $33 a night. It was close to the airport, had a swimming pool, outdoor dining by a canal, and best of all, Thai massage.

Traveling in Bhutan was a little more complicated than traveling in many other places. All travel arrangements in Bhutan had to go through a Bhutanese agent. There was a minimum spending requirement of $250 per person per day. All tourists had to use local guides, because no independent travel was allowed. The king, who'd abdicated, but then was democratically elected president, wanted to protect his country, his people, and his culture. He didn't want an uncontrolled influx of tourists and certainly didn't want his country to be overrun by foreign investors and businesses. I admired him. He coined the phrase "Gross National Happiness" as a response to the rest of the world always focusing on Gross National Product. He knew that the welfare of a country's people and environment had to be calculated as part of the economic equation.

There were no problems with the flight to Paro, in western Bhutan, which had the only airport in the country. Paro was nestled in a lovely valley, with a crystal clear river running through it. Our hotel was located on a mountainside, had an amazing view, and was clean, luxurious and brand spanking new.

I hadn't expected quite so much modernization would be going on. Everywhere you looked something was being built. And everyone had a cell phone. Our guide, a woman named Tshering, and our driver, a man named Sonom, picked us up at the airport in a large shiny new SUV. The four of us were going to be together for a ten day tour.

Both Tshering and Sonom were knowledgeable, fun and relaxed. Bhutanese were asked by their government to wear their traditional clothing when out in public or in any official government building. The women wore a long woven piece of material worn like a sarong with a matching long-sleeved jacket-style top. The men wore a woven cloak that hung to their knees, with a belt, knee-high socks and dress shoes. As geeky as it sounds, it was actually quite sexy. Unfortunately, it seemed that tourists were expected to stay with their guides and not wander out on their own or mingle with the locals. Claudia and I did our best to break that rule.

On our first day we drove northwest from Paro to see the iconic Tiger's Nest Buddhist monastery, built in 1692, which was precariously perched on a cliff high up on a mountainside. We hiked for six hours up steep trails, with dizzying views of the valley below covered in colorful prayer flags floating in the breeze. There were trail horses available to rent, but we declined the offers. There were many tourists on the trail with their guides, and about halfway up there was a rest stop that had drinks, snacks and a toilet. We arrived at the monastery just in time to join in the "puja," a prayer ritual with chanting, horns, drums and small finger cymbals being played by the monks.

Paro looked like a Swiss mountain village, replete with carved wooden buildings and ornately painted homes surrounded by fields being worked by the families who owned them. The food was hit or miss. The main dish was hot peppers (and I mean HOT) with a cheese sauce—just the sort of thing my fragile intestines had trouble with. We managed to find a hidden pizza shop which actually delivered pizzas, but to where, I couldn't imagine. The owners, a young couple, had learned to make pizza and espresso coffee in Nepal of all places. As much as Bhutan's president was trying to ease this country into the twenty-first century, it really looked like they were blasting into it. I even heard Bhutanese rap songs.

The Buddhist tradition in Bhutan was easy to see, with monks wandering the streets in saffron robes. We learned that the monks, and the whole population for that matter, ate meat, but wouldn't kill the animals. The killing was done in India, which was just south of Bhutan. Smoking was illegal, but we frequently saw people partaking anyway and many chewed betel nut. There were two local beers, my favorite being Druk 11,000, which was 8% alcohol and quite tasty.

There was evidence of emerging modern technology juxtaposed with ancient customs. For example, the main sport was archery, and we witnessed a competition where the bows and arrows were made from high-tech shiny metal, not the old wooden ones we'd expected. There was no bank ATM system, so we had to bring enough cash into the country to last the two weeks we were there. But there was Wi-Fi in the lobby of the brand new hotel where we stayed in Paro. Even with all the new buildings being constructed, the roads were tortuous and pretty torn up. The only mass transit was the occasional local bus. It seemed most people had a new car and some sort of employment, even if that was working on the farms. In addition, most classes in their schools were taught in English, even though the native language was Dzong-kha.

After the Tiger's Nest we drove on paved roads to the capital Thimphu, a city of about 100,000 people, about an hour east of Paro. We were told there were only 700,000 people in the whole country. At first we didn't like it in Thimphu because it was so crowded and there was building going on everywhere. I had a bit of a tantrum when we were forced to eat with other tourists in a prearranged restaurant. When I asked why, I was told that other restaurants might not be clean enough for us. I didn't like being forced to be around other tourists or being told where I had to eat.

Then, when our guide left us to make a quick visit with her family who lived in Thimphu, Claudia and I snuck off to wander on our own. We stumbled upon a small film-making studio, and in their one room office we all huddled around a table in front of their computer. The director showed us the film he was working on, and I got an autograph from the film's female star. We also met a monk who was a big fan of hers and he showed us around town a bit. Our guide Tshering began to see that we really didn't want to go to the places tourists usually visited. Just how many monasteries and government buildings can a person see? They were all really beautifully carved and painted, but my favorite part was seeing the young monks and nuns sneaking peeks at their cell phones. I didn't just want to see a building, or even just learn the history of a place. I wanted to see, and better yet, meet the people and learn about their daily lives, hopes, dreams and struggles.

While in Thimphu we also visited a small nature preserve to see an odd Bhutanese animal called the takin. The mythological story of how the takin came into being was that a "god" of sorts ate a goat and a cow, then put the goat's head on the cow's body and created this new bizarre creature. And it did look just like that. We continued to drive around Thimphu and saw the one and only traffic director. He stood in the middle of a roundabout and wore bright white gloves. There were no traffic lights, or even stop signs for that matter, in all of Bhutan. Our guide told us they'd tried to replace the traffic director with a light, but the people complained so they gave the director his job back.

We'd heard there was going to be a Halloween party, of all things, on October 31st, so on our way back to our hotel in Thimphu we stopped to see where the party was going to be held. A big crowd of monks was playing small horns and drums, chanting, and throwing rice to bless the new building where the party was going to be. The unexpected finds like these were what I loved most about travel.

The Halloween party turned out to be an even bigger surprise. Two "famous" male singers had come to perform and the girls went crazy over them. I thought they sang quite well, even though I couldn't understand what they were saying. I was one of the few who "dressed up" for Halloween. Given that I only had whatever was in my backpack, I ended up going as "weird." There were some Canadians at the party, who were in Bhutan teaching English, and they dressed up as *Night Hunters*. They explained that night hunting was a Bhutanese custom, where boys climbed into girls' rooms at night at a prearranged time after the rest of the family had gone to sleep. Other than that, most of the locals just came in Western style clothing rather than the usual traditional dress.

While in Thimphu we also visited the Art & Craft Training School. The government found young people who had some artistic talent and paid them to study the traditional arts of painting, sculpture, embroidery, weaving and woodcarving. Buddhist artwork and carving were so colorful and detailed; it was impressive to see it being made.

I was deeply moved by this wonderful country, which was trying so hard to care for its people and to preserve its culture. We were told that education and healthcare were provided for all, free of charge. They even had schools for disabled children. I didn't get to visit the one and only psychiatric hospital, but I was told they they treated with Western medicine in conjunction with traditional healing methods that were similar to those used in Tibet. The traditional healing method diagnostic procedure checked the pulse, urine, tongue and eyes, and treatment involved the use of herbs, acupuncture, heated packs or stones, and the rituals of Buddhist meditation.

Our guide insisted that serious crime was rare. The more common crimes involved petty theft and some drug or alcohol abuse. Crime had been on the rise though since the county has opened its borders to tourists and foreign laborers. Television had just been introduced to the country in 1999, and some had attributed the rise in crime to that. Television programs included Indian, American and a few Bhutanese shows. Throughout Bhutan Tuesdays were considered "dry days," when no alcohol was sold.

We left Thimphu and headed out, driving on the left-hand side of the road, going east on the one and only major artery crossing Bhutan. We stopped in Chim Lhakhang, a village famous for the phallus paintings on the outside walls of the houses which were supposed to bring good luck in general, and not necessarily with fertility. The paintings were inspired by the "Divine Madman," who was one of Bhutan's favorite saints. He'd lived in a monastery in Chim Lhakhang back in the 1400s and used humor, especially about the topics of sex and wine, to pass Buddhist teachings on to his followers. On the day we visited his monastery many locals were bringing their babies to be blessed because it happened to be a special saint's day of some sort. We also got to be blessed by a monk, which consisted of his tapping us on our heads with a big wooden penis. It was hard to stay serious.

This area was just gorgeous, so gorgeous that I was pretty sure it had all been staged by Walt Disney, who'd planned all the colors, scheduled when the birds would fly by, and planned the props—the fluffy white clouds, the giggling school girls, the painted farmhouses, the light breeze blowing the prayer flags. Then he yelled, "ACTION, bring on the tourists!"

For the first part of the trip the weather had been warm and sunny, but on the day we were driving through a pass where we could have seen the Himalayas, it was overcast. We also missed seeing the famous black necked cranes fly by, because they hadn't arrived yet for the season. But other than that day, it had all seemed perfect.

The road was narrow, winding, and very, very, very high. I think we got up to ten or twelve thousand feet. There were huge road washouts, with thick mud everywhere and traffic jams caused by trucks, SUVs, taxis and even cows. It was a bit nerve-racking at times.

In Trongsa we stayed in another lovely hotel overlooking a valley dotted with red and white government buildings and monasteries. There we had a power outage. All the staff and guests gathered in the main dining hall and waited in the dark with flashlights. The staff and I talked about the different kinds of music we liked and I was able to play for them some of the music I had on my iPhone. They particularly liked Stevie Ray Vaughn.

The best part of the visit to yet another monastery in Trongsa was watching a monk cleaning an altar and being closely accompanied by his cat. I always liked to see cats being treated well, because so frequently they aren't. We continued driving east to Bumthang, around hairpin curves at 12,000 feet. As if that weren't terrifying enough, snow was added to the mix. Claudia and I traded places in the Jeep so that I could sit on the side next to the steep mountain face, while she sat on the side overlooking the sheer drop off without a guardrail. Mostly I kept my eyes closed.

Bumthang, also known as Jakar, had burned down a few years before. So the locals, with government assistance, were in the process of rebuilding it. The town consisted of one roundabout, with three roads coming off of it. Some parts of the road were roughly paved and some parts were still just dirt. There was another power outage, and as we wandered the dark dusty dirt streets at night it resembled a one-horse town from the Wild West.

A festival was being held there, put on by the monks in their monastery. The purpose was to celebrate the monastery's deities, to clear out any demons that might be lingering, and to gain overall good karma. Both the locals and tourists sat on the ground around the edge of the monastery's courtyard. The performances featured either men dressed in elaborate colorful costumes wearing masks and dancing wildly, or women singing demurely while making subtle hand movements. The best part of the festival was the "clowns." Similar to those at an American circus or rodeo, the clowns served as assistants to the performers, and controlled or entertained the crowd during breaks in the show. They wore large masks with creepy oversized ears and noses, and they leapt and crawled around the courtyard waving carved wooden penises, sometimes covered with a condom. They'd come up to someone in the audience and poke or chase them with the phallus. This gesture was made as a "blessing" and was received by the locals with their heads bowed and their hands joined in prayer, and by the tourists with a surprised shriek and peals of laughter.

We stopped for a snack at a place called the Swiss Hotel, run by a Bhutanese and Swiss family. They made cheese and also had REAL coffee, not the usual Nescafé crap, which was made by a Swiss company, Nestlé, oddly enough.

We went to another hotel in Bumthang for an afternoon just to do a "hot rock bath." They heated rocks on an open fire and put them into water that ran into your tub, which was on the other side of the wall. There were little light switches by your tub you could use to let the rock guys know if you needed the water to be hotter, cooler or if it were just right. They added hot rocks or cold water, depending on what you needed, and they were right there on the other side of the thin wooden wall.

After visiting these other hotels, I realized that I loved the one we were staying in even more. It was clean but rustic, with a wood stove to heat our rooms. The food was fresh and well made. But the best part was that they had the most adorable loving kitten hanging out in the dining room. In Bhutan, as in most developing countries, there was the horrible issue of stray dogs everywhere you looked. And in most developing countries you rarely saw cats, and if you did, they were filthy, wild and hungry looking. I didn't know why, but in Bhutan every cat I saw seemed well cared for.

After leaving Bumthang we drove for seven hours on even scarier roads. My shoulders were up to my ears with tension from grabbing onto my seat, as if that would have made a bit of difference if we shot off the side and so far down you couldn't even see the bottom. As we finally descended to Mongar, the terrain changed to more tropical vegetation interspersed with bright golden rice paddies. The weather warmed my aching muscles, but it still took a full bottle of Druk 11,000 beer to calm my nerves after we arrived. While I was relaxing in front of our hotel some school kids stopped to chat and asked me if knew "Julia," a woman they'd met from the "U.S.A." They couldn't quite fathom how many people lived in the U.S. or the fact that I didn't know all of them. I had to remember that there were fewer than a million people in all of Bhutan, whereas the U.S. had over three hundred million. I could understand why they thought I might know Julia.

The following day we drove a quick three hours to Trashigang. Like its name implied, there was more trash there, especially in the town's creek, than what we'd witnessed in this country so far. The trash was just more evidence that we were nearing India. Other clues were the increased humidity, curry in our food, and migrant Indian road workers.

Our hotel in Trashigang only had four rooms and overlooked the town, which had only two streets. Their large monastery stood on the edge of the mountain and overlooked the river far below. The day we visited happened to be the day the monks were allowed to watch cartoons, and they'd all gathered in a large empty room. It was an odd sight to see all the shaved heads and maroon robes crouched on the centuries old wooden floor, with their faces illuminated by the glow of an old style box TV.

I knew that in just a few more days the empty roads, the green natural beauty, the serene, quiet, peaceful interactions with the locals, would all seem like a dream.

Other than the hair-raising road trips the last few days spent in Bhutan were mellow. After having been at such high altitudes driving at only 6,000 feet felt like being at sea level. We passed those last days having picnics by the river, visiting schools and monasteries, and just relaxing on the deck of our cozy hotel overlooking tiny Trashigang. We saw golden langur monkeys and many different birds. Even the famous black-necked cranes finally arrived.

Our last ride in Bhutan was to Somdrup Jonchar, the border town with India. The drive was a bit rushed, as we were trying to make it to one of the "blocks" before they closed. A "block" was when they were doing repairs on the precariously narrow high roads and they scheduled a time when they'd open one lane for traffic to pass through. Everyone lined up ready to race through during the scheduled break.

During a brief roadside stop we did at last see the Himalayas in all their splendor. They were just on the other side of a valley that was dotted with white prayer flags flown on tall bamboo poles. Since we were up so high the Himalayas seemed to be right at eye level. I would have liked to have spent more time contemplating and appreciating their extraordinary beauty, but we had to rush off to the border crossing with India.

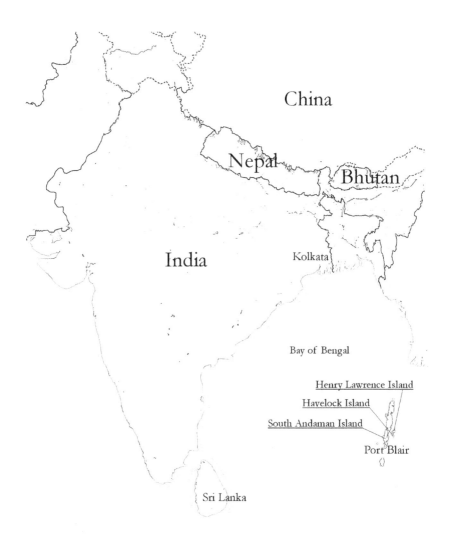

China

Nepal

Bhutan

India

Kolkata

Bay of Bengal

Henry Lawrence Island

Havelock Island

South Andaman Island

Port Blair

Sri Lanka

India
2011

As we came down the pass from Bhutan we could see the flat dusty smoggy plain of India in the distance. At the border crossing there stood only a tiny shack, and we were the only car approaching. Right before we went in to see the immigration agent Claudia and I were transferred to an Indian taxi driver. Tsehring and Sonom had to return home in their SUV by driving along the border of India and Bhutan with a military convoy due to the political unrest in northeastern India's Assam region. Assam was seeking independence from India and there was intermittent fighting. We saw many army trucks and soldiers with big guns. Claudia and I didn't have a military escort as we drove through Assam, just our taxi driver. We seemed to blend in with all the other Indian traffic, including bicycles, tuk-tuks, rickshaws, overcrowded buses, and families piled on mopeds with sari-clad women gracefully balanced sidesaddle on the back. There were also a few yogis and amputees sitting along the sides of the road surrounded by lots and lots of trash. I sighed, remembering that in Bhutan overcrowded buses weren't allowed, plastic bags were illegal, and all its people seemed to be well cared for.

It was a three hour taxi ride south to Guwahati. On the way we got caught up in the traffic generated by a huge memorial service for a famous singer who'd just died. The streets were packed with people and vehicles, and the loudspeakers were blaring words and music we couldn't understand. In Guwahati we caught a quick flight to Kolkata (Calcutta).

At the Kolkata airport we experienced what could happen in a country, especially an over-populated one, where each person had a very specific job. This caused what should have been a simple task, like catching a taxi, to become ridiculously complicated. First you went to a taxi desk in the airport. Someone there took down your information, then another person walked you over to another taxi desk outside, where another person took down your information again, then yet another person went to find you a taxi. Still another person figured out the charge, and another person took the money. Still another returned with the receipt, and so on and so forth. Eventually we made it to the Swissôtel, but it was nothing like the little Swiss place in Bhutan! Wow, did Claudia ever surprise me by booking this place for us. It had a rooftop infinity pool, where it looked like you would swim right off the edge of the building. It was a special place for a night, with great food and coffee.

The next morning we flew south from Kolkata about eight hundred miles over the Indian ocean, to Port Blair, a city on one of India's Andaman islands. We were picked up at the airport and taken to a ferry for a two-and-a-half hour ride to Havelock island. There we were swished off the dock by a tuk-tuk, then driven on the island's one and only narrow asphalt road, passing small thatched roofed villages surrounded by a lush tropical forest before finally arriving at our accommodation called Barefoot Scuba. And voila, we were on vacation. The place was seriously laid back.

When I say "vacation," I mean something completely different from what I mean when I say "travel." Traveling can be hard, even grueling. People have asked me, when I've returned from a trip, "Was it fun?" and I've always had a difficult time answering that. Fun wasn't what I was looking for when I traveled. Bhutan was not a vacation. When I am on vacation, I just want to relax and this island was the right place to do just that.

Barefoot Scuba, as its name implies, was predominantly a scuba diving resort. I use the word "resort" loosely, because this place consisted of a simple open-air kitchen and dining area, a scuba rental office and about twenty huts for guests to choose from. The huts ranged from nice air-conditioned two story wooden structures with ocean view balconies to small thatched shacks with views of the backs of the nice accommodation. Claudia and I had rented two of the nice ones side by side. We'd had separate rooms during the entire trip because one thing that changed as I'd aged was my need for privacy and my own space. Luckily Claudia felt the same way. In my younger days I couldn't afford to stay alone, but now I had a well-paying job as a nurse and we both felt it was worth spending the money to have a break from each other when traveling together for long periods of time. It took a lot of pressure off our friendship.

I could see the water from my balcony. I thought if I were asked the question, "Where were you on 11/11/11 at 11 a.m.?" I'd answer with a happy sigh, "laying on the crystal white sand of Beach #3, watching the clumsy traffic pass on a hermit crab highway, their tiny colorful shells silhouetted by the turquoise water that was as warm as bathwater." It was times like these that I'd wish Carson could join me. But he couldn't take time off work like I could. I appreciated that he didn't mind my traveling without him. In fact he actually saw that it was good and healthy for us to have some time apart. The best part was that we trusted each other's loyalty and commitment. I was a lucky woman.

I spent the next morning exploring on my own, with the goal of finding beer. There was only one store, down by the jetty, in a dark alley. There was a line of men, who were pushing me aside so they could buy their booze through a barred window. I finally asked a rather clean-cut guy, who was neatly dressed and seemed to know what he was doing, if he'd help me. And he did. His name was Joy, which I thought was a good sign. He worked on Havelock island and was my first local "friend." I also hired a tuk-tuk, the three-wheeled open-aired vehicle, with the driver, to tour me around the island for a bit. I was able to find a little Internet café, the Wild Orchid, that just happened to be at the same restaurant where Joy worked. This place also had yoga on the beach every morning, and Ayurvedic massage. I realized I'd found my new hangout.

Before finding this place I'd been up and down the little road, stopping when I saw hand-painted signs that read "High Speed Internet." What I'd find was a shack with a bunch of wires stapled to the walls and a young kid saying that they didn't have any Internet service because the electric bill hadn't been paid since yesterday had been a "holiday." I loved vacation tasks: #1 find beer, #2 watch hermit crabs, and #3 see what happens while searching for a functioning Internet. It never really mattered if the task got done.

There was actually quite a lot to do around Havelock: scuba diving, snorkeling, kayaking, and trekking. I imagined that we'd get around to doing something eventually, but at that moment I thought I heard the hermit crabs calling, and figured the beer would be cold enough.

I went to get an Ayurvedic massage, and the "therapist" was a little fellow with a big mustache. I'd seen him holding hands with another guy right before I went in and since I'd seen men holding hands throughout Asia and the Middle East, I knew it didn't necessarily indicate homosexuality. But when he did the characteristic Indian head wiggle and gestured for me to take off my clothes, he did it in such a way that I felt assured my nudity would mean nothing to him. As I stood in front of him buck naked, perhaps looking a little self-conscious, he said with a big grin, "No worry ma'am, I do this eight years." We were in a little bamboo hut with only a well-used hard wooden bench to lie on. There was no sheet, no pillow, no towel, nothing—just a bowl of warmed oil, burning incense and me. He was good and thorough and even massaged my eyelids. At the end he sat me up and took my hair down to massage my scalp, and then he tied my hair back up so delicately, leaving out one little curl in the front.

I went to the Wild Orchid one morning to do yoga on the beach. There was a petite Indian female teacher and three big men—one from Austria (replete with big muscles, tattoos and sunglasses), one from Sweden (a long blonde-haired hippie), and one from who knew where. All in all it was lovely, and I tried to incorporate the sand, the flies and the occasional spider into my meditation. To run on the beach and out into the ocean after yoga was sublime. Another day I went snorkeling with Claudia. It was an all day trip, with most of the day spent taking a long fishing boat ride through the islands to the snorkeling beaches on the two small islands called South Button and Henry Lawrence. There were hundreds of brightly colored fish. But the coral hadn't fared well because of the tsunami and because of changes in water temperature due to global warming. I could only imagine what it used to look like, since even with the coral damage it was spectacular.

One day Claudia and I rented a moped. Now that was funny! Even though I had a motorcycle license, it was a bit of a challenge because I'd never driven a moped, had Claudia on the back, had to navigate the narrow bumpy roads, and had to continue to remember to drive on the left hand side of the road. We crossed to the other side of the island and found an amazing long white sand beach with little crystal clear waves, as if glass were being melted and blown onto the shore. While we were basking in all that beauty, I heard a ruckus behind me and turned to see Rajan coming toward us, the ocean swimming elephant that was famous on this island. Unfortunately Rajan didn't like waves, even small ones, so we didn't get the chance to swim with him.

We went on yet another snorkel trip, to uninhabited Inglis island, which was only visited by boats from Barefoot Scuba. The reefs were not as colorful or as populated with sea life as what we'd seen on the previous trip. But then we went on a jungle trek. There were hundreds of amazing trees, whose roots were like walls coming out of the ground, with their massive vines so thick that they looked like boa constrictors hanging from the branches. We also saw fruit bats, a couple of deer, which had been introduced by the British for hunting, and an amazing black bird, called a *drongo*, which had long split tail feathers. It looked like a bird of paradise.

After hiking through the jungle we suddenly emerged and were stunned by one of the most, if not THE most, beautiful deserted beaches I'd ever seen. The clean white sand, swaying palm trees, pure clear turquoise water, perfect gentle waves, a soft sandy bottom and hundreds of hermit crabs in all shapes, sizes and shell colors crawling about or meeting in groups to suck on tiny fallen flowers—all made for perfect bliss.

After a lovely day snorkeling we returned to our cabins, and as I was showering I saw that my hair was matted and that there wasn't a spot left on my body that hadn't been bitten, stung or burned. I hadn't a shred of dry or clean clothing left. The air conditioner in my hut had broken on the second day so I'd slept in fits with bugs buzzing and fending off heatstroke. I believed I was now ready for a change. But the experience here had been worth it, all of it.

We took the ferry from Havelock back to Port Blair, where I spent nearly the entire day in my air-conditioned hotel room just to get my core body temperature down to something manageable. In the evening Claudia and I walked around Port Blair and went out to dinner to say good-bye to each other, since the following day she'd be returning to Germany via New Delhi and I'd be flying home to California via Kolkata and Bangkok.

The way my flights had been scheduled, I was going to have an overnight layover in Kolkata, so I'd arranged to stay at the Swissôtel again, and had booked a quick tour of the city. I was met at the airport by my driver, Arun. I asked if he were also my guide for the day, and what followed were a series of miscommunications that led to his erroneously becoming just that. Evidently I was supposed to have stopped by my hotel first and picked up a different car and driver, but I didn't know that, so we just took off as if we were meant to be together. And as it turned out, I was glad we did.

I explained to Arun that I wasn't interested in seeing the usual tourist sites, because I didn't much care for museums or for old British architecture, at least not in this whirlwind tour. So the first place he took me to was an amazing Jain temple that was completely covered with tiny mirrors, mosaics, stained glass, and gold and silver carvings. It was so beautiful it brought tears to my eyes. Jains believed that all living beings, including plants, had souls, and that all deserved equal respect. They lived simply and practiced ahimsa, or non-violence.

Our next stop was at a series of steps, called a *ghat*, leading down to the Ganges River, where they burned dead bodies. This was an intense place, but it didn't make me sad, not really. Indians seemed to have a matter-of-fact, accepting approach to death. There were three bodies aflame and each funeral pyre had a family gathered around it. The ghat overlooked the Ganges, which is sacred to Hindus, but when we walked down to its shore it was absolutely filthy. There were people standing in the river praying, facing the setting sun, and surrounded by mounds of trash, dead flowers and half destroyed statues of various Hindu gods. In the middle of it all a young boy was crouched down taking a dump on the edge of the entry ramp. We saw the dead body of an old woman being unloaded from the back of a rusted out truck. She was encased in a glass coffin like Sleeping Beauty. As the river was sacred, many Indians desired to come here to be cremated. The sky was thick with flocks of crows and billows of smoke. It was all a little eerie, and yet so natural.

Next Arun and I went to a tiny alley in the old part of town to see where they made many of the Hindu sculptures we'd been seeing. The artists started with straw in the shape of a human body or animal, some of which were ten or more feet tall. Then they covered this form with mud, and when it dried it all got painted and decorated. I met three generations of what were called "architects," in a family that designed these sculptures. The family was quite thrilled to show me around and explain which god each statue represented. Hinduism has thousands of gods and its adherents didn't even know all of them.

By now both Arun and I needed to take a break. While I drank a banana lassi, a typical Indian drink made from fruit and yogurt, Arun chewed some betel nut. We sat quietly on a bench on a sidewalk surrounded by throngs of people in what I liked to call "total controlled chaos." Somehow all the people, cars, overloaded buses, animals, and rickshaws piled high with so much stuff all flowed relatively safely, bouncing off each other's invisible protective force fields like rapid molecule collisions in a small Petri dish.

It was getting dark and I was running out of time, so we headed to the hotel via the park surrounding Victoria Palace. I ended up seeing some of the old British architecture after all. Traveling the short distance to the hotel took an hour in stop-and-go Friday evening rush hour traffic in one of the most populated and congested cities in the world.

I had not stopped by the hotel before my tour, and had therefore gone on the city tour with the wrong driver, but instead of being angry with me the hotel manager gave me a complimentary bottle of wine. At times I could indeed appreciate these ridiculously nice hotels. I sipped my free wine by the lovely rooftop pool, had a delicious Aussie burger (made with beets, an egg and pineapple), and contemplated the extremes of life on this tiny planet. I headed back to the airport for my 1 a.m. departure for a short two-hour flight to Bangkok. Without a doubt, the layover in Kolkata was one of the best I'd ever had.

I spent the last night of my month long journey, just like the first night, at The Great Residence hotel in Bangkok. I loved the Thai people, their food, and most of all, their massage. Thai massage had become my favorite type. The little masseuse ladies climbed right up on the low platform with you, then used their hands, elbows, knees and feet to prod and pull and pop and crunch almost every part of your body, as if you were a rag doll.

I got a massage the night I arrived and another in the morning before I left for the airport. I now felt ready for the sixteen hour flight I'd have to endure in order to get home. And, as always, I thought with a sigh just how quickly the awful could turn into the fabulous. And vice versa.

Silver Bank

Dominican
Republic

Samana

Santo Domingo

The Silver Bank
2012

To celebrate my turning half a century old, Carson and I flew to the Dominican Republic, a country that shares an island with Haiti. We'd signed up for a Conscience Breath Adventures whale watching expedition on a 138 foot motor yacht, the Sundancer II. We met the boat in Puerto Plata, a small city on the island's north coast. We were to live aboard Sundancer for a week in the Silver Bank, a special area off the coast where humpback whales come to breed and give birth in the spring.

There were eighteen passengers plus the crew on our beautiful boat, which had three spacious decks. All the staterooms were on the bottom deck, and we stored our snorkeling gear in its stern. The middle deck held the dining area and lecture hall, and the top deck was open and used for relaxing, reading and whale watching.

In every direction we looked from the boat we could see whale blows and dorsal fins between us and the horizon. Every day the passengers got geared up for snorkeling and boarded one of three smaller boats, each of which held six of us and two crew.

When the boat leader told us to get in the water we'd sit on the edge of the boat, hold our masks and fall in. The water was warm and dark blue, and there was nothing else around us but the boat we'd just left. Suddenly I'd be kicking like mad, with my face in the water, following six pairs of churning fins. We were in search of sleeping mother whales and their calves.

When a whale sleeps it does what is known as "conscious breathing", where it shuts down half of its brain to rest, while the other half stays awake to remind the whale to surface so that it may breathe. The mothers stay underwater for twenty minutes or so, but the calves have to come up every five minutes. The water on the Silver Bank is very clear and shallow, so while we were floating at the surface we could look down and see the dim outline of the whales.

The babies, which were already at least ten or fifteen feet long and weighing as much as a Volkswagen Beetle, would slowly rise up to breathe, passing right before our eyes. They were so curious that they would come over to us and hover vertically while staring into our masks. It was absolutely the most amazing thing I'd ever seen. The baby would then play up at the surface, catching a few breaths before heading back down to be with its mother.

After twenty more minutes, the forty or fifty foot mother would ascend. This was like being gently approached, up close and personal, by a semi-truck. We were so close we could stare right into her soulful eye. Because we were all jostling for the position with the best view, each of us at some point was accidentally kicked by another equally excited whale watcher. The mother would seem to tire of our attention and so would calmly flip her tail, and would fade away faster than we could ever hope to swim. The tail, the size of a two car garage door, swept so close to us, but never once hit anyone. We all seemed to have an insane trust in the benevolence and awareness of these immense beings.

The humpback was my favorite whale because they were so playful. They could breach, getting their entire bodies out of the water, making a huge splash as they landed—and they'd do this repeatedly. They also seemed to be communicating when they would slap their tail flukes and pectoral fins on the surface of the water. Each whale has unique markings on their tail flukes, which researchers use to identify individual whales. Their beautiful white pectoral fins, when seen from under the water, simply glow. The most magical thing about these whales is that they sing. It is believed that the different pods actually have their own evolving languages that include local dialects, just as humans do.

Every day, three times a day, for a solid week, we swam with whales. On the last day we got in the water with a female, her calf and an adult male escort. These males were not necessarily the father of the calf, but they liked to hang around the female, with the hope that she might be ready to breed again. When the female is not in the mood to breed she can become a bit agitated and, rather than sleeping, she can start to move around in an attempt to discourage the male. We ended up in the water with three excited whales circling around, slapping their fins and tails on the water. It was a free-for-all, with all of us swimming around madly, wondering if at any moment we might be accidentally rammed by a whale or an ecstatic whale watcher. It was yet another time in my life, my incredibly fortunate life, where I felt compelled to say, "That was the most beautiful and exhilarating experience I've ever had."

Not only was I celebrating turning fifty years old, but Carson and I were simultaneously celebrating seven years together. That was the longest either of us had ever been with anyone. Just as travel wasn't always "fun", love was not always "happy." Through the years I had tried to learn not to expect so much from others, a place or myself. The Twelve Step program had offered a lot of lessons about life. For example, "expectations are future resentments" and that "reasonably content" was probably better than happy anyway. Carson and I had plans to buy a house and a farm in

Texas. We also hoped to continue traveling, perhaps together, but we knew that most of the time I'd probably go alone. We also knew that plans didn't always reach fruition, especially when those of two people were not the same. What I hoped for us was that we would want what was best for the other, even if that meant we no longer shared the same path. I think that is what I had finally learned about love. It wasn't about me.

I was never able to answer the question, "What do you want to be when you grow up?" Without planning it I became a nomad, a bar-stool philosopher, and an unambitious observer of a fascinating world. I will not always know what to do next but I know I will always keep travelling to see what's there.

I wish us all happy trails and, more importantly, a healthy planet in which to find them.

The author, her current husband and their two cats are presently transitioning from their Texas solar organic garden homestead and will carry on with the adage, "home is where you hang your hat–and unpack your bags."

Leslie can be found at http://leslietravels.com

CPSIA information can be obtained at www.ICGtesting.com
Printed in the USA
LVOW02s1203050515

437264LV00003B/3/P